State, Market and Life Chances in Contemporary Rural Chinese Society

Nabo Chen

State, Market and Life Chances in Contemporary Rural Chinese Society

Evidence from Guangdong

中央编译出版社
CCTP Central Compilation & Translation Press

Springer

Nabo Chen
Department of Public Management
School of Government
Sun Yat-sen University
Guangzhou, China

ISBN 978-3-662-45045-1 ISBN 978-3-662-45046-8 (eBook)
DOI 10.1007/978-3-662-45046-8

Library of Congress Control Number: 2015944073

Springer Heidelberg New York Dordrecht London
"Translation from the Chinese language edition: *国家、市场与农民生活机遇 ：来自中国广东农村的经验* (1978–2004) by Nabo Chen, © Central Compilation & Translation Press 2010.

Printed on acid-free paper

Springer-Verlag GmbH Berlin Heidelberg is part of Springer Science+Business Media (www.springer.com)

Contents

List of Figures

List of Map

List of Tables

Chapter 1
Introduction

1.1 Overview of the Study

What are the effects of market reform on social stratification in rural China? This topic has been a focus of sociology, especially comparative stratification research, for more than two decades, because market reform in rural China provides a rare natural experiment involving changes in the stratification order on a scale reminiscent of what was experienced in the West during the rise of capitalism. Earlier researches on Mao's rural China present a state-centered picture: the state[1] and its agents—cadres[2]

[1] By "state," I refer to the governmental hierarchy of the whole state system. The specific level of government being analyzed will be given at the appropriate point—e.g., central government, provincial government, etc.

[2] "Cadre" (ganbu) is a ubiquitous term in the PRC. It originally denoted party and administrative officials holding government positions. In recent years, the meaning of the term has expanded to include white collar workers in managerial positions as well as business leaders generally. The creation of a civil service in the 1990s may help to narrow the definition of the term over time, as functionaries in the bureaucracy are now officially designated as "civil servants." In this study, by "rural cadres" I mean both township cadres and village leaders. Separately, "township cadre" refers to an officer of township government; "village cadres" (cun ganbu) refers to a village leader. As Andrew Walder (2002a, b) points out: "Strictly speaking, village leaders are not state cadres (guojia ganbu). They are not on the state payroll and they do not have an official rank. Salaries of village leaders, if paid, come from funds generated within the village. However, village leaders are still commonly refereed to as rural cadres (nongcun ganbu), making it unclear which of the two definitions a respondent might employ. To make matters more complicated, the status, pay, and power of village leaders also varies greatly across regions. In areas with highly developed economies, village leaders are full-time administrators who may receive high salaries and large bonus for accomplish production and sales targets (Oi 1992, 1999), however, Parish et al. (1995) note correctly that many village officials in areas where agriculture predominates are in fact farmers who work part-time on a volunteer basis and are more analogous to what they call volunteer firemen than administrators" (Walder 2002b, p. 359).

N. Chen, *State, Market and Life Chances in Contemporary Rural Chinese Society*, DOI 10.1007/978-3-662-45046-8_1

controlled all resources and allocated them to peasants[3] according to a "work point" system and to patron-client relationships (Hinton 1984; Kraus 1981; Oi 1989; Shue 1980; Unger 1984; Whyte 1985; Yang 1959; Zhang 1998). Focusing on the changes brought by the Chinese market reform since 1978, in his seminal 1989 article Victor Nee proposes a market transition theory which argues that the transition of the distribution mechanism from the state to the market leads to an erosion of the cadres' advantages (Nee 1989, 1991), while most sequent studies argue the "persistence" or "conversion" of the cadres' advantages (Bian and Logan 1996; Lin 1995; Oi 1992, 1995; Rona-Tas 1994). In the next generation of studies, new institutional analyses contend that the opportunities of cadres and peasants are structured by various institutional frameworks, some of which point to property rights (or economic sector diversity) (Bian and Zhang 2002; Walder 1992; Zang 2002; Zhao and Zhou 2002; Zhou 2000) and others point to regional differences (Nee 1996; Parish and Michelson 1996; Whiting 2001; Xie and Hannum 1996). However, some studies on rural social stratification find that the property rights in rural areas are always ambiguous (Li 1996; Peng 1992; Wank 1999; Goodman 2001). The studies focusing on the regional variation also find that regional variations are similar to other institutional characteristics, so that some researchers try to include them according to the typology of market contexts, under such headings as "institutional transition and structural changes" (Walder 2002b), "typology of market penetration" (Szelenyi and Kostello 1996), and "the scale of firms that dominate the private sector" (Zhao 2004).

Within this line of research, this study addresses the effects of market reform on the life chances of village cadres and peasants by presenting a typology and stages of market penetration of rural Guangdong[4]—the first reform province, located in the coastal region of south China. In this study, "market penetration" is quantitatively and qualitatively defined by level of economic expansion and the development of three market factors: commodity market, capital market, and labor market. The term "life chance" is loosely used and refers to the things open to individuals to better the quality of life for themselves and their families (income, earnings, benefits, opportunities, welfare, and so on) (Dahrendorf 1979). The research is conducted as a comparative case study based on interviews and archival data. It documents how the market penetration processes shape the provincial areas according to three stages, or types, of rural economy according to four township level measurements: average township income, the number of private firms in the township, the number of collective firms in the township, and the amount of wage labor. However, this study doesn't assume that progress from one stage to the next is inevitable or necessary.

[3] In this study, the term "peasant" refers to a person whose household registration records are "nongmin" in Chinese. In the context of China nowadays, this term is interchangeable with the other two terms "farmer" and "villager."

[4] The pinyin system of Romanization, which is widely used in mainland China, is adopted (e.g., Guangzhou, rather than the former transliteration, Canton), except for names of well-known Chinese living in Hong Hong, Taiwan, or overseas, for which I have used the most common transliterations.

The first type, and the highest[5] stage, called "new cooperative economies," refers to the rural economies in the Pearl River Delta region (henceforth, PRD) which surrounds the capital city, Guangzhou. Just as its name implies, the most distinctive characteristic of this type of economy is that almost every village is organized to be a "Rural Shareholding Cooperative Community (*Nongcun Gufen Hezuo She*)." Collective assets (public land, and collective enterprises, etc.), household rights to land use and other household possessions have been taken as the original investments in the Cooperative Community (Hezuo She). Most registered peasants of the community have the right to shares in the profits of the collective economy, while they remain free to operate their own businesses. "Outskirt economies," the second type and the middle stage, refer to the rural economies in fringe areas of the PRD and the outskirt areas of regional cities, where high-value agricultural production is developed to serve the needs of nearby cities. The third type, the lowest stage—"local economies"—is the rural economies in mountain areas of the province. In this type of economy, most young people leave the village for wage labor and private business elsewhere.

This study is based on ethnographic studies of three townships, which are selected as representatives of the three types of economy. Historical and comparative evidence shows how market penetration has affected the life chances of village cadres and peasants in two ways (see Fig. 1.1).

First, market penetration increases the varieties and qualities of earning sources overall, even though village cadres still have advantages in gaining access to the earning sources under their jurisdiction. Historically, accompanying the market penetration processes, peasants' earning sources have increased in quantity from the single source of their crops to that of a large number of agricultural, sidelines and private businesses, and then to a combination of sidelines, private businesses, private enterprises, and wage labor. Comparative data from the three selected townships also shows this tendency: at one extreme, in a new corporative economy, peasants gain their earnings from sharing the profits of collective economies—from housing rentals, wage work, and family businesses and other sources; at the other, in local economies, crops and agricultural sideline are profitless, and therefore migrant work and migrant businesses are the main sources of the peasants' earnings. Between these two extremes is the outskirt economy, in which peasants gain their earnings mainly from high-value agricultural sidelines, as well as from migrant work and migrant businesses.

Second, market penetration lowers the tax rates paid by peasants to state bureaucracies and the amount of local charges retained by local governments—the various fees and ad hoc surcharges, which are considered to be the main burden of the peasants—in rural society and increases the investments of state bureaucracies for social welfare of the community, thereby indirectly increasing the peasants' life chances. (1) At the central level, market penetration gradually decreases the

[5]As mentioned above, the "high or low" stage is defined by level of economic expansion and the development of three market factors: commodity market, capital market, and labor market.

Area	New Corporative Economies		Outskirt Economies		Local Economies	
	Most of Peal River Delta region		The periphery area of PRD region and the outskirt villages of regional cities		Mountain areas of the province	
Market penetration measures						
Level of economic expansion (average township income)	++++		++		+	
Commodity market (number of private and collective firms)	++++		++		+	
Capital market (the amount of capital invested)	++++		++		+	
Labor market (the number of wage laborers)	++++		++		+	
Variety and qualities of earning sources	Variety	Qualities	Variety	Qualities	Variety	Qualities
Crops	-	-	++	++	+++	++
Agricultural sidelines	+	+	++++	++++	++	++
Individual family businesses	++++	++++	+++	++	++	++
Migrant businesses	+	+++	+++	+++	++	+++
Local wage work	++++	++	++	++	+	+
Migrant wage work	-	+	++	++	++++	++
Collective economy	++++	++++	++	+	+	-
Revenue sharing among state bureaucracies and rural society						
Agricultural tax submitted to the state by peasants	-		+		+	
Transfer from higher government levels to local township governments	+		+++		+	
Tax revenues of the township governments	++++		++		+	
Township governments' self-retained funds from peasants	-		+		+++	
Governments' investment in social welfare	+++		+		-	
Dynamics of structure and life chances						
Verities and qualities of earning sources	++++		+++		++	
The aggravation (+) or relief (-) of the peasants' burden	-		+		+++	

Note: A minus sign indicates "none", while plus signs indicate a range from minimal (+) to considerable (++++).

Fig. 1.1 Overview of the study. Note: A *minus sign* indicates "none," while *plus signs* indicate a range from minimal (+) to considerable (++++)

proportion of agricultural tax in the central state's revenue—only 4 % of fiscal income of the central government in 2002. At the same time, the central government tends to decrease the discontent, protest, and even rioting of peasants, who constituted 59.47 % (in 2003)[6] of the population of the country. In 2003, the central government issued the rural fee-for-tax[7] reform over all the rural areas of the country, in order to eliminate local governments' non-tax levies. (2) Generally speaking, the revenue structure of local government consists of three parts: tax revenue, transfer from higher government levels, and self-retained funds. The higher the market penetration level of the local areas, the higher the sharing bases among the various levels of local government and the lower the demands on self-retained funds. The higher the level of market penetration, the more likely that local officials are to oversee community welfare and increase their public investment. The comparative evidence from the three types of market penetration supports this tendency (see Fig. 1.1).

[6] Please refer to http://www.stats.gov.cn/tjsj/ndsj/yb2004-c/indexch.htm.

[7] As a response to the heavy burden on peasants, the central government began a nationwide rural tax-for-fee reform (Nong Cun Shui Fei Gaige) in 2003. According to this reform, fees for rural education, the butchery tax, compulsory labor, and other charges on farmers have been abolished. The ultimate purpose of the reform is to reduce the burdens on farmers and increase their income, as the Chinese central government has identified the slow rise of farmers' income as a major social and economic problem.

1.2 The State, Market and Life Chances: The Puzzles and How They Are Explained

How do the changes of social structure affect people's life chances? In a capitalist state, the market as a resource distribution mechanism is highlighted, where technological change, global competition, and shifting welfare state policies have brought forth significant structural changes. These changes affect individual job mobility and employment exit patterns and thus life chances (Gerber 2002; Lipset and Zetterberg 1959). On the other hand, the socialist state was characterized by very limited private property ownership, a high labor force participation rate (including women laborers), with employment predominantly in state-sector enterprises (in urban areas) and on communes (in rural areas), and a redistribution system by which the socialist party state controlled resources and distributed them to its people according to their political loyalty (Connor 1979; Feldmesser 1953; Mikhalev 2003; Siomdzynski and Shabad 1997, p. 160). Modernization theory argues that the industrial development, whether socialist or capitalist, leads to convergence (Inkeles and Bauer 1959; Inkeles and Rossi 1956, 1957; Treiman 1970). Institutional theory also doubts the absolute dualism of capitalism and socialism. It argues that economies are embedded in various institutional backgrounds and that the studies of social stratification should also take account of underlying differences in institutional forms (North 1981; Polanyi 1957; Polanyi 1965).

An unpredictable great transformation of the socialist states in these two decades has brought more unanswered questions to the above debate. The challenging intellectual task is to figure out how these changes in social structure affect people's life chances. In the former Soviet camp, the answer seems to be clear: the reform is a kind of "shock therapy" which is characterized by large-scale privatization, in various forms (Stark 1992; Stark 1996). Most of the former political elite have given up their positions of power even though some of them have converted their power into forms based on other resources (Rona-Tas 1994). The new petty bourgeoisie did not emerge as the winners of the transition. Instead, the following decade of post communism in the areas previously dominated by the Soviet Union can be understood as a struggle of changing alliances between the different factions of the elites: technocratic-managerial elite, various kinds of intellectuals, and others (Szalai 1989; Szelenyi 2002); the end of the transformation, clearly, is capitalist, even though the ways are varied by country. The reforms didn't bring about obvious economic development but a stagnation or depression for quite a long time (Portes 1994). It means that the reform in these countries didn't enlarge the "pie" but just transferred some quota of the pie from one group to the others.

The story of East Asian Socialism—China and Vietnam, especially the former—is quite complicated: communist parties retain their political monopolies and political elites of the communist parties still hold their positions and influences. A large part of the public sectors still maintain their key functions in the national economies, while most of other sectors are indeed hybrid and cannot be clearly classified as either private or public. In China, the dual structure, of urban areas and rural areas, still maintains its constraining function, a large amount of foreign direct investment floods into the country and the export—process economy, as a main driving force, leads the country to continuous high-speed economic development. The large population and the regional disparities create many various patterns of resource access; the future is ambiguous, with no blue print. A larger pie has been made, but the principles for sharing it are still puzzles (Morduch and Sicular 2000, p. 334).

The ambiguous future and unanswered puzzles of China have attracted many stratification researchers. The seminal article of Victor Nee (1989) triggered a debate on whether the agents of the state, who held the redistributive power in the pre-reform period, will lose their economic and social privileges. The next generation of studies—new institutional analysis—argues that the life chances of different groups of people should be understood under various institutional structures.[8] These studies gave us more in-depth knowledge about the social stratification of reform China: we have learned that urban and rural areas are two very different institutional settings in China (Peng 1992); we have also leaned that property rights (Bian and Zhang 2002; Walder 1992; Zang 2002; Zhao and Zhou 2002; Zhou 2000) and region disparities (Nee 1996; Parish and Michelson 1996; Whiting 2001; Xie and Hannum 1996) are two key institutions to people's return.[9] Some of these studies claim that off-farm employment and rural industry give peasants some chances, while creating new sources of power for rural cadres at the same time (Brauw, Huang, Rozelle, Zhang, and Zhang 2002; Oi 1999; Walder 1995b, 2004; Wank 1999); other in-depth studies point out that the effects of institutional changes and economic growth should be evaluated separately (Walder 2002a, b); yet others consider that the extensiveness of regime change combine with institutional barriers to asset appropriation to give the elite various opportunities to gain assets with diverse characteristics (Walder 2003).

However, there are still three major issues that have not been addressed adequately. Firstly, most existing stratification studies emphasize the broad transition from one type of society to another, while there is little research on specific changes brought about by the transition. Secondly, most former studies are survey researches on income, but we have a much poorer grasp of exactly what kinds of opportunities have been gradually created by market reform, or of people's various access patterns to them. Thirdly, although most researchers agree that both the state and market play important roles in people's life chances in the reform period, how the state and market interact and affect people's life chances still remains a black box. This study tries to contribute to the answers to these puzzles.

To deal with the first puzzle, this study factually describes the changes in rural Guangdong during the reform period from 1978 to 2004 as "a process of market penetration."[10] With this description, I argue that the market reform of rural Guangdong is far away from being a transition from public property right to private

[8] By "institutional structures," Nee points to economic activities embedded in the structure, which consist of customs, social norms, laws, regulations, the state, and so on.

[9] In these studies, "return" mainly points to incomes and employment opportunities.

[10] This term is borrowed from Szelenyi and Kostello (1996).

property right, but is a process of change characterized as the movement of commodities, capital, and labor according to location and to appropriation.

Concerning the second puzzle, two points are emphasized: (1) a detailed picture of what kinds of earning sources have been created by the market penetration process and the opportunities of peasants and village cadres to access these earning sources; and (2) the bringing of the issue of the aggravation or relief of "the burden on peasants" into comparative stratification studies of rural China, with the argument that most former studies have emphasized what peasants "get" but have neglected what they "lose."

As for the third puzzle, this study illustrates how the discrepancy between economic liberalization in the market and continued political authoritarianism in the state leads to the variation of policies and governance of the state and local governments in rural society, which thus affect the rural people' life chances. In this way, this study tries to contribute a state-market interactive view to the stratification studies of rural China.

Some other characteristics of this study should be highlighted. First, this study takes rural Guangdong as the research field. I selected Guangdong for two reasons: (1) it is the first province to undergo the reform policy and one of the most dramatically transforming areas, with increases in GDP of 20 % per year over the last twenty years. Guangdong resembles the whole country in geographic duality (coastal area and inland area) and economic mode (in which most other provinces are copying the economic mode of Guangdong). (2) I focus on rural areas because they are the better places to observe the effects of structural factors on people's life chances, while individual characteristics play more and more important roles in urban China.

Second, the unit of analysis is the township instead of the region, province, prefecture, county or village, because the research on a township can record the face-to-face interaction between local governments and peasants, which is the core of rural politics in China.

Third, the analysis of local governments will focus on the township government and village administration. These two levels of administration should be understood together, since they interact face to face frequently.

1.3 Preview of the Remaining Chapters

Chapter 2 introduces the existing relevant literature and the research framework of this study. Firstly, in Chap. 2, the main features of rural China in Mao's period are presented, which can help readers to understand the departure point of the reform. Then, two generations of studies on reform—China' stratification—market transition debate and the new institutional analysis—are discussed. Based on the unanswered puzzles of the literature, three new directions will be developed as the framework of this study. Lastly, the methodological issues and some basic information of the field sites are presented.

Chapter 3 presents an historical account of the market penetration process in Guangdong. It also depicts the historical thread of two themes of the study: market penetration processes lead to various distributions of the sources of earnings in rural Guangdong; and market penetration affects the inter-governmental revenue sharing and rural society and thus the life chances of rural people.

Chapter 4 focuses on a township located in the PRD region of Guangdong, which is selected as representative of the New Cooperative Economy. The main institutions of the township are introduced, and then I give a detailed picture of the earnings sources of the peasants and the advantages of rural cadres. The cadres' characteristic as the managers of the economy will be highlighted. In sum, the chapter presents how the increasing earning sources, better welfare policies and soft governance of the local governments make the township a more harmonious community.

Chapter 5 presents a township located in the fringe areas of the PRD region, selected as representative of outskirt economies. While I depict the "get" and "lose" of the peasants and cadres, I highlight two characteristics of the township: the high-value sidelines as an earning source, and village cadres as volunteer firemen.

The major task of Chap. 6 is to describe how the township government and village administration act as predators in rural society. I emphasize two things: how cash-starved township government and village administration lead to the aggravation of the peasants' burden and how they extract revenue from peasants in various ways.

In Chap. 7, summary of the findings will be given and interpreted. I will also discuss the implications and limitation of this study.

References

Bian, Y., & Logan, J. R. (1996). Market transition and the persistence of power: The changing stratification system in urban China. *American Journal of Sociology, 61*, 739–758.

Bian, Y., & Zhang, Z. (2002). Marketization and income distribution in urban China, 1988 and 1995. *Research in Social Stratification and Mobility, 19*, 377–415.

Connor, W. (1979). *Socialism, politics, and equality: Hierarchy and change in easter Europe and the USSR*. New York: Columbia University Press.

Dahrendorf, R. (1979). *Life chances*. Chicago: The University of Chicago Press.

Feldmesser, R. A. (1953). The persistence of status advantages in Soviet Russia. *American Journal of Sociology, 59*, 19–27.

Gerber, T. P. (2002). Structural change and post-socialist stratification: Labor market transitions in contemporary Russia. *American Sociological Review, 67*, 629–659.

Goodman, D. S. G. (2001). The interdependence of state and society: The political sociology of local leadership. In C. M. Chao & B. J. Dickson (Eds.), *Remaking the Chinese State: Strategies, society and security* (pp. 132–156). New York: Routledge.

Hinton, W. (1984). *Shenfan*. New York: Random House.

Inkeles, A., & Bauer, R. (1959). *The Soviet Ctizen: Daily life in a totalitarian society*. Cambridge, MA: Harvard University Press.

Inkeles, A., & Rossi, P. H. (1956). National comparisons of occupational prestige. *American Journal of Sociology, 61*, 329–339.

Inkeles, A., & Rossi, P. H. (1957). Multidimensional ratings of occupations. *Sociometry, 20*, 234–251.
Kraus, R. C. (1981). *Class conflict in Chinese socialism*. New York: Columbia University Press.
Li, D. D. (1996). A theory of ambiguous property rights in transition economies: The case of the Chinese non-state sector. *Journal of Comparative Economics, 23*, 1–19.
Lin, N. (1995). Local market socialism: Local corporatism in action in rural China. *Theory and Society, 24*, 301–354.
Lipset, S. M., & Zetterberg, H. L. (1959). Social mobility in industrial societies. In S. M. Lipset & R. Bendix (Eds.), *Social mobility in industrial society*. Berkeley: University of California Press.
Mikhalev, V. (2003). Overview: Inequality and transformation of social structures. In V. Mikhalev (Ed.), *Inequality and social structure during the transformation* (pp. 1–8). New York: Palgrave Macmillan.
Morduch, J., & Sicular, T. (2000). Politics, growth, and inequality in rural China: Does it pay to join the party? *Journal of Public Economics, 77*, 331–356.
Nee, V. (1989). A theory of market transition: From redistribution to markets in state socialism. *American Sociological Review, 54*, 663–681.
Nee, V. (1991). Social inequality in reforming state socialism. *American Sociological Review, 56*, 267–282.
Nee, V. (1996). The emergence of a market society: Changing mechanisms of stratification in China. *American Journal of Sociology, 101*, 908–949.
North, D. C. (1981). *Structure and change in economic history*. New York: W.W. Norton.
Oi, J. C. (1989). *State and peasant in contemporary China: The political economy of village government*. Berkeley: University of California Press.
Oi, J. C. (1992). Fiscal reform and the economic foundations of local state corporatism in China. *World Politics, 45*, 99–126.
Oi, J. C. (1995). The role of the local state in China's transitional economy. *China Quarterly, 144*, 1132–1149.
Oi, J. C. (1999). *Rural China takes off: Institutional foundations of economic reform*. Berkeley: University of California Press.
Parish, W. L., & Michelson, E. (1996). Politics and markets: Dual transformations. *American Journal of Sociology, 101*, 1042–1059.
Parish, W. L., Zhe, X., & Li, F. (1995). Nonfarm work and marketization of the Chinese countryside. *The China Quarterly, 143*, 1–29.
Peng, Y. (1992). Wage determination in rural and urban China: A comparison of public and private industrial sectors. *American Sociological Review, 57*, 198–213.
Polanyi, K. (1957). *The great transformation*. Boston: Beacon Press.
Polanyi, K. (1965). The economy as instituted process. In K. Polanyi, C. M. Arensberg, and H. W. Pearson (Eds.), *Trade and market in the early empires: Economies in history and theory* (p. 248). New York: The Free Press.
Rona-Tas, A. (1994). The first shall be last? Entrepreneurship and communist cadres in the transition from socialism. *American Journal of Sociology, 100*, 40–69.
Shue, V. (1980). *Peasant China in Transition: The dynamics of development toward socialism, 1949–1956*. Berkeley: University of California Press.
Siomdzynski, K. M., & Shabad, G. (1997). Systemic Transformation and the Salience of Class Structure in East Central Europe. *East European Politics and Societies, 11*, 155.
Stark, D. (1992). Path dependence and privatization strategies in East Central Europe. *East European Politics and Societies, 6*, 17–54.
Stark, D. (1996). Recombinant property in East European capitalism. *American Journal of Sociology, 101*, 993–1027.
Szalai, E. (1989). The new elite. *Across Frontiers, 5*, 25–31.
Szelenyi, I. (2002). An outline of the social history of socialism or an auto-critique of an auto-critique. *Research in Social Stratification and Mobility, 19*, 41–67.

Szelenyi, I., & Kostello, E. (1996). The market transition debate: Toward a synthesis. *American Journal of Sociology, 101*, 1082–1096.
Unger, J. (1984). The class system in rural China: A case study. In J. L. Watson (Ed.), *Class & social stratification in post-revolution China* (pp. 121–41). Sydney: Cambridge University Press.
Walder, A. G. (1992). Property rights and stratification in socialist redistributive economies. *American Sociological Review, 57*, 524–539.
Walder, A. G. (2002a). Income determination and market opportunity in rural China, 1978–1996. *Journal of Comparative Economics, 30*, 354–375.
Walder, A. G. (2002b). Market and income inequality in rural China: Political advantage in an expanding economy. *American Sociological Review, 67*, 231–253.
Walder, A. G. (2003). Elite opportunity in transitional economics. *American Sociological Review, 68*, 899–916.
Wank, D. L. (1999). *Commodifying communism: Business, trust, and politics in a Chinese city*. New York: Cambridge University Press.
Whiting, S. H. (2001). *Power and wealth in Rural China: The political economy of institutional change*. New York: Cambridge University Press.
Whyte, M. K. (1985). The politics of life chances in the People's Republic of China. In S. Yu-ming (Ed.), *Power and policy in the PRC* (pp. 244–265). Boulder: Westview Press.
Xie, Y., & Hannum, E. (1996). Regional variation in earnings inequality in reform era urban China. *American Journal of Sociology, 101*, 950–992.
Yang, C. K. (1959). *A Chinese village in early communist transition*. Westport: Greenwood Press.
Zang, X. (2002). Labor market segmentation and income inequality in urban China. *Sociological Quarterly, 43*, 27.
Zhang, Letian. (1998). *Gao Bie Li Xiang: Ren Min Gong She Zhi Du Yan Jiu* [Good bye, Utopia: A study to The Institutions of People's Commune]. Shanghai: Dongfang chuban zhongxin (Dong Fang Press).
Zhao, W., & Zhou, X. (2002). Institutional transformation and results to education in urban China: An empirical assessment. *Research in Social Stratification and Mobility, 19*, 339–375.
Zhou, X. (2000). Economic transformation and income inequality in Urban China: Evidence from a panel data. *American Journal of Sociology, 105*, 1135–1174.

Chapter 2
Literature Review and the Framework of the Study

This chapter focuses on two issues: existing studies of social stratification of rural China and the framework of this study. A background of rural social stratification in Mao's China is first given. Then the recent related studies, according to market transition theory and new institutional analysis, are discussed. Based on the unanswered puzzles left by the existing studies, a research framework is proposed in which three directions are developed to contribute to the literature of comparative stratification studies of China.

2.1 Literature Review

2.1.1 Rural Social Stratification in Mao's China: A Background

It may be helpful to remind ourselves of what prevailed in traditional rural China (A.D. 221–1911). During that epoch, the economy of rural China was autarkic and agricultural. Rural people in traditional China could be divided into two status groups: at the bottom of the society were the numerous peasants and above them were the gentry, including both local gentry and officials, the local agents of the outside government (Chou 1966; Fei 1946; Michael 1955; Weber 1968; Xiao 1960; Zhang 1955).

After the Chinese Communist Party (henceforth CCP) came to power, Chinese rural society was greatly changed. A number of studies of rural politics show how the state destroyed the traditional rural society and rebuilt a new one which was controlled by the party state (Parish and Whyte 1978; Schurmann 1968; Yang 1959). As a result, the state-centered approach prevailed in social stratification studies of Mao's China—the state developed a work organization system to control

N. Chen, *State, Market and Life Chances in Contemporary Rural Chinese Society*, DOI 10.1007/978-3-662-45046-8_2

almost all resources and its distribution. In rural areas, advanced agricultural producers' cooperatives (communes, gong she) were created in 1958. Such a commune governed several brigades, each of which governed several production teams. There were three main features of the commune system: (1) the land in rural areas was claimed to be collectively owned. Every peasant household was distributed a small plot of land, called a "private plot (zi liu di)," which was the only land where private farming was permitted. (2) A household registration system (hu kou zhi du) was instituted in order to strictly control the people's mobility. Rural people could not leave the commune without permission and recommendation letters from the rural cadres of their brigade. (3) Production, exchange, and distribution were controlled by the commune, according to the orders or policies of government at higher levels. Other commercial activities, held at traditional markets, were also strictly controlled by the state and its agents (Hinton 1984; Shue 1980; Whyte 1985; Yang 1959; Zhang 1998).

Under the constraints of the commune system, resource distribution had three characteristics: firstly, distribution between the state and peasants was carried out according to the principal of "the state first, then collectivity, and then the individual (guojia xianxing, ranhou dao jiti, zuihou shi geren)." The members of the cooperatives shared 68.5 % of the total gross production, the remainder after deducting 6.5 % for taxes and 25.0 % for collective expenditures. The latter covered production costs, management expenses, and funds for capital accumulation and its member's welfare expenditures (Oi 1989, p. 17; Yang 1959, p. 225). Other than the tax—the direct extraction from agricultural production by the state—the state also extracted from rural society indirectly through methods such as grain purchase according to contract, compulsory planting of low-profit grains, and control of the grain market (Oi 1989; Shue 1980; Zhang 1998).

Secondly, intra-village distribution of grain involved two principles: the basic grain ration (jiben kouliang) and the work point grain allocation (gongfen kouliang). The former was allocated to all members of the collective organization, while the latter was given according to a bookkeeping system. A work point assessing meeting was held once per year, at which every laborer of the production team was given a basic number of work points through "open assessing (gongkai pingding)," according to his/her physical strength, skills, and work efficiency. The result of the calculation of basic points, time rates, and task rates were one's total work points (Parish and Whyte 1978, pp. 59–72; Shue 1980, pp. 163–171; Zhang 1998, p. 338).

Thirdly, with the work point system, intra-village resources distribution usually depended on three factors. First was the position of the individual in the rural production organization. On the one hand, rural cadres, including office holders of brigades, production team headmen, treasurers, and secretaries, etc., weren't on the state's payroll and officially were required to participate in collective labor. However, they had advantage of being able to profit from the activities of their production teams because they were the leaders of agriculture activities and had the right to distribute the resources and to offer good opportunities (Kraus 1981). Secondly, the quality and quantity of the labor of an individual was important. An educated laborer, or one with technological skills, would have his labor evaluated according to a higher work point standard and thus earn more work points (Zhang 1998).[1] A family with more adult laborers would obviously earn more work points. Thirdly, property-based class categories (shenfen tixi) came into play. The land reform[2] classified the rural populace into property-based class categories: landlords, rich peasants, upper-middle peasants, middle peasants, lower-middle peasants, and poor peasants. This classification distinguished those persons who should receive benefits from those who should lose them. Bad class elements, including landlords and rich peasants, were disadvantaged in a number of ways: it was more difficult for them to attain higher education and they lost chances in employment opportunities, and it was not easy for them to find spouses (Unger 1984).

However, most researchers point out that the function of the class stratification system was limited: for one thing, it played its main role mostly before 1956, during the socialist transformation (Kraus 1981; Unger 1984). Secondly, "bad class elements" were few, "only several people in one brigade (Zhang 1998, p. 149)." Finally, the class system was not strictly set. "The class line could be turned on or off, depending on the local needs of the good-class peasantry (Unger 1984, p. 133)."

A later generation of works on rural social stratification of Mao's China questioned the state's monopolistic effect on individual lives. They paid more attention to the interaction between rural cadres—the state's agents in local society—and ordinary people, focusing on patron-client relationships between the two. They still emphasized the function of political dynamics—assets allocated through the state's hierarchical system, but pointed out that peasants were active in pursuing their interests in many ways. In a study on the grain system during the period from 1955 to 1986, Oi argued that "clientelism" should be the key to understand rural politics, as this sketches the myriad ways in which nonelites try to affect the policy implementation process and to further their particular interests (Oi 1985, 1989). In the clientelist model, "power is routinely exercised through the allocation of opportunities, goods, and various other resources over with the elite have monopolistic control and on which the nonelite are dependent (Oi 1985, p. 240)."

To sum up, the studies of social stratification of Mao's rural China were based on two models—the state-centered model and the clientelist model—presented by two generations of scholars. The former emphasized the dominant influences of the state on peasants, while the latter highlighted the relationship between the state's local agents and the peasants. In their studies, social stratification of rural China in Mao's period can be summarized as involving the state and its agents—cadres controlled all resources and allocated them to peasants according to the work point system and to patron-client relationships.

[1] Nee (1989) assumes that the returns on human capital don't have obvious effects on the people's income. To review the historical facts of rural China in the Mao' period, one can see human capital playing an important role in deciding the people's income. Also see Zhou (2000a).

[2] The land reform was held in 1950, right after the CCP came to power. The main goal of this reform was to reallocate the land. Generally, it consisted of several stages: motivating the people, defining people's class categories, confiscating and reallocating the land, censoring, and summarizing (Lippit 1974).

2.1.2 The Market Transition Debate

The economic reform of China began in 1978. During the following 26 years (1978–2004), the communes gave way to the household production system. Agricultural output grew and rural industry went from almost nothing to becoming the fastest growing sector in the rural economy. The registration system which bound people to residence in cities or in the countryside has now broken down, allowing large numbers of migrant workers to seek higher-paying jobs in different parts of the country; and the frozen wages, work points, and rationing of food and other consumer goods have become things of the past. People's net income rose from less than 150 yuan in 1978 to 400 yuan in 1985 and had increased to approximately 2,000 yuan by 1997. This great transformation has attracted much attention of sociologists, especially comparative social stratification researchers, since it is a great chance to record how the changing structure have affected people's life chances.

One of the most striking questions is whether the advantages of cadres will decline, and the most important part of the related literature is that concerning the market transition debate—the debate on whether the agents of the state, who had held the redistributive power in the pre-reform period, would lose their economic and social privileges. Market transition theory originated in studies of Eastern Europe (Szelenyi 1978, 1982, 1983, 1986–1987), with researchers of social stratification of the states in Eastern Europe who believed that the redistribution economy of state socialism was the foundation of cadre advantages. Thus, the transition from a planned economy to a market economy led to a prediction of an erosion of the cadres' advantages and opportunities, so that the value of political capital would decline, while returns on human capital[3] increases. Based on these studies, Nee developed a market transition theory and applied it to the social stratification of China (Nee 1989). His study generated a lively exchange of opinions among scholars of Chinese social stratification.

The debate over Nee's approach can be largely framed as involving a binary set of opposing claims concerning the issue of whether the shift to market coordination in departures from central planning augments or diminishes the advantages of the political elite. To some, the market mechanism plays more and more important roles in resource distribution, so that the function of the redistribution mechanism according to fixed state determination of social categories will decline. As a direct consequence, the power of cadres will decrease (Nee 1989, 1991). With an analysis of data collected in 1985 in Fujian, a coastal province in Southeast China, Nee's "market transition theory," claims that the emergence of markets in the state socialist redistributive economy causes the most privileged stratum or class, according to state socialism, to lose some or all of their privileges (Nee 1989). Moreover, the

[3] In market transition theory, the human capital variable includes the pooled educational attainment of the household head and spouse, measured by whether someone attended or graduated from primary, junior middle, senior middle, or technical school or college.

transition of the redistributive mechanism from the state to the market will favor human capital over political capital and the direct producer over the redistributors. Based on multi-provincial data of 1989, Nee (1991) found that the income of cadre households was still higher than that of peasant households, but he denies that this is a contradiction to his theory. He explains that it is due to the partial character of the reform and argues that the cadre's privileges will be undermined as the reform progresses (Nee 1991).

On the other hand, some researchers have documented the persistence (Bian and Logan 1996) or conversion of the political elite's power and privilege (Lin 1995; Oi 1992, 1995; Walder 1995b). With a data set collected in Tianjin in 1988 and 1993, Bian and Logan (1996) show that the incomes of Communist Party members and those with high redistributive power have increased more than others. Even though they document a decline in income gaps between party members (especially redistributive power holder) and non-party members in the urban area of Tianjin, they argue that this is not due to market transition but to an egalitarian wage policy. Meanwhile, concerning the changes in the roles of rural cadres, Oi (1992) developed her "local state corporatism" model. In her model, China's fiscal reform granted local governments the right to retain part of the extra tax revenues which they raised. Local governments were therefore motivated to function like large corporations, with diversified businesses, mobilizing and coordinating resources under their jurisdictions to engage in entrepreneurial endeavors. Local state corporatism suggests a loosening of central control in a Leninist system and highlights the coexistence of a strong local officialdom and public enterprise with a thriving market economy and weakened central state. In his study on Daqiuzhuang Village, near Tianjin, Lin (1995) proposed a local market socialism model. In this model, "local" means having sociocultural roots in the locality, with networking as the social axis; "market" means the market mechanism as the economic axis; and "socialism" means the political-ideological experience of the recent past (i.e., socialism as the political axis). While the other studies all focus on the economic dynamics and stratification consequences, Lin's study emphasizes the sociocultural forces that allow the simultaneous and coordinated incorporation of market and collective mechanisms, in order to see how the embeddedness of these forces in the local networks leads to enduring institutions and to see how they function in the transformation (Lin 1995, p. 301).

2.1.3 New Institutional Analysis

After the market transition debate, an increasing number of studies find that market transition has led to various results because of various institutional backgrounds. As a result, beginning with the 1996 symposium of American Journal of Sociology (Henceforth AJS) concerning market transition theory, the binary debates on market transition theory have given way to the "new institutional analysis," which emphasizes that the underlying differences in the mechanism of stratification were caused by changes in the institutional framework that shaped the structure of incentives and opportunities, which hence constrain the choices within which political and economic actors strive to optimize power and resources (Cao and Nee 2000; Nee 1996, p. 919; Parish and Michelson 1996; Szelenyi and Kostello 1996; Walder 1996, 2003; Wu and Xie 2003; Xie and Hannum 1996; Zang 2002; Zhao and Zhou 2002; Zhou 2000a, b). Since then, many studies of the social stratification of China have focused on the effects of various institutions on people's life chances. In brief, these institutions are as follows.

1. **Property rights**

The argument of market transition theory logically leads to a comparison between the returns to people in different sectors with various institutional arrangements, of which property rights of specific economic sectors are the most important. Zang's (2002) comparison of the returns to people in the state sector and in the private sector shows a mixed finding: that political capital is not positively associated with the incomes of workers in the private sector, that human capital is rewarded more in private sector, that firm administrative rank has lost its impact in both collective and state sectors, and that party membership and cadre status retain their effects on the incomes of workers in state and collective sectors (Zang 2002). Zhou (2000a) analyzes the income diversity in various types of work organizations, including governmental agencies, nonprofit organizations in the public domain, central government-owned firms, local government-owned firms, collective firms, and private/hybrid firms. He shows that the relationship between institutional arrangements of work organizations and income distribution in urban China has not changed significantly.[4] However, other researchers find that the work unit rank will affect cadres' abilities to acquire assets (Walder 1992, 1995b). Zhao and Zhou (2002) observe a significant and substantial increase in returns according to education over time, especially in the non-state sector, while Bian and Zhang (2002) find that both the returns for positional power and political capital increase and that the returns to the workers in the state monopoly sector increase, while the workers in the open sector experience a significant relative decline in income.

All of these studies are about urban China. However, the studies of rural China show that property rights do not play significant roles in wage determination in rural industries. For example, Peng (1992) compares the wage determination process for employees in the rural public sector, rural private sector, and the urban state sector and finds that property right cannot explain the different wage determinations in rural areas. One study argues that the imperfect market environment of China makes for ambiguous property rights in the non-state sector, to which most of the rural enterprises—the Township and Village Enterprises (hereafter TVEs)—belong (Li 1996). Indirectly, this study shows that the property rights thesis isn't suitable for application to rural China.

[4] However, he observes the significant and positive effects for private/hybrid firms and also identifies that collective firms have not benefited from market activities.

2. **Regional variation**

Regional diversity is also taken into account to explain wage determination in reform China. The data of Nee (1989) is only from a survey research in the outskirt areas of Fujian Province. However, regional disparities have long existed in China and concern geographical conditions and policy results (Wei 2000). It is thereby necessary to test whether the market transition hypotheses can be applied in different regions. In one of his subsequent studies, Nee (1996) categorizes the provinces of China according to four types: coastal redistributive (Hebei and Shandong Provinces, and Shanghai), coastal corporatist (Jiangsu and Zhejiang Provinces), coastal laissez-faire (Fujian and Guangdong Provinces), and inland. The research results show that market transition theory is only partly supported by the situation of the coastal laissez-faire type, while the findings in other regions still reveal large net advantages for cadres. Xie and Hannum (1996) present regional variations in earning inequality of urban China in the reform era. Their conclusions contradicted market transition theory: economic growth depresses the returns for education and work experience, while the effects of party membership and gender are regionally invariant. They attributed these findings to the lack of a true labor market in urban China. Parish and Michelson (1996a) test parts of the Nee's analysis (1996) of the Chinese countryside, using the 1988 Chinese Household Income Project (CHIP) data set. Their comparative regional analysis focuses on the county level (Nee focuses on the provincial level) and shows that administrators'[5] income advantage had not disappeared by 1988, even in the higher marketized regions.

3. **Changing revenue sharing frameworks and the incentives of local leaderships**

These studies highlight the roles of local leadership in developing economies and resource distribution as a result of the changes in the revenue sharing frameworks by the state hierarchy, paying attention to tax system reform (Oi 1992, 1995, 1999; Wong 1992, 1988) and the cadre evaluation system (Whiting 2001). Some emphasize the effects of local governments at county or township levels, such as Oi's "local state corporatism" model (Oi 1992, 1999) and Walder's "local governments as industrial firms" thesis (Walder 1995b); some others describe the grassroots elite, such as the official village leaders (Lin 1995). Local leaders at various levels play active roles to boost the economic development and increase the bases for revenue sharing.

4. **The variation of industry structure**

Walder and Zhao (2003) argue that rural areas of China can be divided into three types of villages according to their industry structures: agrarian village, industrial village, and entrepreneur village. In agrarian villages, most of the rural people gain most of their income from agriculture, industrial villages are those in which rural

[5] Parish and Michelson replace the term "cadre" with "administrator," which points to "top leaders of townships and villages" (1996, p. 1050).

industrialization has advanced rapidly under public ownership, and entrepreneur villages are those villages in which rural people derive the highest percentage of their income from rapidly developing household enterprises. The average income of rural people drops as one moves from entrepreneur village to industrial village to agrarian village. Another related study, Zhao (2004), presents the effects of "the scale of firms that dominate the private sector" on rural inequality. He argues that transitional economies propelled by the massive entry of small enterprises allow for more equal access, while transitional economies driven by large corporate firms are more likely to favor political and educational elites.

5. **Regime change**

Walder (2003) denotes how the extensiveness of regime change in transforming states and constraints on asset appropriation affect elite opportunities. The extensiveness of regime change refers to the degree to which "Communist Party hierarchies lose their political monopoly and must compete with other organized entities for political power (Walder 2003, p. 901)." "Constraints on asset appropriation" refers to "policy and regulatory environment (the pace of privatization process) and concentration and form of assets (concentrated assets or dispersed assets; liquid assets or tangible assets)". With these two indicators, Walder (2003) divides transforming economies into four types. Rural China is typed as having "low rates of elite turnover. Cadres retain posts, use them to enhance incomes, for themselves and family members, but limits on privatization delays and restricts movement into a new propertied or corporate elite" (p. 907).

6. **Close access to market opportunities (business chances, FDI, etc.)**

Close access to market opportunities can be provided by various factors. Geographical proximity to urban markets provides a community with more chances to develop (Johnson 1994; Nee and Su 1990), as does the number of overseas Chinese of the community (Nee 1989) and the local transportation conditions (Nee and Su 1990).

2.2 Analytical Framework of the Thesis

2.2.1 Unsolved Puzzles and New Directions

From the above studies, we can see that the economic reform has brought diverse changes in Chinese social stratification. Current studies explain some of these, but more substantial empirical studies are needed to explain others. Following the new institutional perspective, this study will adopt three new directions to further the study of the social stratification of rural areas of reform China.

2.2.1.1 The Economic Reform as an Instituted Process of Market Penetration

One of the main theoretical problems of stratification studies in rural China is how we should understand the reform. Market transition theory understands it as a transition from redistributive economy to market economy. However, one of the critical shortages of this understanding comes from the term "market transition": what kinds of markets are referred to, and how do they undergo transition? According to market transition theory, the term "market transition" refers to the transition from a redistributive economy to a market economy. However, studies show that neither redistributive economies nor market economies are monolithic (Bryant and Mokrzycki 1994; Burawoy and Lukacs 1992; Kovacs 1994; Nee 1992; Shirk 1993; Stark 1990, 1992, 1996; Walder 1995a). Polanyi, the creator of these two ideal types, has no analysis of transition from one type to the other. This is why new institutional analyses criticizes that market transition theory lacks the institutional specificity to describe the market reform as a transition from a redistributive economy to a market economy (Walder 1996, p. 1062). Studies according to the new institutional approach go further to denote the effects of various institutions on life chances. But in these studies, institutions play their roles separately. For example, the effects of local leadership on local economic development may be varied depending on whether the community under their governance has close access to market opportunities.

Therefore, the real problem is how these institutions integrate, change, or are "instituted" to form an empirical economy in which people's life chances are embedded. Actually, Polanyi used the terms "reciprocity," "redistribution," and "exchange" not only to denote the mode of economic allocation, which has been emphasized by Nee (1989), but also to refer to "forms of integration," of how empirical economies are actually instituted. He writes:

> A study of how empirical economies are instituted should start from the way in which the economy acquires unity and stability, that is the interdependence and recurrence of its parts. This is achieved through a combination of a very few patterns which may be called forms of integration. Since they occur side by side on different levels and in different sectors of the economy it may often be impossible to select one of them as dominant so that they could be employed for a classification of empirical economies as a whole. Yet by differentiating between sectors and levels of the economy those forms offer a means of describing the economic process in comparatively simple terms, thereby introducing a measure of order into its endless variations. (1965, p. 250)

Because we have no much insight about how these institutions are integrated to form an empirical economy, we are still always debating whether institution A is more or less important than institution B or finding that emphasizing institution A means the neglect of institution B. This study, however, puts this "instituted process" of economy at center stage. As Polanyi has pointed out:

> The economy, then, is an instituted process…process suggests analysis in terms of motion. The movements refer either to changes in location, or in appropriation, or both. In other words, the material elements may alter their position either by changing place or by

> changing "hands"; again, these otherwise very different shifts of position may go together or not. Between them, these two kinds of movements may be said to exhaust the possibilities comprised in the economic process as a natural and social phenomenon...location movements include production, alongside of transportation, to which the spatial shifting of objects is equally essential...the appropriative movement governs both what is usually referred to as the circulation of goods and their administration. (1965, p. 248)

Following Polanyi's analysis, in this study I understand the transition from Mao's China to today's reform China as "an instituted process of market penetration." The term "market penetration" has been used by Szelenyi and Kostello (1996). In their study, three indicators are developed to refer to the institutional aspects of market penetration: commodity market, labor market, and capital market. In their study, the commodity market is measured according to the formula that "the greater the proportion of deregulated prices (prices determined by the mechanisms of supply and demand), the more highly developed commodity markets are" and the labor market according to the formula that "the more the price of labor is determined by supply and demand, the more developed the labor market is"; while capital market refers to "the allocation of capital goods." These three indicators have been revisited and used in some quantitative studies (Bian and Zhang 2002; Shu and Bian 2002).[6] This study integrates the factual situation in rural areas of China, suggesting that the four indicators present the degree of market penetration:

Commodity market. Two indicators are integrated to measure the development of the commodity market. First is the number of private and collective firms in the township: the higher the number, the greater the extent of the commodity market. Second is the development of commercial agriculture—the percentage of commercial agriculture output out of the total agriculture output.

Capital market is measured by the amount of capital invested in the township areas.

Labor market is measured by the number of nonfarm workers in the township areas.

Economic development refers to average township income.

Both statistical data and ethnographic data are taken into consideration in this study to give a qualitative illustration.

By "market penetration as an instituted process," this study presents how the changes occur and endure, with attention paid to two points.

First, market penetration is a location movement of material elements, which usually include capital, commodities, and labor. Market reform usually begins with a petty commodity market, which benefits most people in most places. Then the

[6] Shu and Bian (2002) define commodity market as "the percentage of industrial output by nonstate enterprises out of the total industrial output; labor market is measured by the percentage of employees in non-state firms out of the total number of workers; and capital market is measured by the percentage of foreign investment out of the total investment in the city." In Nee's study (1996), he uses "production market"—the number of private and collective firms in the township—to replace "commodity market." Labor market measures the extent of the market for nonfarm labor by reference to the proportion of the village population engaged in nonfarm work outside the village ... the higher the proportion of off-village nonfarm workers, the greater the extent of the local labor market.

capital market begins to play a key role in determining how far the commodity market can go. Capital can be raised by local[7] or foreign investors.[8] The integrating development of capital market and commodity market attracts large amounts of labor and ultimately accelerates economic development. Market penetration in different places varies during this phase. We can observe this process during the two decades of China's reform: from 1978, the cancellation of collective agriculture and the enforcement of household production benefited rural people as a whole. Then, the coastal areas, especially Guangdong Province, attracted large amounts of capital, both from local and foreign investors, because the gradual reform policy of the CCP gave chances to coastal areas, especially the southeast provinces, and especially Guangdong, to go "one step ahead."[9] The integrated thriving of the commodity market, capital market, and labor market began from coastal cities in Guangdong Province and expanded to the whole coastal area and finally was expected to expand to the whole country. The situation within Guangdong Province is similar to this expected expansion: one can observe a development process from coast to inland within the province. Market reform began with the petty commodity market, stimulated by the decentralization of collective agriculture and the reestablishing of household production. Then the capital market became the driving force to further develop the commodity market; and this contributed to the development of the labor market. Market penetration began in Pearl River Delta Region and then expanded to the inland mountain areas. In Chap. 3, I will offer a comprehensive view of this process.

Second, the location movement of material elements leads to an appropriative movement of material elements from rural cadres to peasants and from the rural population in coastal areas to the rural population inland. At the beginning of market reform, no matter whether cadre or peasant, no matter whether rural in coastal areas or inland, all mainly gain their earnings from crops or agricultural sidelines (there are differences, but they are not obvious). During this phase of the process of market penetration, rural people's opportunities to gain access to material elements become diverse. (1) Rural cadres in coastal areas share the collective benefits from the higher level of market penetration; they also obtain the chances to develop their own family businesses. (2) Peasants in coastal areas can enjoy more chances and better qualities of individual family business; they can also share collective revenue brought about by market penetration in local areas, etc. (3) Local governments in inland areas may lack resources to run the normal administration and are trapped in large amounts of collective debt; they may become predators on rural society by collecting all kinds of fees and penalties from rural peasants in order to help their

---

[7] For example, in Wenzhou city of Zhejiang Province, there are some traditional but effective channels for raising fund for business.

[8] In most developed areas of China, foreign direct investments are main driving forces of economic development.

[9] Guangdong was taken as the first experimental province for the reform because it is near Hong Kong and Macau and the number of state-owned enterprises was small. I will discuss this in detail in the next chapter.

relatives to monopolize some business and to pocket the collective money. (4) Peasants in inland areas face worsening opportunities: the profits from crops and agricultural sidelines become relatively less, and they migrate to coastal areas for wage work and business chances. I will develop these points in the coming chapters.

2.2.1.2 From "Income" to "Life Chances"

Let's try to understand the social stratification of rural China by "who gets what and why" (Lenski 1966). From the findings of previous studies, we know "who" very well: in rural China, the social actors can be grossly divided into "cadres" and "peasants," while the latter can be further divided into "entrepreneurs"[10] and "ordinary peasants." We also know something about "why"—the distribution mechanism from plan to market, even though we may disagree about its effects in various sectors.

However, we still know little about "what." A summary of the empirical survey studies relevant to market transition theory shows that there are nine studies (Keister and Nee 2001; Matthews and Nee 2000; Nee 1989, 1991, 1996; Parish and Michelson 1996; Parish et al. 1995; Peng 1992) focusing on rural areas or on the whole nation of China among a total of 19 studies. However, only "income" and "employment chances of family member" were taken into consideration in these studies (Nee and Cao 2002). Substantive studies of rural China easily demonstrate that the two variables of "income" and "employment chances of family member" not at all cover the facts.

Nee (1996) states that his variable—"income"—includes most profits of rural people and is unlikely to be systematically underreported.[11] However, studies of "income" only focus on what peasants have got, but systematically neglect what peasants have lost. More and more studies in economics and political science show that the life chances of peasants in the post socialist state not only depend on their incomes but also on the relief or aggravation of the "burden" due to the variation of the behavior of local governments, especially township governments and village administrations (Aubert and Li 2002; Lu 1997). Unfortunately, this point hasn't been taken into the new institutional analysis of social stratification of China.

Second, the variable "employment chances of family member" comes from an assumption that rural industry gives cadres advantages for finding jobs for their family members, relatives, and friends. However, rural industry brings cadres many advantages, including profit sharing, easy access to public facilities, power to distribute collective profits, and so on. "Employment chances" undervalues the advantages of rural cadres.

---

[10] Of course, cadres too can become entrepreneurs.

[11] Nee says that his variable "income" includes sale of agricultural products, the cost of food produced by the household, and the contribution of nonagricultural income—private business, cadre salary, factory jobs, service, sidelines, and an unspecified "other" category.

In order to clearly present the "get and lose" of the Chinese rural people, in this study, I use "life chances" to replace "income," the three unique characteristics of which are presented below.

Variations of "The Sources of Earnings"

Market reform creates many new sources of earnings. However, the accesses to these earning sources are not monolithic. In order to understand the question of "who gets and who loses" in the reform period in rural China, we should first illustrate what kinds of earning sources have been created by market. Then we should explain various social actors' opportunities and access patterns to these earning sources. Since market reform began in 1978, the sources of earnings in rural China vary as follows:

Crops
At the beginning of the market reform, the elimination of collective agriculture largely gave peasants incentives to improve their crop production. This happened all over rural China and benefited most of the rural population during the first period of the reform.

Agriculture Sidelines
The plenty of crops and the thriving of rural markets in local areas created chances for sidelines. These sidelines include animal husbandry, fish ponds, vegetable planting, fruit tree planting, etc. At first, the products from agricultural sidelines mainly met the need of local markets. This happened in almost all of rural China and benefited most of the rural people. However, the commercialization and specialization of these sidelines depend on whether the products can be sold to regional markets or even to the world market.

Individual Family Business
Various individual family business activities emerged in rural Guangdong, which included piecework at home; working at short-term jobs as independent construction workers (glazers, plumbers) or as individual repairmen (bicycles, home appliances, tractors); buying tractors for hauling goods; operating buses to haul passengers; and running retail shops, restaurants, guest houses, wholesale businesses, or little manufacturing establishments. The higher the market penetration level, the better the chances for individual family business.

Migrant Wage Work
Migrant wage work becomes a more and more important earning source for rural labor in undeveloped areas when dramatic market penetration in some developed areas provides many chances for wage work. Obviously, migrant wage work is more important for rural people in the areas with lower levels of market penetration, since going outside for higher-paid jobs became a better choice than staying home as peasants.

Migrant Businesses
As for migrant wage work, big cities and rural industrialization in some regions create business chances for people to migrate from less developed regions. These people float to big cities or rural areas of developed regions. Their jobs are various and I will discuss them in Chap. 3.

Rural Industry
Although there are some studies on the booming rural industry of China (Wong 1982, 1988), its effects on life chances of rural people haven't been discussed deeply. Some studies assume that rural industry will bring people employment opportunities (Nee 1996; Nee and Cao 1999, 2002). However, this assumption is far away from the facts of rural Guangdong. Actually, few people will work in TVEs in local areas, even though a limited number of local people will take managerial positions. Instead, rural industry affects rural people's life chances in the following ways: (1) The success of TVEs brings forward collective revenue sharing. (2) The development of rural industry increases the chances for individual family businesses such as house leasing, store operation, and transportation.

In Chap. 3, I will give an overview of the historical and spatial changes of the above earning sources in Guangdong Province. In Chaps. 4, 5, and 6, I will discuss how these various earning sources benefit rural cadres and peasants of different types and at different stages of market penetration.

Explaining the Burden on Peasants

As mentioned above, one of the limitations of survey studies of "income" is that they only focus on what peasants get and neglect what peasants lose. In fact, from the mid-1980s, the problem of the "peasants' burden" has attracted much attention of China specialists, students of comparative politics (Bernstein and Lu 2000; Lu 1997), and even economist (Aubert and Li 2002). However, this hasn't been taken into consideration in social stratification studies. In this study, "the burden on peasants" refers to the fact that, in some places, peasants have to hand over all kinds of taxes, fees, surcharges, and penalties, etc., which are demanded by local governments legally or illegally. The peasants' burden can be divided into three parts:

State Taxes
The state taxes on peasants include three kinds. The first is the *agriculture tax*. Most of the time, agricultural tax has been in kind,[12] by which the state has wanted to ensure food provisions. Agricultural taxes in kind include the following: (1) ordained grain (Zhengliang)—every peasant household has had to hand in part of the yield of its farmland, according to rations set by contract; (2) unified purchase grain (Gouliang)—peasant households have been obliged to sell a certain amount

[12] The agricultural tax was imposed in kind during Mao's period, when the Chinese government implemented a policy of taking grain as a core task (yi liang wei gang) and the agricultural tax was calculated on the basis of grain. In the 1980s and 1990s, peasants began to pay their agricultural tax in cash.

of their crops to the state at fixed prices below production costs; (3) and "purchasing grain above the unified purchase (chaogou liang)"—peasants have been encouraged to sell their grain to the state, even after they have finished the quota of ordained grain and unified purchase grain. The second category of state taxes is the *special agricultural product tax*. This tax is on the agricultural sidelines of peasant households, such as forest products, fruit tree planting, animal husbandry, fish ponds, etc. The third one is the *slaughter tax*—every household who sells its animals for profit has had to submit some revenue to the state. Other state taxes include farmland utilization taxes and various rural business taxes. The abovementioned taxes are all legal.

Local Charges
Local governments (generally township governments) also have the right to tax peasant households. Local charges include (1) *the five township-pooling fees* (Wu Tongchou)—fees for educational subsidy, social help, family planning, road construction, and militia exercises. The five township-pooling fees are used by township governments. Another is (2) *the three village-retained funds* (san tiliu), which include the public accumulation fund, retained to meet the demands of collective production, including sustaining farmland and irrigation works, tree planting, purchasing fixed production assets, and launching collective enterprises; the public welfare fund, retained for investment in social welfare; and administrative funds, retained for salaries of village cadres and administrative costs. The five township-pooling fees and three village-retained funds are also legal.

Other Surcharges
Besides the above two categories, there are other categories of local charges, which include all kinds of administration fees, penalties, local fundraising (jizi) efforts, and the forced apportionment of funds (luan tanpai) in rural China. While the above two categories are legal, these surcharges are always located in the "gray zone" between legal and illegal. These are the main parts of the burden on peasants. There are no strict rules or laws for standardizing these charges. Mostly, the importance of these surcharges depends on the demands of local governments, especially township governments.

These three kinds of taxes and charges became the major burden on peasants. A study of this issue shows that "the first tax is easy, the second tax is heavy, the third tax presses me to death (toushui qing, er shui zhong, san shui ya si ren)." In Chap. 4, this study will document the emergence of the burden on peasants in the late 1980s, its exacerbation in the 1990s, and its cancellation in 2004. The situation of the burden on peasants also varies by townships: in Chaps. 4, 5, and 6, I will illustrate how it has varied according to the various situations of market penetration.

Redefining Rural Cadres' Advantages

Another limitation of market transition theory is that it considers that rural cadres' advantages rely on public assets: the decrease in public assets means the decrease of cadres' advantages. However, as Parish and Mechelson point out, "governments' administrators are not disappearing with marketization but growing with various number and diversity of functions (Parish and Michelson 1996a, p. 1047)." Some recent studies go further and present various forms of rural cadres' advantages: high salaries and bonuses for cadre positions as the managers of collective industry (Oi 1992, 1999; Walder 1995b; Whiting 2001); obtaining salaried positions and managerial posts for family members, relatives, and friends (Parish and Michelson 1996; Parish et al. 1995); developing lucrative alliances with private entrepreneurs that they favor in regulatory and tax matters (Chen 1999; Wank 1999); and even starting their own family businesses (Lin and Chen 1999) using their positional advantages.

In line with the above studies, I try to present how the advantages of village cadres change, accompanying the market penetration process.

Management Advantages

In the context of rural China, rural cadres are always the managers of collective assets. The cancellation of collective farming doesn't mean the vanishing of the collective assets. On the contrary, more or less, a village still owns some collective assets, of which the value can range from several thousands yuan to one billion.[13] As with management positions in companies or governmental agencies, one can imagine that the management of collective assets will bring some benefits for the cadres, which also vary with the amount of the collective assets. Most of the advantages documented in the aforementioned studies belong to this category.

Benefits from Policy Implementation

The implementation of government policies can sometimes become the sources of benefits for rural cadres. The policies for rural society have to be implemented by rural cadres. In order to make sure that the policies are implemented effectively, the higher government levels tend to provide material incentives to rural cadres. However, it is difficult for these higher levels to directly provide rural cadres with enough material incentives, since the number would be titanic. An eclectic solution is to allow the implementers to collect penalties from the violators of the policies. In some places, this kind of authorization sometimes becomes a source of cadres' earnings. To take the family planning system as an example, the violators of the policy will be charged heavily. These kinds of fines sometimes become the main source of administration expenditure in some poor townships. In Chap. 6, ethnographic data from a township of rural Guangdong will provide a detailed description of how this occurs.

Collection of Fees and Penalties

In addition to collecting penalties from policy offenders, which can be considered to be legal, there are also possibilities for cadres to collect fees or penalties with all kinds of other excuses.

[13] The gross production value of some of the richest villages in the east and south coastal areas can reach one billion, while collective assets of some villages in the poorest western areas may be little. For example, the gross production value of Nanjie Village in Shenzhen City was beyond one billion.

To enumerate, the above advantages to rural cadres doesn't mean that all rural cadres will bring them into effect. What I want to point out is that cadres are active in using all kinds of ways to pursue revenue. In Chaps. 4, 5, and 6, with evidence from the comparative cases, this study will show how rural cadres flexibly use their jurisdictions to attain revenue and social support, according to their needs and the situation of market penetration and the revenue-sharing framework.

2.2.1.3 The State-Market Interactive View

The roles of the state and market in resource distribution have been discussed extensively by social scientists (Djilas 1957; Polanyi 1957; Szelenyi 1978). However, in market transition theory, the state and market are antithetical—the rise of one implies the decline of the other (Zhou 2000b). Many researchers criticize that the antithetical state-market view is untenable: from a comparative perspective, studies of other countries show that states and markets are not simply opposed forms of social organization, but are bounded by complex ties. For example, a study on African agricultural policy shows how the marketplace is an instrument of political control: government intervention in the market generates political resources, and these resources are then distributed to build organized support (Bates 1981). Moreover, a series of studies on various countries, including capitalist democracies and Latin Americans and African states, show that the market and the state are interactive in three aspects: (1) the behavior of large firms is the result of internal political processes, (2) the competitive fortunes of firms is based on the extent to which firms bargain and struggle politically instead of merely competing on price and equality, and (3) a "market" is populated by networks of actors, including nominally "state" and nominally "market" institutions (Cawson et al. 1990; Moran and Wright 1991).

The "state-market antithetic view" was also criticized broadly by subsequent researchers of the social stratification of China. Parish and Michelson (1996) suggest three political markets: first, "one type that must be included involves formal and informal bargaining between workers and managers and between managers and the state bureaucracy"; second, the political market between state bureaucracies and state enterprises; and third, the one concerning electoral politics. Lin (2001) argues that the competitive advantages of firms have been formed in two emergent markets, the economic market and the political market. The economic market involves the exchange of goods, services, and factors (capital, labor, and land) among economic actors, whereas the political market includes the exchange of state-controlled resources, opportunities, and exemptions from societal-shared liabilities. Zhou (2000a) proposes a market-politics coevolution model: the market mechanism is treated as just one of the competing processes in institutional changes, while the state actively plays its roles, but not just as a passive recipient. Bian and Zhang (2002) emphasize two points of a state-market interaction view: first, marketization is a multifaceted, historical process; second, the transformation of the Communist Party state occurs because it wants to protect its interest and retain its influence.

Wu and Xie (2003) analyze how the process of sorting workers into labor markets shapes the labor market income and offer a picture of how redistribution and market mechanisms are interactive at the individual level.

Even though all these authors propose a "market-state interactive" view, there are still two things which need to be improved. First, almost all of the above studies' data is from urban China. The "state-market interactive view" hasn't been applied to the study of rural social stratification. My study contributes to the literature by giving an analysis of rural areas of Guangdong Province. Second, the aforementioned studies do not illustrate with empirical data how the state and market interact. The state-market interaction is the precondition but not the subject of the above studies. This means that there is a gap between the macro variable—the state and market—and the micro variable: how people "get" and "lose." As Cao and Nee put it,

> Consequently, we are still left wondering in what sense state policies (or market arrangements) should be understood as the results of the interaction between the state and markets. To the extent Zhou's "coevolution of politics and markets" remains a black box, model indeterminacy cannot be reduced. (Cao and Nee 2000, p. 1182)

This study aims to discover this "black box"—how the state and market interact and affect people's life chances in rural areas. The interaction of state and market is usually caught in a classic chicken-and-egg situation.[14] This study will not try to tell which one is the starting point for analysis. Instead, I argue that the state and market interact with each other and affect the life chances of rural people of China through two mechanisms: on the one hand, the opening and thriving of the market are the foundations of the revenues of the state. As a result, the state tends to protect the operation of the market. On the other hand, market liberation puts people out of the state's control; economically and ideologically, it harms the political support for the state. As a response, the state tends to provide more collective goods to remedy this harm.

The state per se and its agents can be understood as rational actors (Bates 1981; Bates 1988; Evans et al. 1985; Levi 1988a).[15] There are two objects of the state: to

---

[14] As North (North 1979, pp. 249–259.) has said, "the creation of a state is an essential precondition for economic growth (p. 249)"; but also as Marx has said, the economic surplus created classes and then led to the emergence of the state.

[15] The state has been described as a rational actor with its political and economic goals since the state-centered approach was brought up again in the 1980s. There are two groups of state-centered approaches. One is labeled by the famous book title: "bringing the state back in" (Evans et al.1985). Scokpol and her associates insist that state is not neutral—not a passive recipient of demands from the environment—but an actor who has its self-interests and considerable autonomy which is constrained in class-divided socioeconomic structures and an international system of states. With autonomy and capacity, the state can change rules in its own favor and promote policies to strengthen its support, mediating between various interests in society and intervening in economic and social policies. The other group is that of the rationalist state theorists, who argue that the state per se is not the actor but that the actors are the agents who compose the state and the social, political, and economic groups who make demands on the state. As a result, Margaret Levi labeled the impulse behind this approach as "bringing people back into the state" (Levi 1988b). After deducing a plausible set of goals for state actors, rationalist state theorists then focus on the rules and

extract enough revenue and to gain political support.[16] This is true in China: the objects of central government of China are to promote economic development and to maintain social stability (Cao and Dickson 2001; Shirk 1989, 1993; Whiting 2001; Yang 2001). These two objects are also two core evaluation standards for local cadres. The objects are presented in the state's policies as "economic civilization and spiritual civilization, both should be grasped strongly (jingji wenming he jingshen wenming, liang shou dou yao ying)"[17] and "economic development and social stability (jingji fazhan, shehui wending)." In a stable capitalist society, these two objects are maintained by the liberal market and political democracy. However, these two objects are contradictory in China: on the one hand, in Mao's China, in order to preserve power and gain political support, the state tended to control the market and society and distribute resources according to the state hierarchy. The negative effect was that the controlling lead to economic stagnation and in turn decreases the state's revenues. On the other hand, in the reform period, in order to eliminate stagnation and achieve enough revenues, the state loosened its control of the market. However, the liberal market in turn stimulated people to be out of the state's control, economically and ideologically, and this could then harm the political support for the state. This discrepancy between economic liberalization and continued political authoritarianism became the main conflict of the entire post-Mao era. Deng's "four cardinal principles,"[18] in 1979, Jiang Zemin's slogan of the "three representatives,"[19] and in Hu Jintao's advocacy of a "harmonious society"[20] all show that the state's first concern is how to keep the CCP's political support after two decades of reform. The state cannot adopt the centralization policy again since it proved to be a failure in Mao's period. The available way is to provide more collective goods to "buy peace." The penetration of the market in the country makes this possible. This is true enough, both at the central level and the local level. At the central level, three factors contribute to the central state's ability to "buy peace," especially from peasants. First, the continuous market penetration greatly increases the revenue base of the central government. Second, the tax reform issued in 1994 also increases the proportion of the state's revenue sharing. Third, the transforming

arrangements that constitute the state and on the relative bargaining power and influence of non-state actors. This perspective builds on the micro-foundation of constrained rational actors, who face collective action problems and opportunity costs, have only relative bargaining power, and must consider the transaction costs of the policies.

[16] This statement is obviously derived from Weber's classic formulation. But I don't use the term "legitimacy" here, because the "term" is relative to too much theoretical debate and lack of a consensual meaning. Also see Levi 1988a.

[17] This slogan was raised by Deng Xiaoping.

[18] Deng Xiaoping's "four cardinal principals" points to adhering to the socialist road, adhering to the people's democratic governance, adhering to the leadership of the Communist Party, and adhering to Marxism, Leninism, and Maozedong thought.

[19] The "three representatives" was proposed by Jiang Zhemin, the former general secretary of the CCP. It declared that the CCP should always be the representative of Chinese advanced social production, advanced culture, and the interests of most of the population

[20] The slogan "harmonious society" was proposed by President Hu Jintao in 2005.

industry structure decreases the proportion of agriculture in the national economy. As a result, while the peasantry was considered to be the most deprived group in the reform era, a series of policies have been adopted by the central state to relieve "the burdens on peasants." These policies include "direct village elections," "fee-to-tax reform," "opening village affairs," and so on. In Chap. 3, I will give a detailed description of them. More or less, these policies make good the relief of the burden on peasants.

The situation at the local level varies according to the extent of market penetration. In rural areas with a good degree of market penetration, the township governments and village administrations can gain much revenue from the thriving markets and urban areas. Political support is more desirable to local governments than the economic surplus from the peasant. As a result, local governments intend to provide more welfare and subsidies and to implement policies in soft ways, thereby benefiting the life chances of the peasants. On the contrary, for the cash-starved local governments in the rural areas with low levels of market penetration, rural society is their sole source of revenue.

2.3 Methodologies and the Field Site

2.3.1 The Character of the Research Methodology

This study takes Guangdong Province as the field site for the following reasons: (1) Guangdong Province is one of the first reform provinces of China. In the past 20 years, Guangdong Province has become the most successful economic entity in the country. (2) The diverse institutional backgrounds (economical and geographical, etc.) in the province allow an examination of various results of the reform, and this is similar to the situation of the whole country. First, taking geography as an example, Guangdong grossly consists of two geographic areas: the developed coastal areas and the less developed mountain areas, which are similar to the overall nation's coastal areas and inland areas. Second, the economy of Guangdong is a typical export-processing economy, which has been copied by many other provinces. As a result, the study on Guangdong should help us to anticipate the future of some other provinces of China. Of course, this study doesn't claim to use Guangdong Province as a representative of the whole of China.

The methodology is primarily ethnographic and rooted in comparative locales. Ethnography has been proved to be a better method for giving researchers more insight into how processes happen, endure, and change. I prefer ethnography here because this study claims to present the process of market penetration and its effects on rural social stratification. In many recent related studies, the data is from several national survey studies.[21] While these survey studies provide more valuable tests for

---

[21] Most used survey data sets include the 1988 Chinese Household Income Project (CHIP), the 1996 life histories and social changes project of UCLA, and so on.

the hypotheses raised by the market transition debate and the new institutional analysis, they, at the same time, do not produce knowledge of the various ongoing changes in China. Moreover, some quantitative studies of Chinese social stratification have expected that more ethnographic studies can answer the puzzles which are raised by them. As Parish and Micheson have said, "other studies could use more ethnographic methods to access the means by which villagers may still be tied to local administrators, and so on…Governments administrators are not disappearing with marketization but growing number and diversity of functions. The issue for ethnographic research would be to see how often villagers must interact with this increasing diversity of regional bureaucrats" (Parish and Michelson 1996, pp. 1046–47).

The ethnographic research for this study was conduced in three locales of Guangdong Province: Chan Township, Lee Township, and Fan Township. Their locations in the administrative hierarchy are shown in Fig. 2.1, and their geographic locations are shown in Map 2.1. Since the goal of this study is to explore how market penetration affects life chances, these three townships have been selected as representative of three types and stages of economies with various levels of market penetration. The strategy of the case selection is what Glaser and Strauss (Glaser and Strauss 1967) call "theoretical sampling."

This study takes the township as a better analytical level than the region (Nee 1996), city (Xie and Hannum 1996), county (Parish and Michelson 1996), or village (Lin 1995), for rural areas, because the social actors of a township consist of township cadres—the local agents of the state—as well as village cadres and peasants. These three groups of actors can interact face to face. Their interaction is the core feature of the politics of rural China. The analyses of the county and higher levels can only focus on policies and cadres' actions, in which peasants are often absent. In the analysis only base on a single village, the agencies of the state are often absent. The small sample of townships investigated in this study is not intended to

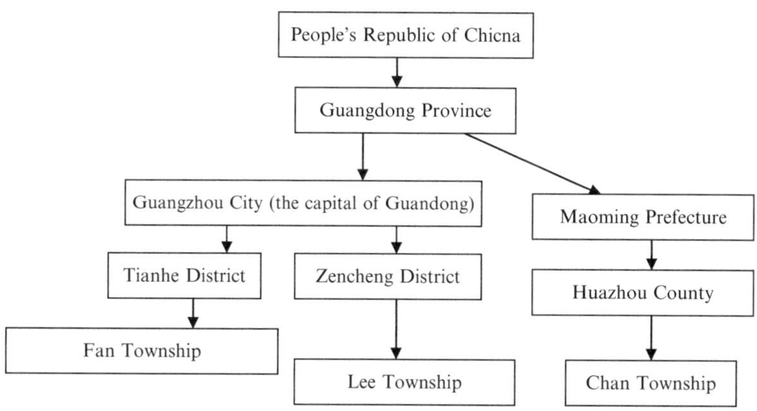

Fig. 2.1 Administrative hierarchy governing townships of the research sites (*Notes:* Guangzhou is the capital city of the province. As a result, its position is administratively higher than that of prefectures)

Map 2.1 Guangdong's location in China

be representative of rural China as a whole. Rather, this study wants to present a tendency of change through various modes of redistribution arrangements and structures of life chances.

The core data has been collected by in-depth interviews, life histories and documentary analyses, socializing and conversations, and nonparticipatory observation. The data collection strategy follows what Clifford Geertz has pointed out as "descriptions, measures, observations, what you will, which are at once diverse, even rather miscellaneous, both as to type and degree of precision and generality, unstandardised facts, opportunistically collected and for the simple reasons that the individuals they are descriptions, measures or observations of are directly involved in one another's lives (Geertz 1983, p. 156)." The content of the data basically includes stories of how peasants make a living in local areas and outside areas; all kinds of income, and payment by peasants and rural cadres; the activities of a normal day of peasants and rural cadres; the setting of houses, transportation vehicles, and other facilities; all kinds of assets through redistributive channels, including money, opportunities, and public services, etc.; the township cadres' attitudes, policies, and actions concerning villages' affairs; and the backgrounds of the townships, including the historical and physical conditions.

I entered the townships in an official way, having been introduced by the prefectural governments. I act as an official assistant in internship—a position often taken by some students who will graduate from university and are looking for a chance to get a job. I also told my informants that my purpose was to collect data for my PhD dissertation. This role made my study go smoothly. In Fan Township and Lee Township, I lived in the township street and went to villages every day. In Chan Township, I lived in peasant's house. These ways provided me with close contact with the informants and more chances to collect "thick data."

Further insights have been gained by documentary research. This includes the chorography (difang zhi)[22] of Guangdong Province and the cities, which govern the three selected townships. It also includes related policy documents, such as grain policies, tax policies, and others. Moreover, I collected annual reports of the local governments, some facilitated documents for policy implementation of rural cadres, agendas, announcements and minutes of meetings, and other written reports of events. Most of the rural studies in Chinese that have been published in academic journals of China have been examined thoroughly.

2.3.2 The Field Sites

Guangdong Province is located in southern China and borders the South China Sea (see Map 2.1). It has an area of 177,901 km^2, presenting merely 1.85 % of China's total areas. The terrain of Guangdong is primarily rolling hills; the vast delta of the Pearl River (Zhu Jiang) is Guangdong's only important lowland. On coastal islands and adjacent mainland territories are Hong Kong and Macao. The population of

[22] Chorography is the study that relates landscape, geography, antiquarianism, and history, showing how forces of the past are reflected on present landscape. In China, governments, ranging from provincial governments to county governments, write chorographies every year, beginning more than one thousand years ago. These data become the most important materials for the studies of China history. For example, a digitized chorography collection databank in Taiwan claims to own chorography materials consisting of 10,000 books, 3,000,000,000 characters, 20,000,000 pages, for the Sung, Yuan, Ming, and Ching Dynasties, covering 2000 counties and cities of the Mainland, Taiwan, Hong Kong, and Macao.

Guangdong reaches 70 million in 2000. In the province's subtropical humid climate, two crops of rice a year are raised.

Guangdong came under Chinese suzerainty during the unification under the Ch'in dynasty (c.211 BC). Located in southeast costal area, Guangzhou, the largest city of Guangdong Province, was the most important port for China to contact the outside world. In modern China, Guangdong has been a center of revolutionary activity, where the Kuomintang was formed (1912) under the leadership of Sun Yat-sen and where Chiang Kai-shek began his drive (1920s) for the unification of the country. In Mao's period, Guangdong wasn't treated as an important province since it is far away from Beijing, and the growth rates of the province's major economic indicators were slightly below the national averages. In 1978, however, Guangdong was selected as the experimental area for the reform policies. In the subsequent 20 years, this province became one of the most striking economic entities in the world: between 1978 and 1998, Guangdong's gross domestic product rose from 18.585 billion yuan to 791.912 billion yuan, showing an average annual real growth rate of 14 %. In the same period, Guangdong's per capita gross domestic product grew from 369 to 11,143 yuan, indicating an average annual real growth rate of 12 %.[23]

However, this economic miracle is not equally distributed in the province. The PRD region, which contains the capital city, Guangzhou, and the two special economic zones[24] of Shenzhen and Zhuhai became the most developed areas of the province. The mountain areas of the province, occupying almost 60 % of the province's terrain, are lagging behind, economically and culturally. Between these two areas are the fringe areas of the PRD and the regional cities.

Three townships were selected separately as representative of the three areas according to four indicators of market penetration: commodity market, capital market, labor market, and annual average income.

Fan Township is under the jurisdiction of Guangzhou City, located in the core of the PRD, with the highest values according to the four indictors. As a suburban township of Guangzhou, Fan Township has a long history as a supplier of resources to the city center. In the recent two decades, Fan Township has been experiencing dramatic changes in economy, urbanization, and population. More detailed descriptions of Fan Township will be given in Chap. 4.

Lee Township is under the jurisdiction of Zengcheng City, which is a county-level city of Guangzhou City. Lee Township is located in the fringe areas of PRD region, 90 km away the city center of Guangzhou.

Chan Township is located in mountain areas of Guangdong Province, under the jurisdiction of Huazhou County, Maoming Prefecture. It is about 500 km away from Guangzhou.

---

[23] See Chen 1999, p. 122.

[24] A special economic zone is a geographical region that has economic laws different from a country's economic law. Usually the goal in creating such a zone is an increase in foreign investment. In Guangdong, three special economic zones, namely, Shenzhen, Zhuhai, and Shantou, were set up in the early 1980s.

2.4 Summary

In the previous sections of this chapter, I have reflected on the dimensions of social stratification in Mao's China. I also discuss two generations of studies of social stratification of reform China—market transition theory and new institutional analyses. Then I have proposed the research framework of this study, in which three new directions are highlighted: In the first direction, I argue that the market reform in rural Guangdong is neither a wholesale transformation from redistributive economy to market economy (as market transition theory has assumed) nor a transformation of property rights from public to private (as some of the new institutional analyses have assumed). Instead, it is "an instituted processes of market penetration," by which I consider that the reform is not only a location movement of material elements from the core (PRD region in Guangdong) to the periphery (mountain areas in Guangdong) but is also an appropriative movement of material elements, from the people in the core to the people in the periphery and from the cadres to the peasants. By the second direction, I argue that survey studies on income, which prevail in social stratification studies of China, neglect two points: first, they neglect what have been created by the reform and people's various access patterns to them and second, they systematically neglect what peasants lose—namely, the burden on peasants. As a result, this study will document the variation of "sources of earnings" created by the market penetration process, the chances of village cadres and peasants to access these sources of earnings, and the aggravation or relief of the burden on peasants. By the third direction, this study aims to contribute two points to the "state-market interactive" view, which has been applied to the studies of Chinese social stratification: to analyze rural cases with the "state-market interactive" view and to bridge the state-market interaction with individual life chances.

References

Aubert, C., & Li, X. (2002). Peasant burden: Taxes and Levies imposed on Chinese farmers. In *Agricultural policies in China after WTO accession* (Collection: China in the global economy, pp. 160–179). Paris: OECD.

Bates, R. H. (1981). *Markets and states in tropical Africa: The political basis of agricultural policies*. Berkeley: University of California Press.

Bates, R. H. (1988). *Toward a political economy of development: A rational choice perspective*. Berkeley: University of California Press.

Bernstein, T. P., & Lu, X. (2000). Taxation without representation: Peasants, the central and the local states in reform China. *China Quarterly, 163*, 742–763.

Bian, Y., & Logan, J. R. (1996). Market transition and the persistence of power: The changing stratification system in urban China. *American Journal of Sociology, 61*, 739–758.

Bian, Y., & Zhang, Z. (2002). Marketization and income distribution in urban China, 1988 and 1995. *Research in Social Stratification and Mobility, 19*, 377–415.

Bryant, C. G. A., & Mokrzycki, E. (Eds.). (1994). *The new great transformation?* London: Routledge.

Burawoy, M., & Lukacs, J. (1992). *The radiant past*. Chicago: University of Chicago Press.

Cao, C.-m., & Dickson, B. J. (Eds.). (2001). *Remaking the Chinese state: Strategies, society and security*. New York: Routledge.
Cao, Y., & Nee, V. G. (2000). Comment: Controversies and evidence in the market transition debate. *American Journal of Sociology, 105*, 1175–1189.
Cawson, A., Morgan, K., Webber, D., Holmes, P., & Stevens, A. (1990). *Hostile brothers: Competition and closure in the European electronics industry*. Oxford: Oxford University Press.
Chen, Minjin. (1999). *Gaige kaifang ershinian chengjiu huigu* [Reflections on the achievements of twenty years of reforms and opening to the outside world]. Guangzhou: Guangdong Nianjian Press.
Chou, J.-t. (1966). *Social mobility in China: Status careers among the gentry in a Chinese community*. New York: Atherton Press.
Djilas, M. (1957). *The new class: An analysis of the communist system of power*. New York: Praeger.
Evans, P., Dietrich R., & Skocpol, T. (1985). Bring the state back in, T. Skocpol (Ed.). Cambridge, MA: Cambridge University Press.
Fei, H.-T. (1946). Peasantry and gentry: An interpretation of Chinese social structure and its changes. *American Journal of Sociology, 52*, 1–17.
Geertz, C. (1983). Culture and social change; the Indonesian case. *Man (n.s.), 19*, 511–532.
Glaser, B. G., & Strauss, A. L. (1967). *The discovery of grounded theory: Strategies for qualitative research*. New York: Aldine de Gruyter.
Hinton, W. (1984). *Shenfan*. New York: Random House.
Johnson, G. E. (1994). Open for business, open to the world: Consequences of global incorporation in Guangdong and the Pearl River delta. In T. Lyons & V. Nee (Eds.), *The economic transformation of south China* (pp. 55–87). NY: Cornell University Press.
Keister, L. A., & Nee, V. (2001). The rational peasant in China: Flexible adaptation: Flexible adaptation, risk diversification, and opportunity. *Rationality and Society, 13*, 33.
Kovacs, J. M. (Ed.). (1994). *Transition to capitalism?* New Brunswick: Transaction.
Kraus, R. C. (1981). *Class conflict in Chinese socialism*. New York: Columbia University Press.
Lenski, G. (1966). *Power and privilege*. New York: McGraw-Hill.
Levi, M. (1988a). *Of rule and revenue*. Berkeley: University of California Press.
Levi, M. (1988b). *Trust and governance*. New York: Russell Sage Foundation.
Li, D. D. (1996). A theory of ambiguous property rights in transition economies: The case of the Chinese non-state sector. *Journal of Comparative Economics, 23*, 1–19.
Lin, N. (1995). Local market socialism: Local corporatism in action in rural China. *Theory and Society, 24*, 301–354.
Lin, Y.-m. (2001). *Between politics and markets: Firms, competition, and institutional change in post-Mao China*. New York: Cambridge University Press.
Lin, N., & Chen, C.-j. J. (1999). Local elites as officials and owners: Shareholding and property rights in Daqiuzhuang. In J. C. Oi & A. G. Walder (Eds.), *Property rights and economy reform in China* (pp. 145–170). Stanford: Stanford University Press.
Lippit, V. D. (1974). *Land reform and economic development in China: A study of institutional change and development finance*. White Plains: International Arts and Sciences Press.
Lu, X. (1997). The politics of peasant burden in reform China. *Journal of Peasant Studies, 24*, 113–138.
Matthews, R., & Nee, V. (2000). Gender inequality and economic growth in rural China. *Social Science Research, 29*, 606–632.
Michael, F. (1955). State and society in nineteenth-century China. *World Politics, 7*, 419–433.
Moran, M., & Wright, M. (1991). Conlusion: The interdependence of markets and states. In M. Moran & M. Wright (Eds.), *The market and the state: Studies in interdependence* (pp. 239–249). New York: St. Martin's Press.
Nee, V. (1989). A theory of market transition: From redistribution to markets in state socialism. *American Sociological Review, 54*, 663–681.
Nee, V. (1991). Social inequality in reforming state socialism. *American Sociological Review, 56*, 267–282.

Nee, V. (1992). Organizational dynamics of market transition: Hybrid froms, property rights, and mixed economy in China. *Administrative Science Quarterly, 37*, 1–27.

Nee, V. (1996). The emergence of a market society: Changing mechanisms of stratification in China. *American Journal of Sociology, 101*, 908–949.

Nee, V., & Cao, Y. (1999). Path dependent societal transformation: Stratification in hybrid mixed economies. *Theory and Society, 28*, 799–834.

Nee, V., & Cao, Y. (2002). Postsocialist inequalities: The causes of continuity and discontinuity. *Research in Social Stratification and Mobility, 19*, 3–39.

Nee, V., & Su, S. (1990). Institutional change and economic growth in China: The view from the village. *Journal of Asian Studies, 49*, 3–25.

North, D. C. (1979). A framework for analyzing the state in economic history. *Explorations in Economic History, 16*, 249–259.

Oi, J. C. (1985). Communism and Clientelism: Rural politics in China. *World Politics, 37*, 238–266.

Oi, J. C. (1989). *State and peasant in contemporary China: The political economy of village government*. Berkeley: University of California Press.

Oi, J. C. (1992). Fiscal reform and the economic foundations of local state corporatism in China. *World Politics, 45*, 99–126.

Oi, J. C. (1995). The role of the local state in China's transitional economy. *China Quarterly, 144*, 1132–1149.

Oi, J. C. (1999). *Rural China takes off: Institutional foundations of economic reform*. Berkeley: University of California Press.

Parish, W. L., & Michelson, E. (1996). Politics and markets: Dual transformations. *American Journal of Sociology, 101*, 1042–1059.

Parish, W. L., & Whyte, M. K. (1978). *Village and family in contemporary China*. Chicago: University of Chicago Press.

Parish, W. L., Zhe, X., & Li, F. (1995). Nonfarm work and marketization of the Chinese countryside. *The China Quarterly, 143*, 1–29.

Peng, Y. (1992). Wage determination in rural and urban China: A comparison of public and private industrial sectors. *American Sociological Review, 57*, 198–213.

Polanyi, K. (1957). *The great transformation*. Boston: Beacon Press.

Polanyi, K. (1965). The economy as instituted process. In K. Polanyi, C. M. Arensberg, and H. W. Pearson (Eds.), *Trade and market in the early empires: Economies in history and theory* (p. 248). New York: The Free Press.

Schurmann, F. (1968). *Ideology and organization in communist China*. Berkeley: University of California Press.

Shirk, S. L. (1989). The political economy of Chinese industrial reform. In V. Nee, D. Stark, & M. Selden (Eds.), *Remaking the economic institutions of socialism: China and eastern Europe* (pp. 328–62). Stanford: Stanford University Press.

Shirk, S. L. (1993). *The political logic of economic reform in China*. Berkeley: University of California Press.

Shu, X., & Bian, Y. (2002). Intercity variation in gender inequalities in China: Analysis of a 1995 national survey. *Research in Social Stratification and Mobility, 19*, 269–312.

Shue, V. (1980). *Peasant China in Transition: The dynamics of development toward socialism, 1949–1956*. Berkeley: University of California Press.

Stark, D. (1990). Privatization in Hungary: From plan to market or from plan to clan. *East European Politics and Societies, 4*, 351–392.

Stark, D. (1992). Path dependence and privatization strategies in East Central Europe. *East European Politics and Societies, 6*, 17–54.

Stark, D. (1996). Recombinant property in East European capitalism. *American Journal of Sociology, 101*, 993–1027.

Szelenyi, I. (1978). Social inequalities in state socialist redistributive economies. *International Journal of Comparative Sociology, 19*, 63–87.

Szelenyi, I. (1982). The intelligentsia in the class structure of state socialist societies. *American Journal of Sociology, 88*(Suppl), S287–S326.

Szelenyi, I. (1983). *Urban inequalities under state socialism*. Oxford: Oxford University Press.
Szelenyi, Ivan. (1986/1987). The prospects and limits of the East European new class project: An autocritical reflection on the intellectuals on the road to class power. *Politics and Society, 15*, 103–144.
Szelenyi, I., & Kostello, E. (1996). The market transition debate: Toward a synthesis. *American Journal of Sociology, 101*, 1082–1096.
Unger, J. (1984). The class system in rural China: A case study. In J. L. Watson (Ed.), *Class & social stratification in post-revolution China* (pp. 121–41). Sydney: Cambridge University Press.
Walder, A. G. (1992). Property rights and stratification in socialist redistributive economies. *American Sociological Review, 57*, 524–539.
Walder, A. G. (1995a). China's transitional economy: Interpreting its significance. *The China Quarterly, 144*, 963–979.
Walder, A. G. (1995b). Local governments as industrial firms: An organizational analysis of China's transitional economy. *American Journal of Sociology, 101*, 263.
Walder, A. G. (1996). Markets and inequality in transitional economics: Toward testable theories. *American Journal of Sociology, 101*, 1060–1073.
Walder, A. G. (2003). Elite opportunity in transitional economics. *American Sociological Review, 68*, 899–916.
Walder, A. G., & Zhao, L. (2003). *Political office, kinship, and household wealth in rural China* (Working paper series of Asia/Pacific Research Center of Stanford University).
Wank, D. L. (1999). *Commodifying communism: Business, trust, and politics in a Chinese city*. New York: Cambridge University Press.
Weber, M. (1968). *The religion of China: Confucianism and Taoism*. London: Collier Macmillan Pub.
Wei, Y. D. (2000). *Regional development in China: States, globalization, and inequality*. London/New York: Routledge.
Whiting, S. H. (2001). *Power and wealth in Rural China: The political economy of institutional change*. New York: Cambridge University Press.
Whyte, M. K. (1985). The politics of life chances in the People's Republic of China. In S. Yu-ming (Ed.), *Power and policy in the PRC* (pp. 244–265). Boulder: Westview Press.
Wong, C. P. W. (1982). Rural industrialization in China: Development of the five small industries as an experiment in the application of intermediate technologies. In R. Barker & R. Sinha (Eds.), *The Chinese agricultural economy* (pp. 137–46). Boulder: Westview Press.
Wong, C. P. W. (1988). Interpreting rural industrial growth in the post-mao period. *Modern China, 14*, 3–30.
Wong, C. P. W. (1992). Fiscal reform and local industrialization: The problematic sequencing of reform in Post-Mao China. *Modern China, 18*(2), 197–227.
Xiao, G. (1960). *Rural China: Imperial control in the nineteenth century*. Seattle: University of Washington Press.
Wu, X., & Xie, Y. (2003). Does the market pay off? Earnings returns to education in Urban China. *American Sociological Review, 68*, 425–442.
Xie, Y., & Hannum, E. (1996). Regional variation in earnings inequality in reform era urban China. *American Journal of Sociology, 101*, 950–992.
Yang, C. K. (1959). *A Chinese village in early communist transition*. Westport: Greenwood Press.
Yang, D. L. (2001). Rationalizing the Chinese state: The political economy of government reform. In C.-m. Cao & B. J. Dickson (Eds.), *Remaking the Chinese state: Strategies, society and security*. New York: Routledge.
Zang, X. (2002). Labor market segmentation and income inequality in urban China. *Sociological Quarterly, 43*, 27.
Zhang, Z. (1955). *The Chinese gentry: Studies on their role in nineteenth-century Chinese society*. Seattle: University of Washington Press.

Zhang, Letian. (1998). *Gao Bie Li Xiang: Ren Min Gong She Zhi Du Yan Jiu* [Good bye, Utopia: A study to The Institutions of People's Commune]. Shanghai: Dongfang chuban zhongxin (Dong Fang Press).

Zhao, Litao. (2004). Paths to private entrepreneurship, Markets and occupational mobility in rural China. PhD thesis, Department of Sociology, Stanford University, Stanford.

Zhao, W., & Zhou, X. (2002). Institutional transformation and results to education in urban China: An empirical assessment. *Research in Social Stratification and Mobility, 19*, 339–375.

Zhou, X. (2000a). Economic transformation and income inequality in Urban China: Evidence from a panel data. *American Journal of Sociology, 105*, 1135–1174.

Zhou, X. (2000b). Reply: Beyond the debate and toward substantive institutional analysis. *American Journal of Sociology, 105*, 1190–1195.

Chapter 3
Market Penetration and the Life Chances of Peasants in Guangdong: An Historical Account

This chapter first presents an historical account for the market penetration processes in Guangdong, followed by an historical account of the two main themes of this study: how the market penetration increases the earning sources and then the life chances of the peasant; and how it increases the fiscal revenue of the state or local governments, leading to the relief of the burden on peasants. As an historical account, a tendency, but not a vested result, will be discussed in this chapter.

3.1 Market Penetration in Guangdong

These two decades have witnessed a transition from formerly planned economics to market coordination. Neoclassical economics emphasizes a wholesale transformation to privatization. However, most empirical studies of East Europe[1] and China depict the complexity of the transition: they document that the pre-transition economies were not simply centralized (Aslund 1992; Berend 1990; Kornai 1992; Oi 1989; Prout 1985; Shue 1988; Szelenyi 1989). They also argue that the post-transition strategies and outcomes were not all of one piece (Bryant and Mokrzycki 1994; Burawoy and Lukacs 1992; Kovacs 1994; Nee 1992; Shirk 1993; Stark 1990, 1992, 1996; Walder 1995a, b). Similarly, market penetration in Guangdong hasn't been a wholesale transformation from one to the other. On the contrary, it has been a changing process without blueprint, which can be described as "Take a step, and then take a look (zou yi bu, kan yi bu)." This chapter documents the market penetration process in rural Guangdong since 1978. In the following sections, I will first give a general picture of the market penetration processes in Guangdong, which consist of two phases marked by different events and then illustrate how the market

[1] I use the term "East Europe" broadly, to include the European countries of the former Soviet Union and its satellites.

N. Chen, *State, Market and Life Chances in Contemporary Rural Chinese Society*, DOI 10.1007/978-3-662-45046-8_3

penetration processes have created the regional disparity between the Pearl River Delta Region and mountain areas. At the end of the chapter, I will classify three types of market penetration in rural Guangdong and illustrate the institutional characteristics of each type.

3.1.1 The Origin of Market Penetration

It may be helpful to remind ourselves of what prevailed before Chinese economic reform. After the Chinese Communist Party (henceforth CCP) came to power (1949), the stratification structure of traditional China and republican China (221 B.C.–1949 A.D.) was destroyed. In its place, the Maoist government (1949–1978) created a centralized planned economy. This centralized planned economy was marked by several polices.

1. The work unit system involved the commune system in rural areas and the *danwei* (work organization) system in urban areas.
2. In the unified purchase and sales (Tonggou Tongxiao) system, the state eliminated almost all self-reliant businesses, controlled prices and wages, subsidized urban dwellers through a state monopoly over the grain trade, and organized industry in state-owned enterprises, which were built without regard to economic or equity factors and operated on a soft budget.
3. The household registration system (Huji Zhidu) rooted people to their place of birth.

Ironically, when Mao tried to develop an egalitarian society with these policies, the results were far from equal. (1) There was no equality between cadres and peasants, as the cadres controlled almost all resources and distributed them to peasants according not only to a work point system but also to clientelist relationships. (2) Rural and urban areas were unequal, as industrialization in urban areas was implemented by extracting the surpluses from the agricultural sectors and sacrificing rural residents' interests, relying on state procurement of agricultural products at lower than market prices and on the monopolistic sale of manufactured products to peasants at prices substantially higher than world prices (Hinton 1984; Shue 1980; Whyte 1985; Yang 1959; Zhang 1998).

Moreover, in Mao's period, two human tragedies occurred: the Great Leap Forward (1958–1960)[2] and the Cultural Revolution (1966–1976).[3] The former threw the economic system into disarray and led to a nationwide famine that

[2]The Great Leap Forward was an economic plan initiated by Mao Zedong during 1958–1960. During that period, the Chinese economic plan aimed at revitalizing all sectors of the economy. The plan emphasized decentralized, labor-intensive industrialization, typified by the construction of thousands of backyard steel furnaces in place of large steel mills. Wildly unrealistic planning, poorly planned communization of agriculture, and a poor harvest in 1959 caused mass starvation.

[3]To read more of the Cultural Revolution, please see Joseph et al. 1991.

claimed more than 20 million lives; the latter plunged China into anarchy and economy stagnation.

The death of Mao in 1976 gave an opportunity for China to change. The negative lessons learned from the Great Leap Forward and the Cultural Revolution made most party leaders realize that there was a strong need for a new direction for China. Party leaders disagreed on what the new direction should be at the beginning, but Deng Xiaoping's experimental, pragmatic views ("take a step, then take a look") won at last in 1978 (Vogel 1989, pp. 76–77). When Deng wanted to find a place for the experiment of reform, Guangdong Province turned out to be a good one because of its three distinctive characteristics. (1) Guangdong is located in the southeast corner of China and is far from Beijing, so that the experiment in Guangdong would not radically threaten the basic national political and economic structure. (2) It is located next to Hong Kong and Macau, which had been the main connection between China and the outside world, as separate colonies of the UK (before 1997) and Portugal (before 1999), respectively. This situation facilitated Guangdong to test the application of foreign technologies and management skills in China. (3) The number of state-owned enterprises in Guangdong was relatively small, so that a failure of the experiment would not affect the nation's heavy industry and national income.[4]

3.1.2 Market Penetrations: Phases and Regional Variations

Market penetration in Guangdong consisted of two phases. During the first phase (1978–1987), there were two outstanding changes: the ignition of the household responsibility system and the consequent thriving of individual family business (geti hu). It can be said that this was the beginning of the development of the petty commodity market mentioned by Szelenyi and Kostello (1996).

The second phase was characterized by the booming of rural industry and the commodity market, together with the development of the capital and labor markets. Guangdong first attracted most foreign direct investment (wai shang zhijie touzi, henceforth FDI) from Hong Kong and later from all over the world. The booming of the commodity market created many jobs and led to the development of the labor market, when rural surplus labor from other provinces flooded into the PRD region, as well as many rural people from the mountain areas of Guangdong Province also went to the PRD region. In this phase, regional disparities within the province emerged—especially, the development gap between the PRD region and mountain areas became outstanding. Three types of market penetration emerged: the new cooperative economy, the outskirt economy, and the local economy.

[4]Actually, the reform first began in some rural areas of Anhui Province, but Guangdong was taken as the experimental province because of its special characteristics mentioned.

3.1.2.1 Phase 1: The Thriving of the Petty Commodity Markets

As Ivan Szelenyi and Eric Kostello (1996) point out, "Market reform usually begins with petty commodity markets: producers are allowed to sell products or services in places, where prices are regulated by supply and demand (p. 1087)." This description can be seen at the beginning of the Guangdong market reform, which can be characterized by the diversification and specialization of agriculture as well as by the development of individual family businesses.

The Thriving of Family Agriculture

When the turmoil of the Cultural Revolution receded, the rural people of Guangdong Province were very poor. There were 11 counties and 98,899 production teams (33.2 % of the total number of production teams of the province) in which peasant annual income was lower than 50 yuan.[5] The de-collectivization and reopening of the markets began from 1978 and provided an opportunity for peasants to pursue family autonomy. Their efforts to do so can be divided into three steps.

First, in the summer of 1978, about one out of a thousand of the production teams adopted a new distribution rule called "three fixes and one reward (san ding yi jiang)"—fixed salary, fixed outputs, fixed costs, and reward for over-fulfilling output quotas. In some production teams, rural cadres approved the new rule; in others, where rural cadres didn't approve the new rule, the peasants tried many "unofficial bargaining strategies"[6] to persuade them to do so. Although this new rule hadn't previously permitted by official documents, it was encouraged and extended to other production teams by the Guangdong Provincial Party Committee in the winter of 1978.

However, the peasants were unsatisfied with the "three fixes and one reward," because the yields still were distributed by the cadres who ran the collective organizations instead of by the peasants themselves, according to "three fixed and one reward." As a result, another rule, namely, "big contract (da bao gan)," was created. According to "big contract," the peasants had the right to operate the land, which was still collectively owned, according to contracts which they made with the collective in exchange for the right to use the farmland. According to the contracts, peasants would guarantee to submit a certain percentage of yields to both the state and the collectives—as captured in the well-known saying, "give enough to the state and to the collective and the rest to ourselves (gei gou guojia de, jiao gou jiti de, shengxia de quanshi ziji de)." In 1983, the State Council promulgated a document[7] to formally recognize all attempts in family farming, which were called by a single

---

[5] The Edition Committee of the Chorography of Guangdong Province 2004, p. 283.

[6] About these strategies, please see Zhou 1996, pp. 53–60.

[7] The name of the document is *Some Problems of Current Reform in Rural Areas* (dangqian nongcun jingji gaige de ruogan wenti) (02 January, 1983).

name, the household responsibility system.[8] The enforcement of the household responsibility system dramatically increased the unit outputs of agriculture.

1. In Guangdong, for instance, although grain-producing areas were reduced by 17.5 % against those of 1978, the yield increased by 20.7 %[9] in 1984 (Chau 1998, p. 89). Crop diversity and agriculture sidelines also increased. Some of the least productive farmlands were converted to agricultural sideline production. Large expanses of former paddy fields were given over to growing of sugar cane, high-quality fruits, vegetables, and flowers. Poultry rearing and fish farming also became popular.
2. With the development of the household responsibility system, specialized households were established as part of the contract system. The precise definition of "specialized household" varied from place to place, but generally it had three characteristics. First, it was specialized in the production of one or several related products (e.g., fish farming and raising ducks could be organized together). Second, production was commercialized, with more than a given percentage sold on the market. Third, income from the specialized production should account for the majority of total household income (Powell 1992, p. 51).

Individual Family Businesses

After the Third Plenum of the Eleventh Party Congress in December 1978, the central government loosened its control on self-operated businesses, so that "laborers (were) permitted to engage in individual industry and commerce (*laodongzhe keyi congshi geti gongshangye*)."[10] By this, the central government wanted to encourage the surplus rural laborers to find a living. As a result, various individual family businesses emerged in rural Guangdong, including piecework at home; short-term jobs as independent construction workers (glazers, plumbers) or as individual repairmen (bicycles, home appliances, tractors); operating a tractor for hauling goods or a bus for hauling passengers; or running a retail shop, restaurant, guest house, wholesale business, or small manufacturing establishment (see Fig. 3.1).

[8] To learn more about this, please refer to Nee 1986, pp. 185–203; Gray and Grey 1983, pp. 151–84; Watson 1983, pp. 705–30; Lu and Selden 1987, pp. 249–289.

[9] Kuang 1991, pp. 332–75.

[10] In 1984, the State Council promulgate a document, named *guanyu nongcun gongshangye de ruogan guiding* (The Regulations Regarding Rural Individual Industry and Commerce), to support household businesses officially.

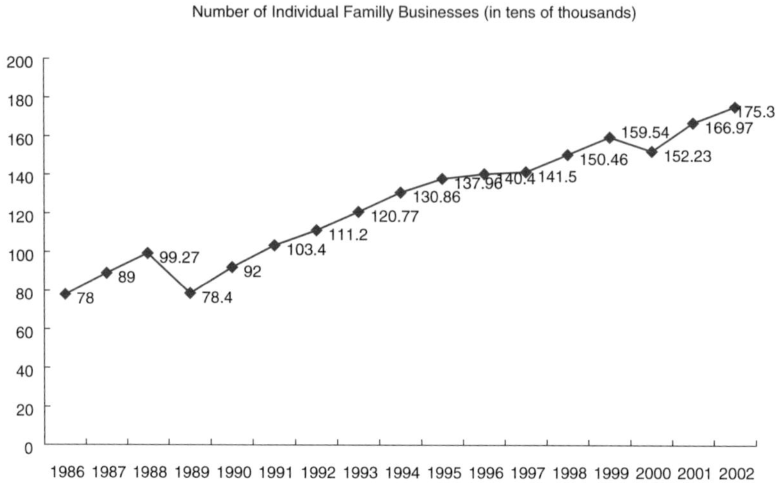

Fig. 3.1 Number of individual family businesses (ten thousands) (Sources: The Bureau of Industry and Commercial Administration of Guangdong, Social Science Academic of Guangdong, and Association of Private Enterprises of Guangdong 2003, pp. 61–84.)

3.1.2.2 Phase 2: The Development of Rural Industry

The development of agriculture reached a record high in the mid-1980s, with diversification and specialization, but since then it has tended to stagnate. Instead, rural industry has tended to play more and more important roles in the market penetration of Guangdong.

Commodity, Capital, and Labor Markets

In the middle of the 1980s, the state began to transfer the focus of reform from rural areas to urban areas, with the core duty being the reform of state-owned enterprises (SOEs). In Guangdong, however, SOEs were not the leading actors in the reform. On the contrary, the importance of state-owned enterprises decreased sharply. The share of state-owned enterprises in total industrial production output dropped from 63 % in 1980 to 39 % in 1990 and to 18 % in 1994. Moreover, most of the SOEs were located in leading cities of Guangdong such as Guangzhou, Zhanjiang, Jiangmen, Zhongshan, etc. Their influence on rural areas was quite limited. Rural industry, including Township and Village Enterprises (henceforth TVEs) and private enterprises, became the new focus of the reform, especially in rural areas.

Related literature emphasizes the two driving forces of the boom in rural industry. For the first, Guangdong benefited from flexible and autonomous policies for economic planning, foreign investments, and tax ratios in Guangdong (Cheng 2000a; Oi 1992, 1999). At the Third Plenum of the Eleventh Party Congress in December 1978—considered the beginning of Chinese economic reform—Xi Zhongxun, the party secretary of the CCP of Guangdong at that time, had proposed that central government grant more autonomous power to Guangdong Province, in order to develop the economy.

In 1979, according to Deng Xiaoping's suggestions, central government accepted the proposal and promised special and flexible policies to accelerate the local economic development[11] of Guangdong and Fujian. These policies included six parts. (1) Guangdong Province could propose its own plan for development if the plan follows the central government's main directions and policies. (2) Guangdong's autonomous rights on foreign trade, price setting, wage standard setting, and company management were increased. (3) The Guangdong provincial government was granted the right to approve direct foreign investment. (4) With a set ratio of the revenue from fiscal and foreign exchange, beginning in 1980, Guangdong Province only needed to submit one billion yuan to the central government per year; the rest of the revenue could be used by the provincial government. (5) Resource distribution and business activities could be transferred from the government to the market, to enlarge the jurisdiction of local government over price setting. (6) Finally, three special economic zones were to be set up.

At that time when other provinces were still under the old system such as "unified purchase and sale (tong gou tong xiao)," these special policies greatly facilitated the development of rural industry in Guangdong (Kueh and Ash 1996; Vogel 1989). The geographic proximity of Hong Kong and Macau also facilitated the economic development of Guangdong (Cheng 2000a; Lin 1997): in 1980s Guangdong needed capital, technology, and productive facilities to develop its economy, while Hong Kong wanted to transfer their industry for cheaper labor and land costs. The cooperation between Guangdong and Hong Kong boosted the development of the capital market of Guangdong.

In the 1990s, Guangdong attracted a large amount of FDI from Hong Kong. Moreover, the success of Hong Kong's investment in Guangdong then attracted foreign direct investments from many other districts and countries, including Taiwan, the USA, the European Union, Japan, etc. (Cheng 2000b, p. 87), until FDI in China constitute over one-third of the world's FDI flowing to developing countries (Zeng 2000, p. 103).

As the selected experimental province for attracting foreign investments, Guangdong has occupied a significant position in the utilization of FDI among China's provinces since the 1980s (see Table 3.1).

The development of the capital market boosted the petty commodity market of Guangdong to go a long way at high speed, which led to the boom of rural industry.

[11] These policies were promulgated in 1979 by the State Council Document (Document No. [1979] 202), which was named *dali fazhan duiwai maoyi zenjia waihui shouru ruogan wenti de guiding* (The Regulation Regarding the Energetic Development of Foreign Trade to Increase Income from Foreign Exchange).

Table 3.1 The distribution of FDI in China and Guangdong

Year	China's total	Guangdong	%
1986	1874.89	722.68	38.5
1987	2313.53	602.99	26.1
1988	3193.68	957.86	30
1989	3392.57	1156.44	34.1
1990	3487.11	1460.00	41.9
1991	4366.34	1822.86	41.7
1992	11075.1	3551.5	32.1
1993	27514.9	7498.04	27.3
1994	33766.5	9397.08	27.8
1995	37520.5	10180.3	27.1
1996	41725.5	11623.6	27.9

Sources: Zeng (2000, p. 104)

In 1998, the 721,600 TVEs in Guangdong generated 737.4 billion yuan of gross output value. They employed 9,874,000 staff and workers, accounting for 26.1 % of the total employment in Guangdong.[12]

Most of the enterprises located in rural Guangdong are of four types: township-owned enterprises, village-owned enterprises, private enterprises, and cooperative enterprises (see Table 3.2).[13] However, property rights have not been strictly set in rural Guangdong. For one thing, township cadres have their influence on all kinds of enterprises. For the other, private enterprises in rural areas have close relationships with TVEs. Actually, many private enterprises have registered as township-owned or village-owned in order to share some advantages: to pay less in taxes, avoid political risks, escape the strict regulations on private enterprises, and have the facility to get loans from local banks (Lau 1998).[14] As a result, many studies use "TVEs" to put all these enterprises under a joint name.

The combination of capital market and commodity market needed the development of a labor market. It absorbed surplus rural laborers from the poorer regions of Guangdong in the economically prosperous Pearl River Delta Region. It also created many jobs for migrants from the interior parts of China, especially Hunan, Sichuan, Jiangxi, Guangxi, etc.

[12] Guangdong Provincial Statistical Bureau 1999, p. 309.

[13] The emergence of TVEs began with the Great Leap Forf in the 1950s and was boosted by the so-called five small industries (iron and steel, chemical fertilizer, farm machinery, cement, and energy—coal and electricity) in 1960s, when Mao triggered the industrialization movement. All over the country, people took part in the movement. People contributed their valuable materials and capital to build up factories. In rural areas, these factories were under collective ownership—owned by townships or villages. However, most of them were poorly conceived, uneconomic, and soon closed down. In 1978, the number of township and village enterprises was 85.7 thousand. The number of employees was 1,800 thousands. The gross income was 30.55 billion (Also see Perkins 1977; Riskin 1971, pp. 245–73; Riskin 1978, pp. 77–98; Sigurdson 1977).

[14] For example, in Foshan, there were 458 private enterprises registered as collective enterprises which accounted for 32.2 % of total TVEs in the areas in 1988. See Zhu 2003.

Table 3.2 Various enterprises in rural areas of Guangdong

Ownership	Township	Village	Cooperative	Private	Total
No. of establishments	27.4	106.3	66.3	1257.5	1457.5
(%)	1.9	7.3	4.5	86.3	100
No. of employees	2180.5	3279.6	705.1	4000.9	10166.1
(%)	21.4	32.3	6.9	39.4	100
Total revenue (RMB billion)	131.7	105	24.3	94.9	355.9
(%)	37	29.5	6.8	26.7	100
Gross output value (RMB billion)	137.4	99.6	25.1	90.4	352.6
(%)	39	28.2	7.1	25.6	100

Sources: Guangdong Provincial Statistical Bureau (1995)

The Formation of Three Types and Stages of Market Penetration

As I have pointed out above, the developments of capital market, commodity market, and labor market are not equally distributed in Guangdong. The province was divided officially into four economic regions: the PRD region, the mountain areas, the west wing (the western coastal areas of the province), and the east wing (the eastern areas of the province). However, in regard to the market penetration in rural areas, the province can be grossly divided into three regions: (1) the Pearl River Delta Region, including the special economic zones (henceforth, SEZ) of Shenzhen, Zhuhai, and the so-called four little tigers—Nanhai, Panyu, Shunde, and Dongguan; (2) the mountain areas, including 51 counties, which contains almost half of the province's population and more than half of the province's area[15]; and (3) between the above two regions, the fringe areas of the PRD region and the suburban villages of regional cities of the west and east wings.

The disparity between these three regions was not so outstanding at the beginning of the reform. People could observe the increased yields of grain in all rural areas of the province. However, the PRD region had two advantages in agriculture development: the delta areas are more fertile than the mountain areas and the proximity to Hong Kong and Macau made the commercial agriculture of the PRD region more successful than that of other areas of the province.

The regional disparity became obvious gradually, accompanying the market penetration process. Most FDI has been invested in the PRD region. As Table 3.3 shows, in 2001 over 90 % of FDI was invested in the PRD region. Labor from all over the country and from the other regions of the province flooded into the PRD region.

As Table 3.4 shows, the PRD region attracted 18,450,000 migrants, of which 6,050,000 were from the mountain areas of Guangdong and 12,400,000 were from other provinces. As a result of FDI, most of the rural industries of the province were located in this region. For example, the share of Guangdong's total industrial output

[15] See The Edition Committee of the Chorography of Guangdong Province 2004, p. 192.

Table 3.3 Contribution of PRD to the GDP of Guangdong

	The contribution of PRD in Guangdong (%)		
Year	GDP	Export	Used FIC
1980	47.7	28.4	47.2
1985	52.6	55.2	70.4
1990	55.9	76.7	76.0
1995	68.0	81.5	70.9
2000	76.4	92.2	86.0
2001	78.6	95.2	90.1

Source: The Center of Urban and Region Studies (2002), Guangdong Provincial Statistical Bureau (2002, pp. 538, 626), State Statistical Bureau (2002, pp. 586, 599)

Table 3.4 Guangdong sheng di wu ci renkou pucha zong renkou yu 1999 nian nianmo huji zong renkou bijiao (A comparison between the population in the fifth population census and the population in 1999 of the prefectures in Guangdong (in ten thousands)

Region	City	Population in fifth population census, 2000	Registered population at end of 1999	Increase/decrease
PRD region	Guangzhou	994.3	685	309.3
	Shenzhen	700.84	119.95	580.99
	Dongguan	644.57	150.82	493.75
	Foshan	533.79	329.24	204.55
	Zhongshan	236.35	132	104.35
	Zhuhai	123.56	71.4	52.16
	Jiangmen	395.03	378.84	15.15
	Huizhou	321.63	271.82	49.81
SEZ	Shantou	467.11	448.94	18.17
	Subtotal			1845
Other cities	Shaoguan			−31.59
	Yanjiang			−30.83
	Qingyuan			−62.91
	Heyuan			−88.11
	Zhanjiang			−49.85
	Chaozhou			−2.3
	Meizhou			−95.93
	Maoming			−94.76
	Jieyang			−45.13
	Shanwei			−23.95
	Zhaoqing			−44.13
	Yunfu			−35.56
	Subtotal			605

Notes: (1) The Fifth Population Census (held in December 2000) included migrant workers, while the registered population of 1999 did not. The deduction of the latter number from the former is the number of the migrant population. So the big cities in the PRD, including Shenzhen, Dongguan, Guangzhou, Foshan, and Zhongshan, attracted 18,450,000 migrants, of which 6,050,000 were from the mountain areas of Guangdong and 12,400,000 were from other provinces.
(2) Source: Yang and Xian (2001)

that came from the PRD region was 79 % in 1997 (Lau 2000, p. 84). Based on the abovementioned advantages, the annual income per capita of the PRD region became much higher than that of the other two regions. The disparity in the extent of market penetration also led to variations of the institutional characteristics of these three regions.

New Cooperative Economy

In the PRD region, the forms of rural industry are diverse. In some cities, like Dongguan City,[16] most TVEs were so-called "three supplies, one compensation (san lai yi bu)" enterprises.[17] In Shunde,[18] the leading actors in rural industry were large-scale township enterprises. However, in Nanhai the so-called "six wheels" model was put into practice, meaning that enterprises at six levels (county-owned enterprises, township-owned enterprises, district-owned enterprises, administrative village-owned enterprises, natural village-owned enterprises, and private enterprises) were all developed greatly. In some rural areas of Guangzhou City, tertiary industry played a more important role than secondary industry. However, no matter in what form it was carried out, rural people benefited from the development in similar ways. First, their collective assets increased dramatically because of the ongoing market penetration process, which thereby increased the values of rural people's sharing in the collective revenue. Second, the development of local areas increased opportunities for rural family business. Third, more or less, rural people in this region had more possibilities to find jobs than their counterparts in mountain areas. Among these benefits, the sharing of collective economy became the most outstanding characteristic. I thereby call the rural areas of in the PRD region the "new cooperative economy" (see Fig. 3.2).

Local Economy

In most of the mountain areas of the province, the economy presents a totally different picture than that of the new cooperative economy. I call the economy of rural mountain areas "local economy," by which I point out that the economy in these areas is still marked by an agricultural orientation and by substantial pockets of poverty (see Fig. 3.3).

[16] The third largest prefecture city in Guangdong, located in the PRD region.

[17] The term "three supplies, one compensation" points to a kind of export-processing industry that requires the overseas investors to supply raw materials (lailiao jiagong), components or parts (laijian zhuangpei), and models for what is to be processed (laiyang jiagong), while the participators in China provide labor, land, buildings, electricity, and other local facilities necessary for production. After that, the products are to be sold to foreign markets through compensation trade (buchang maoyi). The investors make contracts with participants in Guangdong, who generally are representatives or organizations of the townships or villages. According to the contracts, investors don't hire or pay workers directly. Instead, they give lump-sum payments to the Chinese participants for the contracted goods.

[18] A city of Foshan Prefecture.

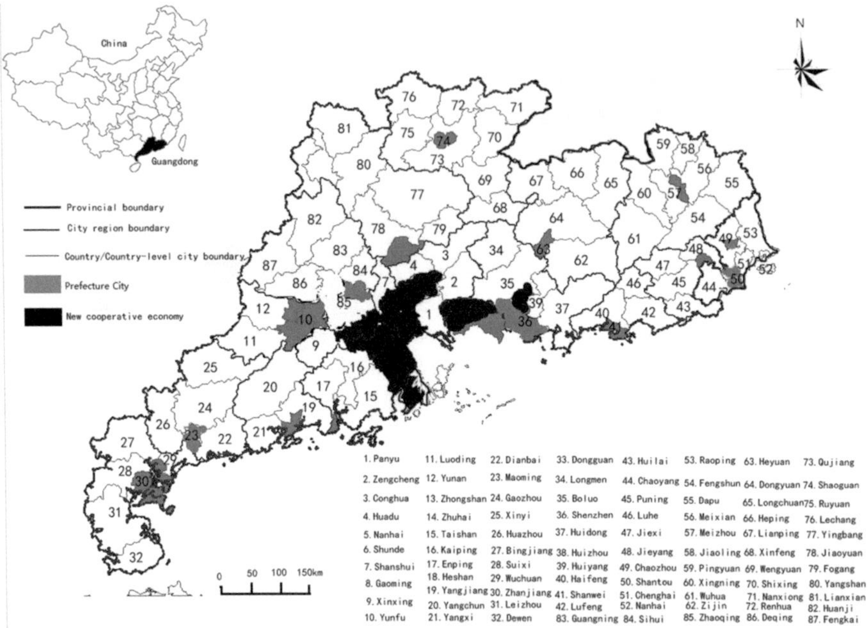

Fig. 3.2 New cooperative economy in Guangdong Province

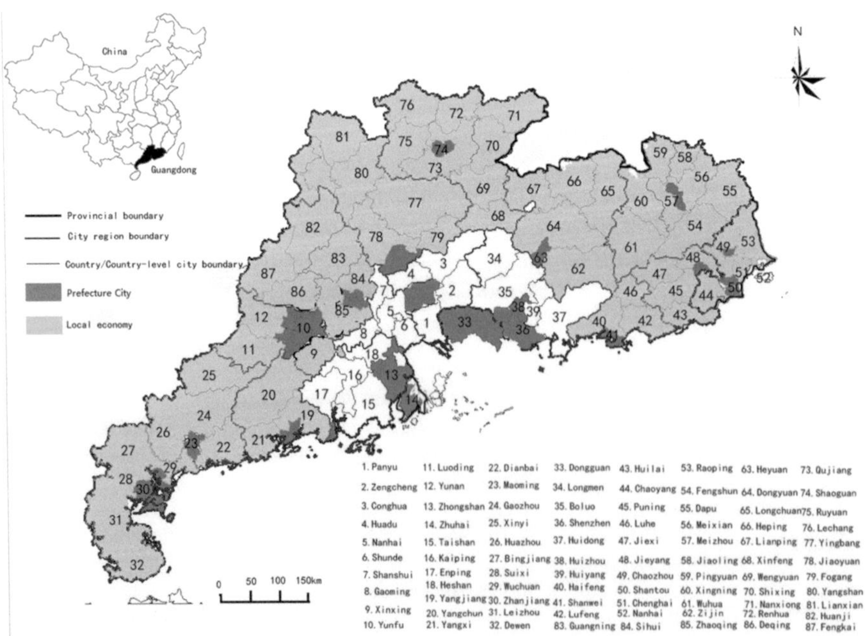

Fig. 3.3 Local economies in Guangdong Province

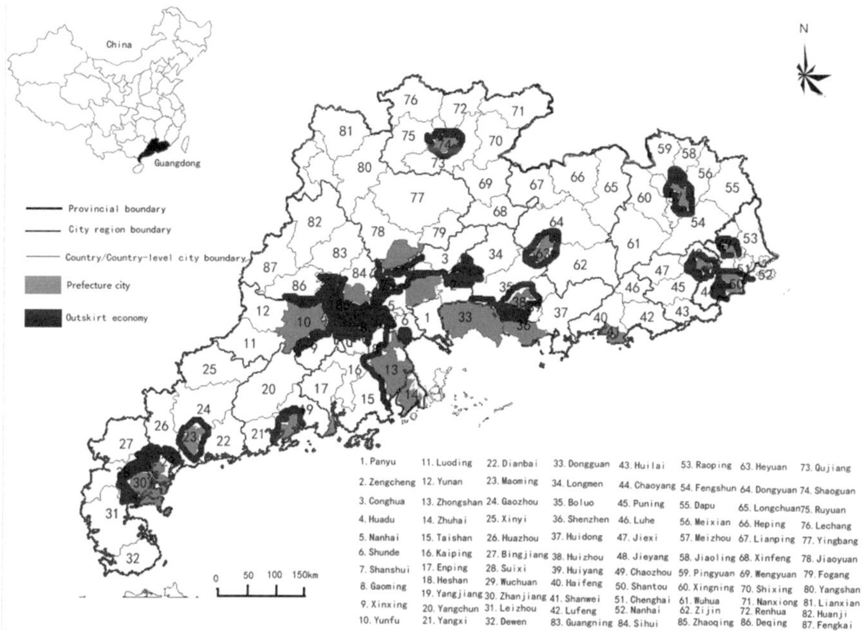

Fig. 3.4 Outskirt economies in Guangdong Province

Outskirt Economy

Between the PRD region and mountain areas of the province are the fringe areas of the PRD region and the suburban villages of regional cities of west and east wings (see Fig. 3.4). I label this economy the "outskirt economy," because one outstanding characteristic of this kind of economy is its proximity to the big and middle cities. This proximity has made the commercialization and specialization of agricultural sidelines possible.

3.2 The Increase and Distribution of Earning Sources

During the collective period (1956–1978), under the constraints of the planned economy, natural resources were the main determinants of income differentials among villages of Guangdong. Cash income was obtained mainly from sales of vegetables from the private plots and from minor farm products. Severe restrictions on the scope and size of family nonagricultural activities and very limited access to urban labor markets did not permit much differentiation of economic activities or of sources of off-farm income.

Market penetration in Guangdong dramatically changed this situation. Accompanying the introduction of private farming and the booming of both urban and rural economies, the earning sources available to the rural population increased tremendously.

Crops As I have mentioned in the previous section, the rural people of Guangdong directly benefited from the thriving of family agriculture. For one thing, the earnings from crops increased. Although the price of grain was set by the state till 1998, the average output of crops increased. This happened all over rural China and most of the rural population benefited from it. Ordinary peasants and cadres had equal abilities to access this source of earnings because of the low entrance costs and the few political restrictions. In Guangdong, people could observe the increased yields of grain in all rural areas of the province.

However, although the PRD region had its fertility and its proximity to Hong Kong and Macau for agricultural development, the market penetration process was accompanied by the retreat of crop planting, and the role of crops as earning sources for peasants has described an inverse U curve. The following discussions will explain why.

Agricultural Sidelines The thriving of crops and local rural markets in local areas in the early period of Reform Era created opportunities to engage in agricultural sidelines, which greatly increased the sources of cash income for peasants (please see Chap. 2 for categories). The distribution of agricultural sidelines shared a similar logic with that of crops: at first, the products from agricultural sidelines mainly met the needs of local markets. This happened in almost all of rural China, and most rural people benefited. However, the further development of agricultural sidelines varied according to varying levels of market penetration. Whether the products of agriculture sidelines could be sold in the larger market (regional or world markets) became a key factor. In Guangdong, agricultural sidelines too are gradually retreating from the core areas of the PRD region, although they are developing dramatically in the fringe areas of the PRD region and in the suburban villages of most regional cities because of geographic proximity to the core cities. However, the situation in mountain areas is different: the development of agriculture sidelines there is limited, lacking connections with outside markets.

Individual Family Businesses Various individual family businesses have increased, as mentioned above (see Sect. 3.1.2.1 of this chapter). These activities spread over almost all of rural Guangdong during the first stage of reform (about 1978–1985), because of the low entrance investment requirements and the great market needs triggered by the open policy. Then the degree of market penetration and of diverse areas led to different degrees of opportunity for individual family businesses—the greater the degree of penetration, the greater the opportunities. In the PRD region, the thriving of the commodity and labor markets provided rural residents with many chances for leasing, services, and other businesses, which were seldom available to the rural residents in fringe areas of the PRD region and in the mountain areas.

Migrant Wage Work Two factors decided whether migrant wage work became a major source of earnings for some rural people. Firstly, the household responsibility system led to the emergence of a great number of rural surplus laborers[19]; secondly, the high degree of market penetration in some regions attracted this surplus labor from rural areas with lesser degrees of market penetration. In Guangdong, migrant wage work was the main source of earnings for rural people in mountain areas at the end of 1980s, when the market penetration in the PRD region created great needs for cheap labor. One thing is noteworthy: rural cadres in mountain areas are disadvantaged for migration wage work, because they can't leave their positions for jobs elsewhere outside the township.

Migrant Businesses Migrant businesses shared similar distribution logic with migrant wage work. The chances in some developed regions attracted people from less-developed regions. These people floated to big cities or rural areas of developed region, developing businesses that variety from junk collection to restaurants and big factories. Like migrant wage work, migrant business has become more important earning sources for the rural people of mountain areas than for the rural people in the PRD region. Rural cadres in mountain areas also are disadvantaged for accessing this kind of earning source.

Rural Industry Rural industrial activities are not ubiquitous in Guangdong. As mentioned in the first section of this chapter, more than 80 % of TVEs are located in the PRD region. However, the rural people of mountain areas also benefit from rural industry, which provides them with chances for migrant wage work. Rural people in the PRD region, on the other hand, benefited from rural industry as well. First of all, their successful TVEs brought collective revenue sharing. In their development processes, many township-owned or village-owned enterprises needed to utilize collective assets, land, and the peasants' capital. The peasants thereby became stockholders in the collective economy. Secondly, the development of rural industry increased the chances for individual family businesses such as house leasing, running stores, transportation, etc. Rural cadres in the PRD region had advantages in sharing the revenue brought by rural industry because of the managerial positions they assumed in it.

3.3 Intergovernmental Revenue Sharing and Peasants' Life Chances

This section provides an historical account of how market penetration affects the revenue sharing between the state, local governments and rural society, and thus the peasants' earnings. It highlights that the aggravation or relief of the burden on peasants is constrained by the framework of revenue sharing, and how market

[19]The household responsibility system greatly increases production efficiency. As a result, the number of rural laborers became much larger than the number needed for agricultural production in rural areas. The State Statistics Bureau reports that China had an 807 million rural population in 2000.

penetration changes this sharing framework and then the life chances of rural people. Market penetration has lowered the state's economic reliance on rural society and has increased the state's ability and intention to relieve the burden on peasants. This section presents how the disparity of market penetration in different regions of rural Guangdong has led to various revenue-sharing frameworks, which thereby affected the local governments' aggravation or relief of the burden on peasants.

Chinese fiscal policy has been at the center of academic attention in the last two decades and has rapidly become one of the most researched areas regarding China. Many publications of economics or political science point to the great changes in revenue sharing in China (Li 2005; Oksenberg and Tong 1991; Whiting 2001; Wong 1991; World Bank 1990). In this section, an overview of changes and the characteristics of the tax system in China will first be given, after which the revenue-sharing framework within the state hierarchy will be described. Thirdly, this study will discuss the revenue-sharing framework within Guangdong Province. Lastly, how market penetration affects the revenue-sharing framework and thereby the life chances of rural people will be illustrated.

3.3.1 Intergovernmental Revenue Sharing in China—An Overview

The Chinese fiscal administrative structure can be divided into six levels. From the highest level to the lowest are central, provincial,[20] prefecture, county, township, and village[21] levels. The Ministry of Finance pays little attention to revenue sharing between sub-provincial governments and leaves it to provincial governments. Therefore, in this study, the discussion of revenue sharing among these five levels of governments consists of two parts: central-Guangdong Provincial sharing and sub-provincial-local government revenue sharing.

3.3.1.1 Central—Guangdong Revenue Sharing

Fiscal policy in China is a complicated issue, given the broad territory and great changes in the last several decades. Actually, the revenue sharing between the Central Government and Guangdong Province often changed. On average, the fiscal

[20] Between the province level and prefecture level is the associate province level. Most often, the capital city of the province and some other special (special because of economic success, or political importance, etc.) cities will be assigned to this category. For example, in Guangdong Province, Guangzhou, the provincial city, and Shenzhen, the SER with economic success, are associate province-level cities. As a result, the districts and townships under their jurisdiction are also higher in the hierarchy than their counterparts under the jurisdiction of prefectures.

[21] Most studies of Chinese revenue sharing don't take the village level into account. However, the special roles played at the village level have to be addressed to analyze Chinese revenue sharing. Although the village level isn't a formal level of the government of the state, it has its own revenue function and its own revenue, which is set by law.

system of China has undergone a big change every 10 years (in 1953, 1963, 1973, 1983–1984, 1994),[22] and smaller changes were even more frequent. For example, during 1969–1978, the central government changed the fiscal system 6 times.

However, more generally, China's fiscal policy can be grossly divided into three phases. The first phase was the fiscal system in Mao's China, characterized as "tong shou tong zhi (unified income and unified expenditure)." This policy could be considered an integral part of the system of centralized planning and allocation of resources. The characteristics of this policy were three. (1) It was centralized: local governments enjoyed little budgetary autonomy. The Ministry of Finance approved not only the consolidated budget but also annual revenue and expenditure plans at the provincial level. (2) It was simple: revenues from rural society were transferred to the industrial sector via "price scissors"[23]; tax revenue heavily depended on industry, especially state-owned enterprises; and the fiscal bureaucracy was unified, but with all revenues actually collected by local agencies. (3) It provided poor incentives: local governments had little incentive to increase the revenue base or to use funds frugally (Oksenberg and Tong 1991; Wong 1991; World Bank 1990).

The second phase began in the 1980s with the economic reform. The old centralized fiscal system was replaced by the new contracted fiscal system with intergovernmental sharing of revenues and specific expenditure assignments. The major task of the new tax system was to offer better incentives to local governments and enterprises for revenue mobilization. The reform involved two major changes. (1) The central government started to share revenue with provincial governments according to various contracts (Wong 1992), with a fixed or adjusted quota arrangement applying to provinces such as Guangdong and Fujian. Most other provinces shared revenue with the central government according to agreed ratios, which were set annually. (2) The tax-for-profit reform was made in state-owned enterprises. By this reform, state-owned enterprises didn't need to remit all their revenues any more. Instead, enterprises turned over parts of their revenue through taxation. The amount of the tax was subject to the negotiation between the central government, local governments, and enterprises. With this reform the central government wanted to encourage both local governments and state-owned enterprises to enlarge the total amount of the revenue so that they could retain more. This tax reform has been used to explain the success of the Chinese economy by some researchers (Byrd and Gelb 1990; Oi 1992, 1999; Wong 1988, 1992).

Thirdly, in the middle of 1990s, the state issued a fiscal reform which is usually called the "tax assignment system (*fen shui zhi*)." While the fiscal reform of the 1980s encouraged local governments to increase their revenues and granted them more power over their own finances and resources, it also weakened the central government's macroeconomic control. As a result, the major tasks of the 1994 reform were three: (1) to provide adequate revenues for governments, especially the central government; (2) to make the tax structure non-distortionary and more trans-

[22] Please refer to http:www.guangdongdz.com 2006-8-21 14:05:07.

[23] "Price scissors" refers to the government's use of pricing policy to systematically discriminate against agricultural and raw materials producers in favor of industry.

parent; and (3) to revamp central-local revenue-sharing arrangements.[24] These tasks were to be carried out by: (1) reduction of types of taxes from 32 to 18; (2) tax source separation according to three categories: central government revenue, local government revenue and shared revenue (Table 3.5 shows the taxes in each of these categories); and (3) division of administration of the collection of central and local tax revenues. The 1994 reform program established a national tax system (NTS) to collect central government revenues and a local tax system to collect local taxes. For this purpose, existing tax bureaus were split into national and local tax offices. The 1994 tax reform greatly increased central government's *share* of all taxes, which grew from 22 % (in 1993) to 52.2 % (in 1995).[25] At the same time, fiscal transfer from the central government became an outstanding fiscal instrument to correct regional disparities in income and maintain provincial governments' dependence on the central government (Wedeman 1999).

Revenue sharing between the central government and Guangdong was regulated by the national revenue-sharing framework, with some special characteristics. Generally, it can be grossly divided into four phases:

1. In 1950, together with other provinces, fiscal sharing with Guangdong was under the "unified income and unified expenditure" principal.
2. From 1951 to 1979, the central-Guangdong fiscal relationship can be labeled "income and expenses classification, managed hierarchically (huafen shou zhi, fenji guanli)." The central state still controlled most of the revenue. Central-local revenue sharing was set by ratios, which were often changed. For example, Table 3.6 shows that from 1954 to 1957, revenue-sharing ratios between the central government and Guangdong Province changed almost every year.
3. From 1980 to 1993, in order to help Guangdong to go "one step ahead," revenue sharing between the central government and Guangdong was under what was called "big contract (da baogan)." As far as income was concern, the central state received tariffs, the income of railways, harbors, enterprises, and public organizations under the direct jurisdiction of central government. All other incomes belonged to the Guangdong provincial government. The central state was responsible for the expenditure for enterprises and public organizations directly under its jurisdiction, while all other expenditures were the provincial government's duty. Under this classification of income and expenditure, Guangdong was required to remit one billion yuan to the Central Government per year from 1980 to 1987. This policy allowed Guangdong Province to save much money to develop its provincial economy, while most other provinces remained under the framework of the "unified income and unified expenditure" principal.
4. The fiscal reform in 1994 removed the special revenue-sharing framework between the central government and Guangdong Province. After years of high-

[24] The reform was issued at the Third Plenum of the 14th Party Congress in November 1993. The tasks of the reform were present in the provisions of the "Decision on Issues Concerning the Establishment of a Socialist Market Economy."

[25] Please refer to http://news.xinhuanet.com/fortune/2004-10/27/content_2144238.htm.

Table 3.5 Tax separation between central and local governments

Central government revenue	*Tariffs*
	Consumption taxes and value-added taxes collected by customs
	Consumption tax
	Income tax on local banks, foreign banks, and nonbanking fiscal institutions
	Revenue from railways, headquarters of banks, and insurance companies (including business tax, income tax, profits, and urban maintenance and construction tax)
	Profits remitted by state-owned enterprises under the central government
Local government revenue	Business tax (excluding the business tax paid by the railway sector, headquarters of banks, and insurance companies)
	Income tax on local enterprise (excluding the income tax of the abovementioned local banks and foreign-funded banks and nonbanking fiscal enterprises)
	Profits remitted by local enterprises
	Individual income tax
	Land use fees in cities and townships
	Levies on capital investment in low priority areas
	Urban maintenance and construction fees (excluding railways, headquarters of banks, and insurance companies)
	House property tax
	License fees for vehicles and ships
	Stamp duties
	Tax on slaughtering animals
	Agricultural tax (including special agricultural product tax)
	Farmland occupation tax
	Land value-added tax
	Levies on the use of state-owned land
Shared central and local government revenues	Value-added tax—75 % of the value-added tax was assigned to the central government and the remaining 25 % to the local governments
	Resource tax—apart from the oceanic petroleum resource tax that was assigned to the central government, other resource taxes were assigned to the local governments
	Stamp tax levied on securities transactions
Others	The central government also reassigned part of the tax collected to local governments—for every 1 % increase in the value-added tax and consumption tax in each province, autonomous region and municipality, the central government would increase the tax revenues reassigned to the province by 0.3 %

Sources: Zhu (2003a, pp. 17–18)

speed development, the fiscal income of Guangdong Province greatly increased. In 2005, tax incomes (both central government revenue from Guangdong Province and local government revenue) reached 420.261 billion in 2005. During the past 14 years, the tax income of Guangdong has always been the highest of

Table 3.6 Revenue sharing between the central government and Guangdong, 1954–1957

	1954		1955		1956		1957	
	Central	GD	Central	GD	Central	GD	Central	GD
Business tax	93	7	95	5	94	6	80	20
Excise	93	7	95	5	94	6	80	20
Sales tax of industry and commerce	83	17	88	12	90	10	70	30
Income tax of industry and commerce	83	17	88	12	90	10	70	30
Agriculture tax	83	17	75	25	70	30	70	30
Public debt					60	40	60	40

Sources: Edition Committee of the Chorography of Guangdong Province (1999, p. 282)

all the provinces of China.[26] However, like other provinces, Guangdong Province also needs the state's transfer to meet its expenses.

3.3.1.2 Revenue Sharing of Sub-provincial Governments

Revenue sharing of sub-provincial governments refers to the revenue sharing among provincial governments, prefecture governments, county governments, township governments, and village administrations. Because this study focuses on rural society, the analysis of the fiscal situation of township governments, which directly govern the rural society, should be put at the center of the analysis of intergovernmental sharing. Before we come to the analysis of fiscal arrangements of township governments, this study will introduce the characteristics and principals of the revenue sharing between various tiers of local government.

1. *The composition of the revenue of sub-provincial governments.* Most studies of the fiscal system of China divided fiscal revenue into "budgetary (yusuannei)" and "extrabudgetary (yusuanwai)." However, at local levels, especially at the township level, this typology of governmental income is blurred. The specialized vocabulary of finance is not appropriate to describe the situation of rural China. As a result, this study divides the fiscal income of local governments according to their sources. At every level of local government, the revenue structure consists of three parts: local fiscal revenue, allocation (transfer) to the government from higher-level government, and self-retained revenue. Local fiscal revenue includes all kinds of tax income the government can get from the areas under its jurisdiction. Fiscal allocation (transfer) from the governments at higher levels (henceforth fiscal transfer) consists of above-target remittances, all kinds of transfers, subsidies, earmarked funds, and so on, which come from the higher levels of government. Self-retained revenue refers to various income collected by the government in all kinds of ways, such as administrative fees, penalties, funds, etc. This is the most complicated part

[26] Please refer to http://news.xinhuanet.com/fortune/2006-01/02/content_4000383.htm.

of the fiscal income of local governments. Some methods are officially sanctioned and reported, while others are unsanctioned and unreported. Some are legal while some others are "gray" or illegal.

2. *More importantly, the amounts of these three kinds of fiscal income are the result of different factors.* First, local tax revenue, of course, depends on the local economic development. The more developed the local economy, the larger the revenue bases, and the more the tax income.

Second, the amount of fiscal transfer depends on several factors. (1) If a local government itself can get much income from its local area, it will not get much in fiscal transfers from the governments at higher levels. (2) The higher the revenue of a government, the more likely that it subsidizes governments at lower levels and the less likely it is to intercept money which should be distributed to the governments at lower levels. For example, a rich county government is less likely to intercept money allocated to township governments by the provincial government or prefecture government. (3) If a local government leader has a close relationship with the leaders at higher levels of government, his government can more easily get fiscal transfers from the latter. (4) The shorter the physical distance between a government with its higher levels of governments, the more possible it is for it to get fiscal transfers and subsidies from them.

Third, concerning self-retained revenues, (1) a cash-starved government is more likely to create various ways to collect self-retained income; and (2) the longer the distance between the local government and their higher levels of governments, the more likely it is that it will extract all kinds of money from society.

3. *Dependence on the allocation of governments at higher levels is one salient characteristic of Chinese revenue sharing.* After the 1994 tax reform, the revenue sharing of the government at higher level is always set as large as possible (e.g., the sharing of the central government is larger than province government's; the sharing of province government is larger than prefecture government's). Then, through the revenue sharing, the higher levels of government can "buy" the dependence of the inferior governments by allocating all kinds of earmarked funds or subsidies. In Guangdong Province, there are 66 counties that receive transfers from higher levels of government. In many counties, the amount of transfer is higher than the amount of revenue from local sources; the areas under the 66 counties' jurisdictions occupy 46.4 % of the total area of Guangdong.[27] Transfers not only occur between local governments but also between the central and provincial governments.[28] Even Guangdong, one of the "richest" provinces of the country, still needs the transfer from the central government to cover its expenditures. In rural areas, earmarked funds are another way for superior governments to buy the dependences of governments at lower levels. The main uses of earmarked funds are for agricultural support, investment in agricultural infrastructure (including TVEs), welfare assistance and disaster relief, urban maintenance, and so on. Most of such transfers are pass-through funds from central and provincial grants. Such earmarked funds sometimes

[27] Please refer to http://www.gdstats.gov.cn/tjfx/t20040406_10565.htm.

[28] Wedeman 1999, pp. 103–22

can be very important to some local governments. Wong's study in Shandong and Guizhou Provinces shows that the proportion of earmarked funds in total expenditures there ranged from 13 to 56 % (Wong 1997, p. 184).

3.3.2 *Market Penetration and Revenue Sharing Between the State and Rural Society*

The previous section has presented an overview of revenue sharing between the various levels of government in China. With this background, this section will show how market penetration affects the revenue sharing between the state, local governments, and rural society.

3.3.2.1 The State's Needs from Rural Society

The attitudes and policies of the state toward peasants depend on what it needs from rural society. The peasants, who lived in rural areas of China and occupied almost 80 % of the Chinese population, were the key element in the CCP's coming to power. The army of the CCP mainly consisted of peasants. All the CCP's revolutionary bases (geming genjudi) were built in rural areas during the 1930s and 1940s. The CCP could not have defeated the KMT (Kuo Min Tang or Nationalist Party) in the civil war without the supports of the peasants (Benton 1999; Bernhardt 1992; Chen 1986). After the CCP came to power, rural society became the CCP's source of economic surplus and political legitimacy. Under the boycott of the capitalist countries and with the severing of the diplomatic relationship with Soviet Russia, the state had to extract much revenue from rural society by "price scissors," to support the development of industry. This policy continued until the mid-1990s, when the state released control of the prices of most agricultural products to the market. On the other hand, one main element in the CCP's propaganda has been to claim that the CCP has made the peasants the masters of the state. In the standing rules of the CCP, the main slogan is "to serve the people (wei renmin fuwu)"—and "the people" mostly means the peasants.

These two needs—economic surplus and political legitimacy—are not only needs for the central state, run by the CCP, but also for its agencies at local levels. To meet the economic goals and maintain political stability are also two main goals of, and evaluation standards of, local governments. These two needs of the state from rural society help us explain the changes of the state's policies toward rural society. In the coming paragraphs, this study will give an historical account on how these changes have happened.

Mao's China In Mao's China, under the "self-reliance" principal and the planned economy, agriculture and rural society were the main sources of the state's revenue and were extracted by the "price scissors" and transferred to the industrial sector, where high profits are artificially created.[29] Table 3.7 shows that the state's purchase prices for agricultural and sideline products was lower than market prices from 1960 to 1978. Taking agricultural taxes into account, before 1978, rural society turned over 10–30 billion yuan to the central government per year (Zhu 1992).

Table 3.7 Contribution of rural society to the state by "price scissors"

	The price index of market (taking 1952 as 100)	The state's purchase price for agricultural and sideline products (taking 1952 as 100)	The gross purchase by the state of agricultural and sideline products of rural areas (billions of yuan)	The balance between the state's purchase prices and market prices	The balance of gross purchase between the state price and market price (billions of yuan)	The retail price index of industrial products in rural areas
1955	106.1	111.1	18.09	−5.0	−0.90	102.0
1956	105.9	114.5	18.06	−8.6	−1.55	101.0
1957	108.9	120.2	20.81	−11.3	−2.35	102.2
1958	117.5	122.9	22.22	−5.4	−1.19	101.0
1959	119.0	125.1	26.52	−6.1	−1.62	102.2
1960	136.6	129.4	20.80	7.2	1.49	101.5
1961	491.8	165.6	19.60	326.2	63.94	102.5
1962	319.6	164.6	20.3	115.0	31.47	105.3
1963	241.2	159.9	23.2	81.3	18.69	110.5
1964	167.8	155.8	26.3	12.0	3.16	115.4
1965	173.2	154.5	29.9	18.7	5.59	114.2
1966	175.3	161.0	33.6	14.3	4.82	112.0
1967	178.2	160.8	33.5	17.4	5.84	107.9
1968	178.2	160.5	32.8	17.7	5.82	104.8
1969	178.1	160.3	31.4	17.8	5.60	104.0
1970	178.1	160.4	33.7	17.7	5.98	103.7
1971	193.8	163.1	35.8	30.7	10.99	102.2
1972	209.6	165.4	36.4	44.2	16.10	100.5
1973	220.7	166.8	42.1	53.9	22.71	99.9
1974	224.8	168.2	43.0	56.6	24.38	99.9
1975	233.8	171.6	45.7	62.2	28..44	99.9
1976	243.1	172.5	44.88	70.6	31.69	99.9
1977	237.2	172.0	47.80	65.2	31.17	100
1978	221.6	178.8	53.01	42.8	22.69	100.1
1979	211.6	218.3	67.76	−6.7	−4.54	100.2
1980	215.8	233.9	79.77	−18.1	−14.44	101.0
1981	228.3	247.7	90.80	−19.4	−17.62	102.0
1982	235.8	253.1	103.10	−17.3	−17.84	103.6
1983	245.7	264.2	120.60	−18.5	−23.31	104.6

Sources: Department of Price Statistics of the State Statistical Bureau (1984, p. 258)

[29] To learn more about the "price scissors," please refer to Gregory and Stuart 1986; Schultz 1978.

Although much of this revenue was taken away from rural society, the state still maintained the political control of the peasants through the collectivization of agriculture and by controlling ideological propaganda.

The Early Reform Period In the beginning of the 1980s, when the reform had just started, the family responsibility system quickly increased peasants' production incentives. There were various earning sources of peasants also because of the thriving of the petty commodity market in agriculture, agricultural sidelines, and individual family businesses. Moreover, the state increased the purchase prices for agricultural products. At the same time, the ratio of the "price scissor" descended. Taking Ningxia province as an example, the extent of "price scissors" descended from 64.7 to 36.65 % between 1977 and 1982 (Duan 2000). Table 3.5 shows the same tendency from 1979 to 1983.

3.3.2.2 The Reemergence of the Burden on Peasants

The situation mentioned above didn't last for a long time. The burden on peasants gradually became heavier again from the end of the 1980s. The burden on peasants refers to an array of formal and informal exactions on peasants which are greatly beyond what the peasants can accept, so that they become a burden. In order to understand the burden on peasants, we should first understand what peasants had previously submitted to state and local governments.

Revenue remitted by peasants consisted of three parts. The first part was *the state tax*, which included agricultural tax and surcharges, special products tax, slaughter tax, and farmland utilization tax. The second part was made up of two kinds of *local charges:* the five township-pooling fees (wu tongchou) and the three village-retained funds (san tiliu). The former was collected for five issues: education subsidy, social help, family planning, road construction, and militia exercises. The latter was collected mainly for three issues: collective production, public welfare fund, and administrative funds.

These two parts of the revenue remitted by peasants were set according to laws and regulations. The structure of the third part, *other local surcharges* however, was far more complicated. It usually came from four sources:

1. *Fees.* In rural areas, township government provides peasants with public services, although these services are not all free. Moreover, township governments create some compulsory services. For example, in Chan Township, which will be presented as the representative of the local economy in Chap. 6, a waterworks is being constructed and the peasants there are compelled to pay more than 70 yuan per month.[30]
2. *Fundraising.* For all kinds of reasons, including road construction, educational development, cultural development, and so on, some township governments will "amass capital (jizi)" from peasants, requiring them to make so-called voluntary

[30] Informant Chan200407.

contributions (juankuan)" and pay "unsanctioned levies (tanpai)." These are the so-called three unrullies (san luan), which have attracted the attention of the central government.

3. *Fines and property confiscation.* Fines and property confiscation are also frequent in some rural areas. Some crimes are punished by fines in rural areas. Moreover, all tiers of local government promulgate many regulations every year, and violations of these regulations will lead to fines or property confiscation. For example, violations of family planning policy can lead to up to 10 thousand yuan in fines, and the property of peasants who cannot pay the fines can be confiscated.
4. *Hidden burdens.* There are also other hidden burdens that occur unsystematically, such as the pocketing of loans from peasants, the confiscation of peasants' land without enough compensation, the issuance of new fines or penalties, etc.

All abovementioned tax, charges, and surcharges together constitute of the burden on peasants. But the three parts play different roles in the formation of the burden on peasants. As a peasant saying goes, "The first tax (the state tax) is easy, the second tax (local charge) is heavy, the third tax (other local surcharges) presses me to death (yi shui qing, er shui zhong, san shui ya si ren)." Obviously, the various local surcharges are the main sources of burden on the peasants, especially as there are no specific rules and regulations on these local surcharges.[31] As a result, township governments can use these methods according to their needs.

From the beginning of the reform to 1988, the growth of peasants' incomes was higher than the growth of the burden on peasants, but from 1988 the situation was reversed. From 1994 to 1999, the average tax on peasants went from 25.3 yuan to 45.9 yuan, an increase of 50 %, while the average income of peasants increased by only 10.43 %. In 1999, average burden on peasants increased 5.8 %, while the average income of peasants only increases 2.2 % (Ma 2002).

Three main factors led to the emergence of the peasant's burden. Firstly, the state's focus for the economic reform was transferred from rural areas to urban areas at the end of the 1980s. The state's special policies for rural areas became fewer (He and Wang 2005).

The second factor was the continuation of revenue extraction of the state from rural society. The state began to levy a farmland utilization tax in 1987 and a tax on special products of agriculture and forestry in 1989, in order to remedy the loss of tax revenue because of the structural adjustment of the mix of agricultural production and better quality, high-value-added products.[32] This also contributed to the emergence of the burden on peasants.

[31] In the middle of 1990, the central government promulgated a regulation in order to relieve the burden on peasants. According to the regulation, the total of taxes, local charges, and other surcharges may not exceed 5 % of the total income of the peasants' households. However, this regulation didn't make much difference since it is hard to calculate how much the 5 % ratio represents.

[32] The agriculture tax was calculated according to staples at first. Therefore, if the land is used for high-value-added products, the tax (according to grain) would be underevaluated.

The third factor consisted of the fiscal constraints on local governments, especially county and township governments. After 1994 tax reform,[33] the local governments' revenue share decreased. This was especially true of local governments in the less developed areas. Many studies (in Chinese) bear witness to the heavy debts of county and township governments in the middle and west parts of the country (Guo 2002; Duan 2000; Jiang 2004). Under such fiscal constraints, a cash-starved local government will have more motivation to extract money from the society to meet the needs of administrative operation and/or personal interests.

3.3.2.3 Market Penetration and the State's Policies on the Relief of the Burden on Peasants

The aggravation of the burden on peasants led to numerous complaints and dissatisfactions of peasants expressed in various ways: appeal to the upper levels of government (shangfang), protests, and even riots. Some studies by researchers of comparative politics reported that the situation was becoming serious (Aubert and Li 2002; Lu 1997; Wedeman 1997; Thomas 1999). The burden on peasants gradually attracted the attention of the central government. What the former president Jiang Zemin said may fully present the worries of the central state over this issue:

> To decrease or increase peasant burden is not the problem of money, but the problem of protecting or destroying peasants' positivity, the problem of accelerating or blocking the productivity of rural society, and the problem of gaining or losing the peasant' trust and support. We have to understand the problem of the burden on peasants from the perspective of politics, from the perspective of the theme of our party and the stability of rural administration. Rural areas were the cradle of the Communist Party's revolution. Peasants are the main force of our revolution. We couldn't have won the revolution without the great sacrifice of the peasants. "Serving the people" with full hearts' is the persistent tenet of the Communist Party. 80 percent of the Chinese people are peasants. The CCP's relationship with the peasants directly determines whether the CCP can gain the people's support. If there is any wrong in this relationship, we may lose the largest, most accountable body of confederates. Our state's base will be risky and our idealism will be ruined.[34]

However, market penetration in China has empowered the central government to relieve the burden on peasants. First, accompanying the market penetration process, the state's economic dependence on rural society is decreasing. Figure 3.5 shows that the state's tax income has increased very quickly, but the agricultural tax has contributed little to it. Second, the political dependence of the central state on rural society has gradually come to outweigh its economic dependence. With this understanding, the central state has promulgated many policies to decrease the burden on peasants, among which two should be highlighted here.

---

[33] The "tax assignment system (*fen shui zhi*)" was initiated by the central government in 1994.

[34] Important Literature Since the Fourteenth Representative Conference of the CCP (zhongguo gongchandang shidi ci daibiao dahui yilai de zhongyao wenjian), Beijing: People Press, 1999.

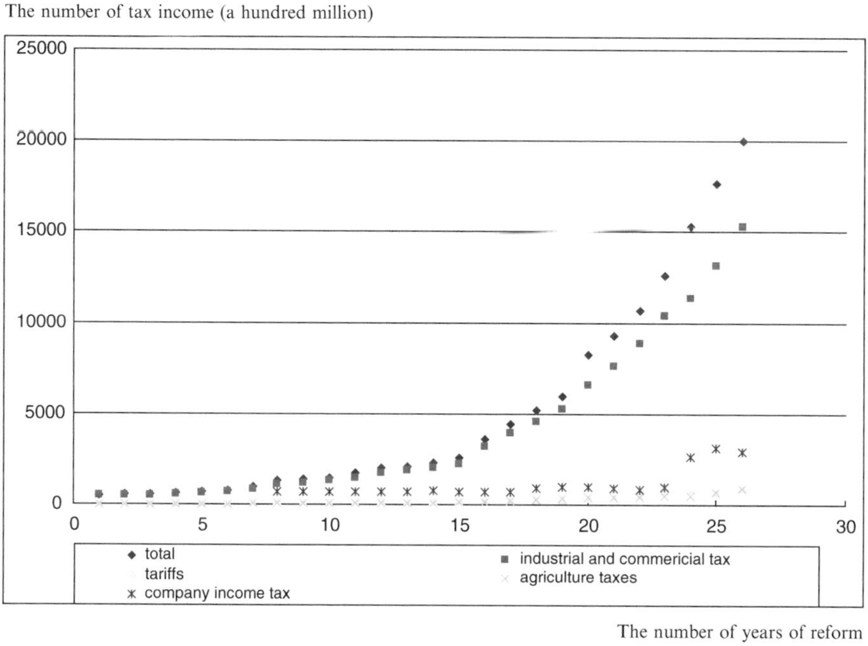

Fig. 3.5 The contribution of the five main taxes to the state's tax. Notes: The main revenue of the state can be divided into five types: industrial taxes, commercial taxes, tariffs, agricultural taxes, and company income taxes. From 1978 to 2003, the total revenue of the state increased more than 20 times, but agriculture contributed very little to the increase (Source: State Statistical Bureau 2004, pp. 334–35)

Direct Village Election The central state believes that the main cause of the burden on peasants is the unchecked extraction power of the village administration. Therefore, in 1998, The Villagers Committee Organization was enacted to implement direct village elections. Direct village election had been proposed in 1987 by the central government (Kelliher 1997; O'Brien 1994). However, the regulation wasn't implemented fully by local governments, for many reasons,[35] so that the new law was enacted in 1998. Even since then, however, how local governments, especially township governments, implement this law depends on their needs from rural society. Cash-starved township governments have a greater tendency to influence village elections than their counterparts in rural areas with developed economies because their control over elections facilitates their economic extraction from the villages.

Tax-for-Fee Reform As a response to the heavy burden on peasants, the central government tried to prohibit the extra tax collection and to compensate rural finance by reforming the agricultural taxation system. This is the essence of the tax-for-fee

[35] There are many studies on this issue by comparative politics and China specialists; please refer to O'brien and Li 2000, pp. 465–489; Shi 1999, pp. 385–412; Pastor and Tan 2000, pp. 490–512.

experiment. The reform was implemented gradually: the experiment of the tax-for-fee reform first emerged in Anhui Province in 1995, and in 2000 Anhui Province was designated as an experimental site for the tax-for-fee reform by the central government. In 2003 the Central Council decided to extend this reform to the whole nation.[36]

The content of the tax-for-fee reform is as follows. (1) The "three cancelations" (san ge quxiao) cancel the slaughter tax, the five township-pooling fees, and labor obligations. (2) "Two readjustments" (liang ge tiaozheng) compensate for the loss of revenue from the three cancelations by readjusting the agricultural tax to 7 % on average and by readjusting the special agricultural tax by integrating it with the agricultural tax. (3) Finally, the "one reform" (yi xiang gaige) replaced three village-retained funds with one surtax, limited to 20 % of the adjusted agricultural tax; this surtax was to be collected by the township and used by the villages (Yep 2004; Li and Wu 2005).[37] After 5 years of testing and extension, in 2005, when I began to research this thesis, the State Council decided to cancel all agricultural taxes[38] for the coming year. This meant that the state and local governments would no longer levy any taxes on the peasants. This reform indirectly increases the peasants' earnings.

3.3.3 Market Penetration, Intergovernmental Revenue Sharing, and Peasant's Life Chances

Although a series of policies have been adopted by the central government to relieve the burden on peasants, the local governments' attitudes to these policies are various. To explain these variations, market penetration and the intergovernmental revenue-sharing framework should be taken into consideration. Economic and political dependence is not only an issue for the central state but also involves the local governments (Cao and Dickson 2001; Whiting 2001), and this helps us to explain the local governments' attitudes toward the relief of the burden on peasants. Local governments are of four levels: provincial, prefecture, county, and township. This study focuses on the township level, because the township governments directly govern rural society and all revenue from rural society is extracted by them.

[36] In 2003, the State Council issued a document entitled *The State Council's Ideas for Extensively Boosting the Testing of the Rural Tax-for-Fee Reform* (Guowuyuan guanyu quanmian tuijin nongcun shuifei gaige shidian gongzuo de yijian) to extend the reform to the whole nation.

[37] Document of the State Council (No.7, 2002), *Notice of the CCP center and the State Council for enforcing the rural tax-for-fee reform* (zhonggong zhongyang, guowuyuan guanyu jinxing nongcun shuifei gaige shidian gongzuo de tongzhi).

[38] In January 2005, the state council promulgated a document entitled *The ideas of the State Council of the CCP center on some policies for enforcing the work in rural areas and improving the general production capacity of agriculture*. This document accelerated the exemption from the agricultural tax. As a result, 22 of 31 provinces had announced that they would exempt peasants from all agricultural taxes, as of February 2005. Please see http://news.xinhuanet.com/focus/2005-01/24/content-2491449.htm.

3.3.3.1 The Revenue Structure of Township Governments

Under the commune system, the income and expenses of communes were regulated by the "unified income and expenditure" system (Huang 1988; Chen and Chen 2004). In 1983, accompanying the abolition of the commune system and the establishment of township governments, the Central Committee of the CCP and the State Council considered that the township governments should have their own revenue management organization. As a result, the Treasury Department of the State Council promulgated a document entitled *The regulation on treasury management of township governments* in 1985.

As at every level of local government, township governments' revenue consists of three parts: fiscal revenue, allocations from higher government, and self-retained funds.[39]

Fiscal Revenue Fiscal revenue was of two sorts. The first was the sharing of state-set taxes, including agricultural tax, agricultural special products tax, farmland utilization tax, animal slaughter tax, and the title tax. The second was that from local charges, which included the five township-pooling fees (wu tongchou), the profits of township-owned enterprises, the fee for maintenance and construction of the town, the exchange tax at fairs, the tax for trade in livestock, and the fee for vehicle licenses. All these taxes were set by law or by higher government regulations. It is easy to see that fiscal revenue really depended on the extent of local market penetration.

Transfer from Higher Government As mentioned above, dependence on transfer of funds from higher levels of government is a characteristic of Chinese revenue sharing. As far as township governments are concerned, transfers from higher government consist of many kinds of funds, subsidies, earmarked funds, etc. The stable earmarked funds from the central government include subsidies to soldier's family, funds to guarantee a minimum standard of living (zuidi shenghuo baozhanjin), funds for "five guarantee households (wu bao hu),"[40] and welfare funds for medical treatment. There are also other kinds of earmarked funds according to yearly needs.[41] For the township government, which is the lowest level of the governmental hierarchy, its share of the transfer depends on the fiscal situation of all higher levels of government. It is also closely related to the market penetration level of the territory under higher government jurisdiction. The richer higher levels of government have lower remittance requirements, so that more is left for transfer and vice versa.

[39] Susan Whiting (2001) divided the township's revenue structure into three parts: budgetary, extrabudgetary, and self-retained fund. However, the budgetary and extrabudgetary revenue is quite blurred in rural China. This study classifies township governments' revenues according to the source of the revenue.

[40] As stipulated in the Chinese Constitution, the state promises to provide food, clothing, housing, and medical care to those individuals or households with no capacity to work, no family to help them, and no means of support.

[41] Informant Lee2004: 23.

For example, the township government can get little from the county government if the fiscal situation of the latter is bad. Furthermore, transfer from central, provincial, and prefectural governments can be bitten off by county governments.

Self-Retained Revenue This included all kinds of administration fees, penalties, apportionments, and raised funds. Revenue raised by township government merits special attention because it presents the most distinctive phenomenon of the fiscal arrangement in rural areas: the unchecked revenue-mobilization power of the township government. As I have mentioned, every level of government has its self-raised revenue, but the revenue-mobilization power of the township government is more unchecked, as the tax base consists of the individual peasant household, which has little bargaining power with the township government. To challenge the government power according to law can hardly be afforded by an ordinary peasant household. As a result, self-raised revenue is the most important source of revenue for some cash-starved township governments. Such revenue can be raised with many excuses and from many items, but generally there are three categories: (1) funds raised for various purposes, such as road construction, the construction of primary or middle schools, and so on; (2) loans from other sources such as rural credit cooperative, other local agencies of the state, and even individuals; and (3) various penalties. This self-retained revenue is the most important cause of the burden on peasants.

The role of the village administration in raising township government revenue should be pointed out here. A village is not a formal level of government. The village has inherited its framework of governance from the collectives, including the Villagers Committees and a party branch. As a result, although the village administration doesn't have independent budgetary status, it had its own exclusive revenue, namely, the "three village-retained funds (san tiliu)," which is collected for three issues: collective production, public welfare, and administration. These funds are collected from households by village cadres and turned over to the township for unified allocation. The revenue function of village administration is always integrated with that of the township government, as the village is partly responsible for the collection of tax, local charges, and even many self-raised funds for the township government. Moreover, all earmarked funds to individual households come through village cadres. As a result, village administration also shares a given proportion of all kinds of self-raised revenue with township government (Wong 1997, p. 174). A village with a high level of market penetration can be a large economic entity, and village-owned revenue can be very considerable. Revenue sharing between township government and village administration will thus be one of the key points in discussion of the cases in the following chapters.

3.3.3.2 Market Penetration, Intergovernmental Revenue Sharing, and Peasants' Life Chances in Guangdong

From this discussion of fiscal structure, one can see that there are three ways for a township government to improve its fiscal income: (1) by developing the local economy to increase the tax revenue; (2) by bargaining with higher government for more subsidies, funds, or other help; and (3) by extracting more revenue from peasants with various excuses and for various purposes. A township government's economic and political needs from rural society decide how it selects among these ways.

This selection by the township of means for raising revenue also depends on the extent of market penetration, both locally and within the territory under higher government' jurisdiction. In regions with high market penetration, taxation will be the main source of revenue for township government and village administration. For example, in the PRD region, the thriving of rural industry has enlarged the tax base of township governments. In this situation, local governments tend to provide more welfare and subsidies, in order to gain the political support of the peasants.

However, for township governments in outskirt areas, bargaining with higher government for more subsidization, funds, or help will be a preferred way. For example, for a township located in the fringe rural areas of the PRD region or in suburban areas of other regional cities, higher levels of governments can provide much revenue extracted from the city center and other developed areas under their jurisdiction. The large transfers from higher government to the township governments and village administrations in outskirt areas thereby become possible. As a result, in many such townships, the amount of transfer is often much higher than the amount of local tax revenue.

In most of the mountain areas of Guangdong, which have what I call "local economies" in this study, township governments' main revenue sources are from self-retained funds. To increase the tax base by developing the local economy seems difficult because of the low level of market penetration, while county and even prefectural governments are also cash-starved, so that it is difficult to get much money from them as these cash-starved governments at higher levels themselves become the township governments' competitors for the limited revenue sources available. As a result, extraction of revenue from the peasants becomes the only available way for the township governments to meet their economic needs.

In the subsequent chapters, I will analyze this variation with detailed ethnographic data from the comparative cases.

3.4 Summary

This chapter has depicted how the reform in rural Guangdong has progressed as a market penetration processes and how this process affects the life chances of rural people in Guangdong. Firstly, an historical account of the market penetration processes in Guangdong has been presented, consisting of two phases: (1) the reintroduction of family farming and the open market leading to the development of petty commodity markets, which was common to the whole province, and (2) the flood of FDI into the PRD region and its boosting of the commodity market and labor market there. From coastal areas to mountain areas, regional disparities came into being in the province.

Secondly, the chapter has documented how market penetration has increased the earning sources of the peasant. Market penetration has increased the number of earning sources for all rural people in Guangdong, from crops only to a variety of other sources. However, the distribution of sources of earning depends on the level of market penetration: the higher the level of market penetration, the greater the diversity of sources of earnings for rural people.

Thirdly, market penetration has also increased the fiscal revenue of the state and local governments, which has led to relief of the burden on peasants. Market penetration decreases the state's economic dependence on rural society and increases the state's ability and intent to strive for the peasants' political support. As far as local governments are concerned, the higher the level of market penetration, the more is the possibility that local governments will relieve the burden on peasants.

Market penetration in rural Guangdong has created three kinds of economy: new cooperative economy, outskirt economy, and local economy. In the following chapters, I will discuss how these three kinds of economies are varied in two aspects: the distribution of the sources of earnings and the local governments' attitude and behavior within the communities.

References

Aslund, A. (1992). *Market socialism or the restoration of capitalism*. Cambridge: Cambridge University Press.

Aubert, C., & Li, X. (2002). Peasant burden: Taxes and Levies imposed on Chinese farmers. In *Agricultural policies in China after WTO accession* (Collection: China in the global economy, pp. 160–179). Paris: OECD.

Benton, G. (1999). *New fourth army, communist resistance along the Yangtze and the Huai, 1938–1941*. Berkeley: University of California Press.

Berend, I. T. (1990). *The Hungarian economic reforms, 1953–1988*. New York: Cambridge University Press.

Bernhardt, K. (1992). *Rents, taxes, and peasant resistance, the lower Yangzi region, 1840–1950*. Stanford: Stanford University Press.

Bryant, C. G. A., & Mokrzycki, E. (Eds.). (1994). *The new great transformation?* London: Routledge.

Burawoy, M., & Lukacs, J. (1992). *The radiant past*. Chicago: University of Chicago Press.

Bureau of Industry and Commercial Administration of Guangdong, Social Science Academic of Guangdong, and Association of Private Enterprises of Guangdong. (2003). *Guangdong sheng shehui kexue yuan lanbi shu xilie: Guangdong saying qiye de fazhan* [The series of blue books of the social science academy of Guangdong province: The development of private enterprises in Guangdong]. Guangzhou: Guangdong jingji chubanshe.

Byrd, W. A., & Gelb, A. (1990). Why industrialize? The incentives for rural community governments. In W. A. Byrd & Q. Lin (Eds.), *China's rural industry: Structure, development, and reform* (pp. 358–387). New York: Oxford University Press.

Cao, C.-m., & Dickson, B. J. (Eds.). (2001). *Remaking the Chinese state: Strategies, society and security*. New York: Routledge.

Chau, K.-C. (1998). Agriculture and forestry. In D. K. Y. Chu (Ed.), *Guangdong: Survey of a province undergoing rapid change* (pp. 87–112). Hong Kong: Chinese University Press.

Chen, Y.-f. (1986). *Making revolution, the communist movement in eastern and central china, 1937–1945*. Berkeley: University of California Press.

Chen, Yongzheng, & Chen Jiaze. (2004). An analysis on township level fiscal in china. *The Observation on Rural China (Zhongguo nongcun guancha), 5.*

Cheng, J. Y. S. (2000a). *Guangdong in the twenty-first century: Stagnation or second take-off?* Hong Kong: City University of Hong Kong Press.

Cheng, J. Y. S. (2000b). Guangdong's challenges: Organizational streamlining, economic restructuring and anti-corruption. In J. Y. S. Cheng (Ed.), *Guangdong in the twenty-first century: Stagnation or second take-off?* (pp. 17–54). Hong Kong: City University of Hong Kong Press.

Department of Price Statistics of the State Statistical Bureau. (1984). *Zhongguo de maoyi he jiage tongji ziliao* [The statistical materials of trade and price of China]. Beijing: Chinese Statistical Press.

Duan, Q. (2000). Bu fada diqu nongmin fudan wenti yanjiu—yi Ningxia wei li (The studies on peasant burden of underdeveloped region—evidences from Ningxia). *Management World (Guanli shijie), 7.*

Edition Committee of the Chorography of Guangdong Province. (1999). *Guangdong Shengzhi—caizheng pian* [The chorography of Guangdong—Fiscal]. Guangzhou: Guangdong renmin chubanshe.

Edition Committee of the Chorography of Guangdong Province. (2004). *Guangdong Shengzhi—zongshu* [The chorography of Guangdong—Summary]. Guangzhou: Guangdong renmin chubanshe.

Gray, J., & Grey, M. (1983). China's new agricultural revolution. In S. Feuchtwang & A. Hussein (Eds.), *The Chinese economic reforms* (pp. 151–184). New York: St. Martin's Press.

Gregory, P. R., & Stuart, R. C. (1986). *Soviet economic structure and performance* (3rd ed.). New York: Harper and Row.

Guangdong Provincial Statistical Bureau. (1995). *Guangdong tongji nianjian* (Guangdong statistical yearbook). Beijing: Zhongguo tongji chubanshe.

Guangdong Provincial Statistical Bureau. (1999). *Guangdong tongji nianjian* [Guangdong statistical yearbook]. Beijing: Zhongguo tongji chubanshe.

Guangdong Provincial Statistical Bureau. (2002). *Guangdong tongji nianjian 2001* [Guangdong statistical yearbook 2001]. Beijing: Zhongguo tongji chubanshe.

Guo Yongzhong. (2002). Dangqian zhongguo nongmin fudan wenti yanjiu [A study on the peasant burden in contemporary China]. *Journal of Peking University (Philosopy and Social Sciences), 1*, 47–54.

He, Xuefeng, & Wang, Ximing. (2005). *Nongming fudan de xianzhuang yu zhengjie* [The current situation and crux of the peasant burden]. Available at http://www.usc.cuhk.edu.hk/wk.asp

Hinton, W. (1984). *Shenfan*. New York: Random House.

Huang, Yuguang. (1988). *Sheshui zhuyi xiang caizheng* (Township fiscal of socialism). Beijing: Economics and Science Press.

Jiang, C. (2004). Xian xiang caizheng kunnan jiqi dui caizheng zhi nong nengli de yingxiang (The fiscal constraints of county and township governments and their effects on the ability to giving fiscal supports to peasants). *Guanli shijie, 7*, 61–68

Joseph, W. A., Wong, C., & Zweig, D. (1991). *New perspectives on the cultural revolution.* Cambridge, MA: Harvard University.

Kelliher, D. (1997). The Chinese debate over the village self-government. *China Journal, 37*, 63–86.

Kornai, J. (1992). *The socialism system.* Princeton: Princeton University Press.

Kovacs, J. M. (Ed.). (1994). *Transition to capitalism?* New Brunswick: Transaction.

Kuang, Ji, (Ed.). (1991). *Dangdai Zhongguo de Guangdong* [Contemporary China: Guangdong]. Beijing: Dangdai zhongguo chubanshe.

Kueh, Y. Y., & Ash, R. F. (1996). The fifth dragon: Economic development. In B. Hook (Ed.), *Guangdong: China's promised land, regional development in China* (Vol. 1, pp. 149–192). Hong Kong/New York: Oxford University Press.

Lau, P.-k. (1998). Industry and trade. In D. K. Y. Chu (Ed.), *Guangdong: Survey of a province undergoing rapid change* (pp. 127–172). Hong Kong: Chinese University Press.

Lau, P.-k. (2000). Industrial structure and industrial policy in Guangdong province. In Y. S. Joseph Cheng (Ed.), *Guangdong in the twenty-first century: Stagnation or second take-off?* (pp. 79–102). Hong Kong: City University of Hong Kong Press.

Li, L. C. (2005). Understanding institutional change: Fiscal management in local China. *Journal of Contemporary Asia, 35*, 87–109.

Li, Linda Chelan, & Licai, Wu. (2005). 'Daobi' haishi 'fan daobi'—nongcun shuifei gaige qianhou zhongyang yu defang zhijian de hudong ('Force from Below' or 'Force from Above'—The interaction between the central government and local governments before and after the reform). *Shehuixue yanjiu, 4*.

Lin, G. C. S. (1997). *Red capitalism in South China: Growth and development of the Pearl River delta*. Vancouver: UBC Press.

Lu, A., & Selden, M. (1987). The reform of land ownership and political economy of contemporary China. *Peasant Studies, 14*, 249–289.

Ma, Xiaohe. (2002). *Wo guo nongcun shuifei gaige yanjiu* [A study on rural tax and fee reform of our country]. Beijing: Zhongguo jiahua chubanshe.

Whyte, M. K. (1985). The politics of life chances in the People's Republic of China. In S. Yu-ming (Ed.), *Power and policy in the PRC* (pp. 244–265). Boulder: Westview Press.

Nee, V. (1986). Peasant household economy and decollectivization in China. *Journal of Asian and African Studies, 21*(3–4), 185–203.

Nee, V. (1992). Organizational dynamics of market transition: Hybrid froms, property rights, and mixed economy in China. *Administrative Science Quarterly, 37*, 1–27.

O'Brien, K. J. (1994). Implementing political reform in China's villages. *Australian Journal of Chinese Affairs, 32*, 33–59.

O'Brien, K. J., & Li, L. (2000). Accommodating 'Democracy' in a one-party state: Introducing village election in China. *China Quarterly, 162*, 465–489.

Oi, J. C. (1989). *State and peasant in contemporary China: The political economy of village government*. Berkeley: University of California Press.

Oi, J. C. (1992). Fiscal reform and the economic foundations of local state corporatism in China. *World Politics, 45*, 99–126.

Oi, J. C. (1999). *Rural China takes off: Institutional foundations of economic reform*. Berkeley: University of California Press.

Oksenberg, M., & Tong, J. (1991). The evolution of central-provincial fiscal relations in China, 1971–1984: The formal system. *China Quarterly, 125*, 1–32.

Pastor, R. A., & Tan, Q. (2000). The meaning of China's village elections. *The China Quarterly, 162*, 490–512.

Perkins, D. (1977). *Rural small-scale industry in the People's Republic of China*. Berkeley: University of California Press.

Powell, S. G. (1992). *Agricultural reform in China: From communes to community economy 1978–1990*. Manchester: Manchester University Press.

Prout, C. (1985). *Market socialism in Yugoslavia*. New York: Oxford University Press.

Riskin, C. (1971). Small industry and the Chinese model of development. *The China Quarterly, 46*, 245–273.

Riskin, C. (1978). China's rural industries: Self-reliant systems or independent kingdoms. *The China Quarterly, 73*, 77–98.

Schultz, T. W. (1978). *Distortions of agricultural incentives*. Bloomington: Indiana University Press.

Shi, T. (1999). Village committee elections in China: Institutional tactics for democracy. *World Politics, 51*, 385–412.

Shirk, S. L. (1993). *The political logic of economic reform in China*. Berkeley: University of California Press.

Shue, V. (1980). *Peasant China in Transition: The dynamics of development toward socialism, 1949–1956*. Berkeley: University of California Press.

Shue, V. (1988). *The reach of the state: Sketches of the Chinese body politic*. Stanford: Stanford University Press.

Sigurdson, J. (1977). *Rural industrialization in China*. Cambridge, MA: Harvard University Press.
Stark, D. (1990). Privatization in Hungary: From plan to market or from plan to clan. *East European Politics and Societies, 4*, 351–392.
Stark, D. (1992). Path dependence and privatization strategies in East Central Europe. *East European Politics and Societies, 6*, 17–54.
Stark, D. (1996). Recombinant property in East European capitalism. *American Journal of Sociology, 101*, 993–1027.
State Statistical Bureau. (2002). *Zhongguo tongji nianjian 2001* [China statistical yearbook 2001). Beijing: Zhongguo tongji chubanshe.
State Statistical Bureau. (2004). *Zhongguo caizheng nianjian* [Chinese fiscal yearbook]. Beijing: Zhongguo tongji chubanshe.
Szelenyi, I. (1989). East Europe in an Epoch of transition: Toward a socialist mixed economy? In V. Nee, D. Stark, & M. Selden (Eds.), *Remaking the economic institutions of socialism: China and Eastern Europe* (pp. 208–32). Stanford: Stanford University Press.
Szelenyi, I., & Kostello, E. (1996). The market transition debate: Toward a synthesis. *American Journal of Sociology, 101*, 1082–1096.
The Center of Urban and Region Studies. (2002). *The study of the economic interaction between Hong Kong, and the Pearl Delta Region* (pp. 1, 34). Guangzhou: Sun Yat-sen University Press.
Thomas, B. (1999). Farmer discontent and regime responses. In G. Merle & M. F. Roderick (Eds.), *The paradox of China's post-Mao reforms* (pp. 195–219). Cambridge, MA: Harvard University Press.
Vogel, E. F. (1989). *One step ahead in China: Guangdong under reform*. Cambridge, MA: Harvard University Press.
Walder, A. G. (1995a). China's transitional economy: Interpreting its significance. *The China Quarterly, 144*, 963–979.
Walder, A. G. (1995b). Local governments as industrial firms: An organizational analysis of China's transitional economy. *American Journal of Sociology, 101*, 263.
Watson, A. (1983). Agriculture looks for 'Shoes That Fit': The production responsibility system and its implications. *World Development, 11*(8), 705–730.
Wedeman, A. (1997). Stealing from the farmers: Institutional corruption and the 1992 IOU crisis. *The China Quarterly, 152*, 81–107.
Wedeman, A. (1999). Agency and fiscal dependence in central-principal relations in China. *Journal of Contemporary China, 8*, 103–122.
Whiting, S. H. (2001). *Power and wealth in Rural China: The political economy of institutional change*. New York: Cambridge University Press.
Wong, C. P. W. (1988). Interpreting rural industrial growth in the post-mao period. *Modern China, 14*, 3–30.
Wong, C. P. W. (1991). Central-local relations in an era of fiscal decline—The paradox of fiscal decentralization in post-Mao China. *The China Quarterly, 128*, 691–714.
Wong, C. P. W. (1992). Fiscal reform and local industrialization: The problematic sequencing of reform in Post-Mao China. *Modern China, 18*(2), 197–227.
Wong, C. P. W. (1997). Rural public Finance. In C. P. W. Wong (Ed.), *Financing local government in the People's Republic of China* (pp. 167–209). New York: Oxford University Press.
World Bank. (1990). *China: Revenue mobilization and tax policy*. Washington, DC: World Bank.
Lu, X. (1997). The politics of peasant burden in reform China. *Journal of Peasant Studies, 24*, 113–138.
Yang, C. K. (1959). *A Chinese village in early communist transition*. Westport: Greenwood Press.
Yang, Qinxi, & Pin, Xian. (2001). *Guangdong xiao chengshi fazhan he nongye laodongli zhuanyi yanjiu* [The study on development of little cities and rural labor transferring of Guangdong]. Unpublished document of the Center for Development Studies of the Guangdong Provincial Government (Guangdong Sheng zhengfu fazhan yanjiu zhongxin). In Chuanyi Cui. (2004). *Zhongguo nomin liudong guangcha* [The observation on the mobility of Chinese peasants]. Shangxi: Economic Press.

Yep, R. (2004). Can 'Tax-for-Fee' reform reduce rural tension in China? The process, progress and limitations. *The China Quarterly, 177*, 42–70.
Zeng, K. (2000). Retrospect and prospects of foreign direct investment inflow: The case of Guangdong province. In J. Y. S. Cheng (Ed.), *Guangdong in the twenty-first century: Stagnation or second take-off?* (pp. 103–128). Hong Kong: City University of Hong Kong Press.
Zhang, Letian. (1998). *Gao Bie Li Xiang: Ren Min Gong She Zhi Du Yan Jiu* [Good bye, Utopia: A study to The Institutions of People's Commune]. Shanghai: Dongfang chuban zhongxin (Dong Fang Press).
Zhou, K. X. (1996). *How the farmers changed China: Power of the people*. Boulder: Westview Press.
Zhu, Q. (1992). *The application of social indexes*. Beijing: Chinese Statistical Press.
Zhu, G. (2003). Intergovernmental fiscal relations and budget deficits. In C. Findlay, A. Waston, E. Cheng, & G. Zhu (Eds.), *Rural financial markets in China* (pp. 13–34). Canberra: Asia Pacific Press.

Chapter 4
A New Cooperative Economy

In Mao's China, after the establishment of the commune system, villages were organized as cooperative communities, in which the collective ownership and redistribution of resources constituted the main features. The collective agriculture was later replaced by family farming soon after the market reform began. However, the reemergence of family farming hasn't necessarily led to the vanishing of the collective characteristics of rural China, as assumed by market transition theory. For one thing, the collective administration units, as instruments of political control, still remained. For another, in most rural areas, village administrations still more or less possess some collective assets, as all farmland, except for the land of the peasant's estate (zhai ji di), which inherited from family members,[1] is still owned collectively, as well as some other collective assets that are not be distributed to individual families (e.g., fish ponds, forests, etc.).[2]

The reform in rural China led to various results. The new cooperative economy is one of them. As implied by its name, the outstanding characteristic of this kind of economy is its institutions of cooperation. On one hand, peasant households have cooperated in a new way—the individual family contributes capital, user rights to

[1] According to the Chinese Land Laws, the land in rural areas is separately owned by township governments, the brigade (called administrative village after 1984), and the production team (the natural village after 1984) [it is the so-called the policy of three levels of owner (san ji suoyou zhi)] except for the land for house construction (zhaijidi), which usually is inherited by peasants from their parents. The land in urban areas is owned by the state. But there is no clear definition of what is rural land and what is urban land. Moreover, the state has the right to confiscate the land in rural areas for public goals.

[2] In 1985, after the family responsibility system came into force, 53.5 % (113.58 billion yuan) of gross fixed material production assets were owned by peasant households and 46.7 % (99.43 billion yuan) were owned by collective organizations. Please see *The tendency and countermeasure to the structural reform of the property institution of our nation*, unpublished document of the Policy Study Office of the State Council.

N. Chen, *State, Market and Life Chances in Contemporary Rural Chinese Society*, DOI 10.1007/978-3-662-45046-8_4

land[3], and other assets to the collective organization as the original capital for collective economic enterprises; on the other hand, the individual family still runs its own business, including its farming business and other individual family businesses. In most of the rural areas of the PRD region of Guangdong, the village economies were developed in this way when market penetration provided chances for the development of local economies, beginning at the end of 1980s. This chapter takes Fan Township, which is located in the middle of the PRD region bordering the Guangzhou City center (see Fig. 4.1), as an example of the new cooperative economy. Firstly, I will summarize the market penetration process in Fan Township and the revenue sharing between the township government and higher levels of government. Secondly, this chapter will introduce the institutions of the new cooperative economy. Thirdly, the various sources of earnings of peasants will be presented in detail. Fourthly, I will introduce the village administration and the advantages of village cadres as the managers of the new cooperative economy. Lastly, the results of the stratification of the new cooperative economy will be discussed.

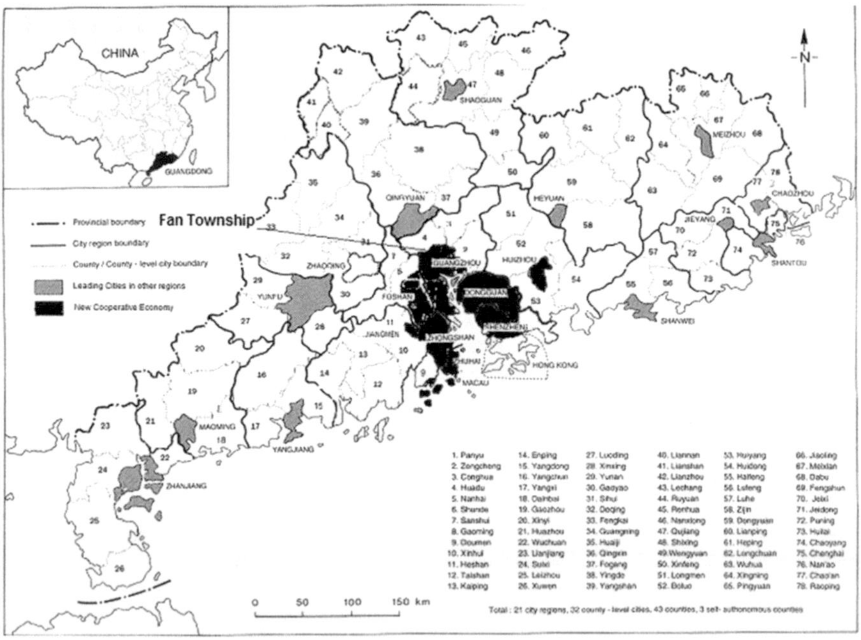

Fig. 4.1 The location of Fan Township

[3]According to the household responsibility system, the individual household contracts out the land. As a result, in order to use the land collectively for economic development, peasant households in Fan Township were required to give up user rights to the land.

4.1 An Introduction to Fan Township

4.1.1 Market Penetration in Fan Township

Fan Township, representative of the new cooperative economy, is located in Tianhe, a district under the Guangzhou City administration. Fan Township has an area of 46.27 km^2. Its population in 2004 reached 50,000. Fan Township governs seven administrative villages. As in many other townships of the province, peasants in Fan Township were very poor in the mid-1970s, when the annual average income was only around 100 yuan.[4] With the reestablishment of family agriculture in the early period of the reform, the peasants gained their earnings mainly from agriculture and sidelines production. However, because Fan Township was located near the Guangzhou City center, the agricultural sidelines played a more important role than other sources of income for the peasants. These agricultural sidelines include vegetable gardening, animal husbandry, fishing, etc.[5] As a result, the economy of the township can be considered to have been an outskirt economy at that time.

However, this situation changed very quickly along with the market penetration of the PRD region. As I have discussed in Chap. 3, capital from Hong Kong, and from other countries, flooded into Guangzhou and its suburban areas, accompanying the thriving of the commodity market and labor market. In the middle of the 1980s, the number of enterprises at the township level reached 1,445 and was of both the "three supplies, one compensation (san lai yi bu)" and "three capital (san zi qiye)" types.[6] The employees of these enterprises reached 21,047, and the total income amounted to 421.03 million yuan. By 1990 income had reached 646.75 million yuan. At the village level, the number of enterprises (mainly shoe factories, costume factories, feed factories, paper factories, etc.) reached 401 in 1990, employing 8,764 persons, with a total gross income of 351.169 million yuan. At a lower level of organization were the 111 jointed-household enterprises, most of which were garages, with 1,105 employees and a total gross income of 3,461 million yuan (also see Table 4.1). Market penetration in Fan Township improved greatly the lives of the rural people. In 1994, the gross production value of secondary industry in the township totaled 1,288,542,000 yuan. The gross production value of agriculture was 105,800 yuan. The average annual income of the rural population was 7,345 yuan, and the average annual income per laborer was 11,375 yuan.[7] The data from Tianhe District also shows an obvious increase in annual income of the rural area during the periods discussed (see Table 4.2).

---

[4] *Guangzhou shi tianhe qu difangzhi (The Chorography of Tianhe District of Guangzhou City)*, Guangzhou: Guangdong People's Press, p. 121.

[5] Informant No. Fan 200403.

[6] "Three capital enterprises" refers to three kinds of enterprises: those established by foreign businessmen alone, those invested by both foreign capital and local capital, and those established in cooperation between foreign business and copartners from local areas. The latter, foreign businessmen generally provide capital, while local copartners provide land, labor, and other production materials.

[7] *The Chorography of Tianhe District of Guangzhou City*, p. 121.

Table 4.1 The commodity market in Fan Township in the late 1980s

	The number of employees of TVEs	Gross production value (units of ten thousand)	Net income (units of ten thousand)
1985	5,873	3,920.18	370.14
1986	6,866	5,700.97	536.04
1987	9,192	8,663.64	711.68
1988	10,332	12,273.42	1,221.49
1989	12,676	19,857	1,880
1990	14,744	19,174	3,014

Sources: *The Chorography of Tianhe District of Guangzhou City*, p. 222.

Table. 4.2 The annual income of rural people in Tianhe District, 1985–2000

Year	Annual income per capita (yuan)	Annual income per laborer (?) (yuan)
1985	1,240	2,217
1986	1,448	4,305
1987	2,185	4,645
1988	3,134	5,220
1989	3,430	5,909
1990	3,437	4,435
1991	3,542	7,248
1992	5,833	8,349
1993	6,573	10,587
1994	9,042	13,538
1995	9,831	14,840
1996	10,584	15,788
1997	11,967	19,794
1998	13,040	22,388
1999	13,605	24,284
2000	14,481	24,781

Sources: Zhuang and Zheng (2002, p. 289)

4.1.2 The Emergence of the New Cooperative Economy

This dramatic market penetration process affected Fan Township in several ways: firstly, the market penetration process in Guangzhou City center increased demands for land for economic expansion. Fan Township is located at the east of the city center and naturally became an object for land requisition. According to the state's regulations, governments and their agents have to pay compensation for their requisitions. The compensation of Fan Township was divided into three parts. One was compensation to the peasants who lost the user rights to the land [the so-called green seedling fees (qingmiao fei)]. Natural villages and administrative villages collectively shared the other two parts according to negotiated contracts. When more and more land was requisitioned, the amount of the compensation fees collected by the two levels of village administration[8] increased. How to share these collectively owned revenues became a serious issue. Moreover, without land, peasants no longer had their original means of production. How to use the compensation fees to support their future became a critical problem, and there were strong needs to design a new institution to deal with the changing situation.

Secondly, market penetration in the PRD region in the middle of the 1980s also provided many business opportunities for Fan Township. However, these called for cooperation among individual family households. For example, more and more businessmen wanted to lease the farmland of Fan Township to enlarge their production. To change the farmland to warehouses or workshops required the common agreement of many individual family households. Moreover, the village also needed investment capital to develop better facilities to attract investment from outside. Usually, the original investment funds for constructing these facilities also came from individual family households.

Cooperation seemed a good way to solve the above issues. Cooperative economy was nothing strange to Chinese rural people, who had experienced the Maoist years. As a result, after complicated bargaining processes, the new cooperative economy was built. One of my informants,[9] a leader of a natural village in Fan Township, told me how they had persuaded villagers to develop collective business.

> There are 300 villagers in our production team. Now our economy is better. We have constructed some workshops, and rent them out. Some others do some sidelines. Our gross income has improved. It reaches 900 thousands. At first, the people didn't agree to build up the workshops. But we persuaded them. I told them that farming can earn little and building workshops to rent is an earning source with better return. They accepted my idea at last.... we told them that we would give up our year-end bonuses if we can't improve our economy...The work was quite hard at the beginning. We needed cash capital to build workshops on the land. To collect capital, we invited public bidding from every individual family household. We also set the price (for the bids). We collected 2 million at last. Now the money has been spent to build 4000 m^2 of workshops. Because the workshops were built at high quality, they were rented for good prices. Now our villagers can get money without doing anything. The income is quite good. (informant No. Fan200409)

The new cooperative institution was built first in Deng Village in 1987 and in the six other administrative villages at the end of 1990. In this circumstance, the district government gave official support to the cooperative institutions, promulgating a regulation *entitled Concerning the promotion and improvement of the rural stock cooperative economy* (guanyu cujin he tigao nongcun gufen hezuo zhi). In 1991, all 22 administrative villages (196 natural villages) of Tianhe District adopted the institutions of the cooperative economy.[10]

The new cooperative economy has been a great economic success. I haven't found recent statistical data on the economic results of Fan Township, but the data

---

[8] The administrative village (brigade) and natural village (natural village).

[9] Informant Fan2000401.

[10] Zheng et al. 1996.

for Tianhe District in 2000 shows that the annual income per capita of the rural people of Tianhe District was 14,481 yuan, which is 140 times the peasants' income in the 1970s (see Table 4.2).

4.1.3 An Introduction to the New Cooperative Economy

As Fig. 4.2 shows, the administrative structure of Fan Township is quite complicated. There are 16 offices at the township level, each of which has its jurisdiction. The township governs urban areas and rural areas. In the urban areas, the lowest-level administrative office is the residence committee (jumin weiyuanhui). One point is noteworthy: since Fan Township is near the city center, the urban part of Fan Township is larger than that of the ordinary townships in the province. In the rural areas, the administrative villages and natural villages are under the jurisdiction of township governments.[11] Administrative villages and natural villages are the counterparts of brigades and production teams before 1984, when the commune system was still running (see Fig. 4.2).

4.1.3.1 The Structure of the New Cooperative Economy

The new cooperative economy is built at the village level. The exact name of the new cooperative economic institution is the "Rural Economic Stock Cooperation (nongcun jingji gufen hezuoshe)," and the stock and their administrative institutions constitute the main structure of the cooperative economy.

Stock Holders and Other Social Actors

Not every peasant in Fan Township is a stockholder. Before the market reform, almost all of the people who lived in the rural areas of Fan Township were peasants whose main jobs were working on the farmland. However, this situation changed dramatically along with the market penetration. The people of Fan Township now are of five types.

1. Some urban work units have moved to the rural areas of Fan Township, and their members are urban residents living in the suburban rural areas.
2. Immigrant laborers (dagong zai/dagong mei) from other provinces or other areas of Guangdong working for factories or companies located in rural areas of Fan Township. Most of them are young and single and live in dormitories provided by the factories.

[11] The role of the administrative village has to be explained in detail: according to the Village Committee Organization Law (Cun min weiyuanhui zuzhi fa), the administrative institution is the villagers committee, an autonomous institution, to which members are elected by the peasants of an administrative village. The township government only has the right to direct and help. But unfortunately, this law does not tell what and how much should be directed.

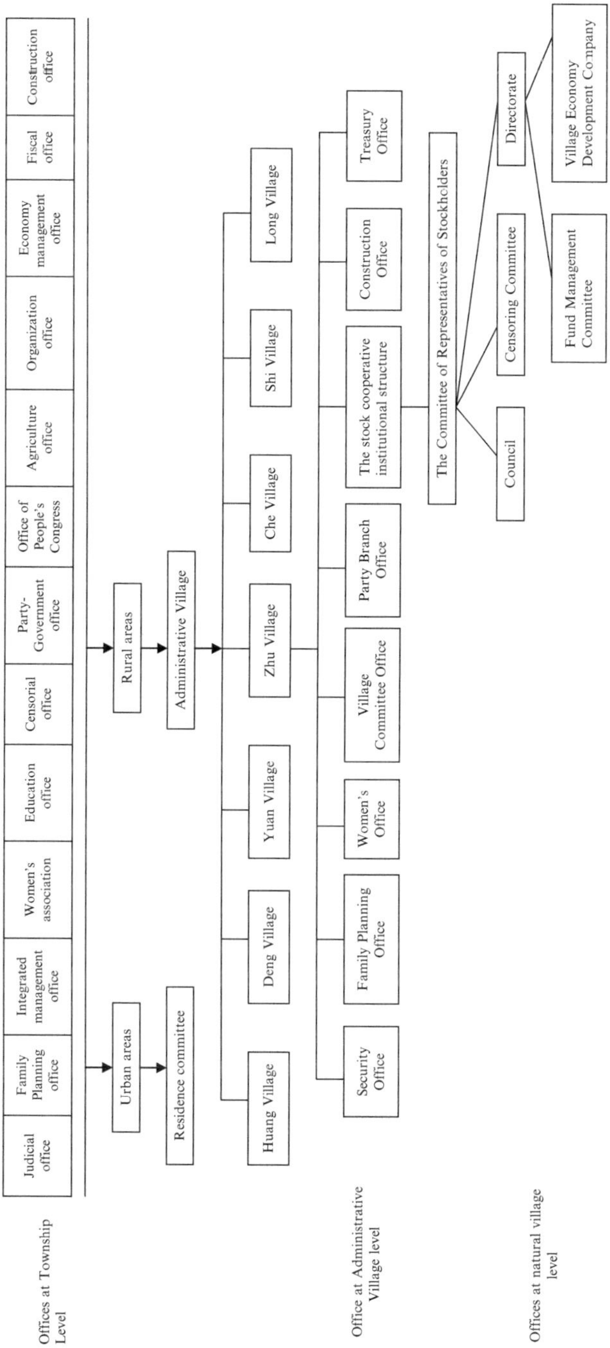

Fig. 4.2 Administrative structure of Fan Township

3. Those who rent the houses of peasants in Fan Township. These, include young college graduates and immigrants who have come from all over the country for all kinds of business, such as peddlers, construction workers, shop owners, etc.
4. Accompanying the process of land confiscation, some peasants of Fan Township were arranged to work in some urban institutions (mostly factories). As a result, their household statuses were changed to urban, [the so-called rural to non-rural (nong zhuan fei) change]. They are the so-called residents (jumin).[12]
5. The original inhabitants who didn't transfer to become jumin are still the peasants of Fan Township. The stockholders of the cooperative are mostly of this last type.

Although there are a variety of definitions of stockholders in the different administrative villages of Fan Township, we can take one example to grossly portray who the stockholders are. According to the constitution of the stock cooperative of Zhu Village, a stockholder is defined as follows:

> The reference period for setting stock was from June 1, 1971 to December 31, 1996. In this period, those who were registered as villagers of Zhu Village, who had participated in the collective work, and had taken the responsibility as members of the collective economy, and other villagers who fulfill the condition of stockholders, can become the stockholders of the stock cooperative economy.[13]

The Committee of Representatives of Stock Holders (gudong daibiao dahui, henceforth CRSH)
As implied by the name, the CRSH consists of representatives of stock holders. CRSH has the right to deliberate, pass, and revise the constitution of the stock cooperative economy. The other functions of CRSH also include deliberating the work report of the Directorate and deciding the important issues of the village. The representatives are elected in the conference of stockholders, which is held annually. To be a representative of the stockholders, a person must be currently participating in the economic activities of the village and be 18 years old or above. Representatives are elected by all stock holders. The electees are not only the representatives of the natural village but also of the administrative village. No matter how many stocks he (she) has, a stockholder can only have one vote. It is different from a stock company, where stockholders have votes proportional to their shares in the corporation. Decisions are made according to democratic principals.

Directorate and Council The Directorate is the standing decision-making institution of the CRSH, while the Council is the administrative institution of the CRSH. Their functions include preparing and holding the CRSH; executing the decisions of the CRSH; reporting to the CRSH; and taking responsibility for the strategies, production, management, administration, and treasuries of the natural and administrative villages. The Directorate consists of 9 directors and the Council

[12]The term *jumin* (residents) is comparable to the term *nongmin* (peasants), referring to those whose household registration record identifies them as urban residents.

[13]The Constitution of Rural Economic Cooperation of Zhu Village.

had 5–9 members. All of them can gain reappointment. The Directorate makes decisions in a collective manner. Every member has the right to vote. When the number of approvers and objectors is equal, the chairperson of the Directorate will be authorized one additional vote.

The Directorate has two sub-institutions. One is the *fund management committee*, whose main functions range from finance and the treasury to auditing. The other is the *economic development company*. This is the economic administrative institution of the cooperative economy rather than an independent company. The staff of the company is nominated by the Directorate and approved by the committee of villagers and the village party branch. The Directorate also assigns the functions, roles, and tasks of the company.

Censorial Committee The Censoring Committee is also a sub-institution of the CRSH, to which the members are elected by the representatives of the stock holders. One cannot be a member of both the Directorate and the Censorial Committee. The main functions of the Censorial Committee consist of (1) supervising the members of the Directorate, fund management committee, and economic development company; (2) preventing any behavior harmful to the collective economy and the interests of the stock holders; (3) supervising and auditing the finances of the administrative village; (4) executing the right to request the Directorate to report on special and critical issues.

The Principals of Profit Sharing Five principals guide the profit sharing of the cooperative economy. (1) More than 60 % of the annual profits should be spent to enlarge the reproduction of the collective economy and collective welfare. (2) Only net profits can be shared. (3) Compensation fees for land requisition should be kept as collective assets instead of being distributed to individuals. (4) Profit sharing should take both the rights and incumbencies (contributions) of stock holders into consideration. (5) Administrative costs of the villagers committee and village party branch should be paid by the collectivity; and this has to be discussed and approved by the CRSH.[14]

The Types of Stock The stocks can be divided into collective stocks (jiti gu), individual stocks (geren gu), and cash stocks (xianjin gu), according to ownership. (1) Collective stock is accumulation stock, which won't be distributed to individual villagers. In general, the proportion of collective stocks is above 60 %.[15] (2) Individual stock is like a voucher of the individual stockholder. The number of individual stock shares a peasant can own depends on his (her) contribution to the village (counted according to years of labor, the level of labor skills, and the amount

[14] Zheng et al. 1996.

[15] There are two ways to deal with the collective assets. One is to set collective stocks, which occupy over 60 % of the total amount of the stocks. In this way, the cooperative institutions can retain enough funds for further development. The other way is to divide the collective parts among all individual villagers so that every village knows his (her) share of the collective assets. The collective share of the profit is made according to profit sharing regulations, which require that over 60 % of the profits should be retained as collective accumulation.

of contracted farmland).[16] Individual stock can't be sold or withdrawn and can be inherited. (3) Cash stock refers to capital directly invested in the cooperative institutions by the villagers, other residents in the village, and sometimes investors from outside the village. This kind of stock can be sold and cashed in.

The Procedure of Profit Sharing The interest on the stocks is shared once at the end of every year. Only part of the profits can be shared. The administrative costs of the village and the capital for developing the collective economy and collective welfare are first retained. Then the Directorate proposes a sharing project for the rest of the profits. The project should be approved in the CRSH. The stockholder will get the interest in February of the following year.

From the above description, one can see that the institutions of the new cooperative economy are quite complicated. As a result, the relationship between cooperative institutions and other administrative institutions of the villages is noteworthy. According to the official document promulgated by Tianhe District in 1990, *Concerning the promotion and improvement of the rural stock cooperative economy*, the relationship is prescribed as follows: (1) The village branch of the CCP still possesses the highest power. It has the duty of political leadership of the new cooperative economy. All cooperative economic institutions should voluntarily accept its political lead and follow its guidelines, strategies, and methods. (2) The villagers committee is the autonomous administrative organization. It is responsible for the programming, organizing, and management of the development of the village's economic, social, and spiritual civilization. As a result, the villagers committee should administer the cooperative economic institutions. (3) The individual family household is the basic production unit of the village and operates according to its contract with the state. The cooperative economic institutions should give some guidance to these individual family households and create a good environment for the production of family households.

Although the roles of these main institutions are set by the official document, this doesn't mean these institutions will be exactly governed according to this scenario. In fact, the official regulations are enforced by unofficial political artifice. The overlap of the directors of these institutions is a good way to realize the goals of the local government. In general, the director of the villagers committee will take the chair position of the Directorate of the CRSH.

[16]According to the Constitution of Zhu Village Stock Cooperative, individual stocks consist of two kinds: the headstock (rentou gu) and working age stock (nongling gu). The headstock refers to the stock of each individual, who has the right to share in the collective revenue. It is counted by the years the stockholder has been in the village. The maximum of headstock for one stockholder is 15 shares. The working age stock is counted by the years the stock holder has worked in the village. The maximum is 53 shares.

4.2 Peasants' Lives in the New Cooperative Economy

One of the two main themes of this dissertation is how the market penetration increases the sources of earnings of rural people. This section not only presents a detailed picture of the earnings of peasants in Fan Township but also introduces their everyday lives, by which we can tell the peasants' true feelings.

4.2.1 The Sources of Earnings of Peasants

Market penetration in Fan Township provides many sources of earnings for the villagers. For one thing, they can share profits from the quickly developing collective economy. For another, market penetration brings in many business opportunities for Fan Township's peasants. The sources of earnings of peasants in Fan Township can be placed in three main categories: the stock bonus from collective profits, private business, and wage work:

Sharing of the Collective Profits

The profits of the cooperative economy play a very important role in the earnings of the peasants of Fan Township. Most important is the stock bonus. A woman in Long Village gave me detailed information about the stock bonus of her family:

> Stock, stock is like this–every villager has stock. The bonus was 200 yuan per share last year. Take my family as an example: I have 19 shares. Counting the shares of my sons and my husband, the total number of our shares is 49. Taking all bonuses together, it is more than 300 yuan per share. Totally, we can share 17,000 yuan per year. Moreover, there are some other collective programs, in which you can invest money. We can also gain bonuses from these collective programs. (Informant Fan200408)

There are also some other kinds of subsidies besides the stock bonus. For example, every laborer whose job is not assigned by the village administration has a "labor bonus (jiuye butie)" of 150 yuan per month (I will discuss this in the next section) in Long Village. Of course, the stock bonuses and welfare sharing of a family depend on the profits of the collective village economy. The bonus of each share varies from 30 to more than 100 yuan[17] in different villages. The totals of stock bonuses of a family also depend on the number of family members, the number of years they have worked, and the amount of the original investment of the family members. During an interview, the director of Long Village told me that the bonus of the collective economy of his village can reach 6,000 yuan per person per year.[18] An informant also told me that the stock bonus of a peasant in the richest village of Fan Township could reach 30,000 yuan[19] per year. In Zhu Village, where

[17] Informant Fan200413.

[18] Informant Fan200407.

[19] Informant Fan200430.

the collective economy is at its beginning stage, the stock bonus is less than that of Long Village:

> How to say! For example, my son has 5 shares. I have 40 shares. My husband has almost 40 shares. Our family totally owns 97 shares. This is 22 yuan per share. It means that it is less than 2,000 yuan. It is not enough. But the situation is better this year, our stock bonus cashes in twice. (Informant Fan200410)

The comparison of these two villages vividly shows us the effects of market penetration on the peasant's life chances. Long Village is near the Guangzhou city center. The compensation for requisitioned land is higher than in other areas. The collective economy is better, with more business chances for peasants. But Zhu Village has potential, since it still has many lands for development.[20]

Leasing Trade[21]
The second important earning source is house leasing. The market penetration in Fan Township has attracted many people from outside, and this has boosted the house leasing business. Housing is leased at about 6–12 yuan per square meter in Fan Township. Some peasants build new houses to rent; some add floors to their own houses to rent.

> My house has six floors. Our family lives on the fifth and sixth floors. The second to fourth floors have been leased out. Every floor has two apartments. Each apartment is 30 square meters, equipped with washing room and water heater. The price of each apartment is about 200 yuan. The first floor is leased out to be a store and the price is higher. (Informant 200408)

Besides the lease of the peasant's own house, there are other chances to engage in the leasing trade. In Long Village, the Village Economic Development Company developed a program to build a mart to lease. Some peasants have invested money in this program in order to share in the profits. Some have bought one or two stalls in the market to rent. There are 2,000 households and 2,600 houses in Long Village, of which 700 houses have been leased out.

Wage Work The market penetration also provides many work opportunities for the peasants in Fan Township. Most of them are in service industries and include waiting tables, driving, providing security, and so on. Moreover, the collective economic institutions also offer some work opportunities for the young people of the village. Most of these jobs are in security, cleaning, and driving.

> Interviewer: What are the peasants' occupations?
> Interviewee: Some old men will do something in farmland. Some young men carry passengers by motorcycle. Of course, the people who can find jobs outside will go outside.[22]
> Interviewer: What kind of jobs do they get?
> Interviewee: Some of them work in factories. Some are typists, some are salesperson, some work for their relatives or friends, etc. (Informant Fan200413)

[20] Informant Fan200427.

[21] Leasing trade can be considered as part of private business. It is emphasized because of its importance in the peasants' lives.

[22] In his words, the "outside" mostly refers to the city center of Guangzhou.

Working for the village as a security guard is one of the major jobs for the young men of the village, if they can't find a better job outside. Pan Junyan, a 27-year-old man of Zhu Village, talked with me about his life.

> I haven't done any work on the farm, even though my family has some farmland. Mostly, my parents, brother and sisters would do the farm work. I don't need to do it because I am the youngest one in my family. At that time, the work on the farm were very hard. My family woke up at 4:00 AM every day and began to work. At noon, they came back to have lunch. After having a rest, they went to the farm again. They worked more than 13 h every day. There were no good things to eat. It was extravagant if a person could get enough to eat at that time. After the land was requisitioned, our lives got better. The farmland was getting smaller. No one wants to do farm work now. But my parents still do some vegetable planting now, because they are used to doing it. The life of my family is better now. We don't need to work so hard now. I work for the administrative village as a security guard. I wake up at 7 AM every day. After my breakfast, I am on duty at 8:00 AM. We have three shifts and we work for 8 h per day, without holidays, even during Spring Festival.[23] But this job isn't hard. We just go around in the village, taking care of the security issues. If there is any bustup or hooligan we should deal with it, do some mediation or send them to the police. We don't have the right to lock up anybody. In fact, our village is quite secure. Most of the time, we just walk around and have a chat together. All my colleagues are the "brothers" of the village. We care about each other. We go out for a drink and play cards sometimes. If I want to have some holidays, I can apply for them. I am on holiday for 2 days every month. We take these two days off in turn. But we won't be paid in the holidays. I feel this job is OK for me. Without good education, it is difficult to me to find a better job. This job is easy and free. But if there are other chances, I want to have my own business and be a boss. I don't have extra money to invest. As a result, I can't change my job now. … The salary is 800 yuan per month. My stock bonus is about 700 yuan per year. The income is not very good. Some is spent on having tea, dinner with friends. Some is spent on clothes and other necessary commodities. Some money is spent on going out with my girlfriend. The house of my family is a building with two and a half floors. It is 150 square meters. As an ordinary household in our village, my family has a TV, Hi Fi, refrigerator, VCD, motorcycle. Although the economy now is not very good, it is much better than before. I don't need to pay for the expenses of our family. My parents have a stock bonus. My older brother and sister will give some money to the family. My salary is just enough for my expenses. I want to save the stock bonus for my marriage…I am at home when I am off duty. Most of the time, I watch TV or enjoy music at home. Sometimes, I read some novels, especially love stories. I will go outside if friends call me. We play snooker sometimes. Most of the young men in the village like playing snooker. My technique is not very good. It is just for fun. Sometimes we go out to have some tea, to have a dinner together, to go to karaoke, to discos. When we are together, we talk about some funny things. We also talk about our life goals. If someone has any difficulty, he can tell and see if there is any help he can get from friends. We pay the bill in turn. I have played on the football team and dragon boat team of my village. (Informant Fan200421)

Private Business

Accompanying the expansion of the city center, most of areas of Fan Township have been integrated as a part of the city center. This integration gives many business opportunities for rural people of Fan Township. In addition to the leasing trade, in which many of families have participated, there are other private businesses,

[23] Spring festival is at the end of the Chinese lunar year and is the most important festival for the Chinese.

including restaurants, salons, stores, motorcycle repair shops, etc. A successful businessman told me his story.

> I was born in 1956 and I am 44 years old. I began to work on our farmland when I was seven. I began to be a full-time peasant in 1975 (19 years old). But I became a "fake peasant" in 1985 when I began to do some business--to sell agricultural products in the periodic market. Now I run a garage. I wake up at 6:00 AM every day. After having morning tea,[24] I go to my garage. I don't have fixed work. Mostly, I just need to allocate jobs to my employees. I employ about 30 people, including villagers in Zhu Village. I pay them according to their contribution. They can do their jobs well. So, my job is easy. We don't have holidays. Every day there are people who need their cars repaired. So I have no "weekend". It is the same for my employees. Sometimes, they work to midnight. Now the business is highly competitive and we need to do our work as well as possible. I am satisfied with my business. In sum, my life is OK right now. I think my life is at the middle level for Zhu Village. My house is more than 200 square meters. I also have two old houses. I have more than ten airconditioners, five TVs, two computers, four motorcycles, and three cars. My income is mostly from my garage and the stock bonus. The stock bonus is 600 yuan per month. I am enthusiastic about public affairs. I contributed 5,000 yuan to a school this year. When I am off duty, I like to go out to have a tea, chatting with friends. I don't like gambling and I don't like whoring. I like to travel very much. This year I have been to Beijing, Xiamen, Yunnan, Sichuan, Singapore, Malaysia, Thailand, and so on. Only in Spring Festival I go out for a tour with my family. At other times, I go out by myself. (Informant Fan200426)

Agricultural Sidelines In some villages, there is still some farmland where some old villagers continue to work in agricultural sidelines. Almost all of them are vegetable planting. For example, in Long Village, there is still 1,000 mu[25] of farmland and several hundreds of fruit trees. Some of the fruit trees have been contracted out[26] to migrant workers from other areas of China. These agricultural sidelines don't mean too much to the villagers of Fan Township. It isn't difficult to forecast that the farmland will be swallowed by the expanding city center very soon.

4.2.2 The Welfare of Rural Fan Township

Welfare in Fan Township is very good compared to most other rural areas of China. I strongly feel this during my observation in Long Village. A hospital with quite good facilities is located there (see Fig. 4.3). The Culture Activity Center (wenhua huodong zhongxin) is a three-floor building, with beautiful gardening, airconditioners, and other good facilities (see Fig. 4.2). The center has many function rooms, including a gymnasium, a reading room, etc. I saw many old people watching TV, playing cards, reading newspapers, and chatting there. There is a plaza in the middle of the village. The main part of the plaza is an open theater. A big screen was

---

[24] In southern China, especially Guangdong and Hong Kong, some people will go to a restaurant to have some dim sum and tea in the morning. It is called "morning tea."

[25] Chinese unit of area (1 mu = 1/15 of a hectare).

[26] By "contracting out," the contractor has the right to run the orchard and sell the fruits of the trees.

Fig. 4.3 The culture activity center of Long Village

established there in front of many stone seats. Every night, there were TV programs shown in the plaza. Many migrant workers gather there to watch movies. A village cadre told me that the facilities of the village include a primary school, a kindergarten, a nursery, an activity center, and a hospital (Fig. 4.4).

> In Zhu Village, the villagers' welfare is good. For one thing, almost every one can have a stock bonus at the end of the year. Every old person in the village gets 50 yuan of annuity per month. They can also get some presents in each festival. A building will be built up very soon and every four people can be assigned an apartment in this building. We also plan to organize our villagers to go out on a tour twice per year (a one-person quota per household) without any charge. There are three free nights of courses for villagers every week. The persons who have attended the course can get some subsidies. More than that, the village also provides promotion of agricultural technologies, and set up a team of security guards to take care of the security of the community. (Informant Fan200422)

A more detailed picture of the welfare shared by the villagers of Fan Township follows.

Cooperative Medical Care System In Long Village, there is a village medical care center that handles common diseases. Villagers need to pay only 1 yuan per visit for their medical treatment. All medicine is free at the center. In order to cure serious diseases, villagers can go to the hospitals outside in the city center, which have signed a contract with the villages as appointed hospitals. Every time a villager goes to see a doctor in those hospitals, he (she) can get a 50-yuan subsidy from the village. A villager who has to stay in the hospital for treatment will get a 50 % reimbursement from the village. Moreover, every year, the village arranges for all the villagers to have a physical examination.[27]

[27] Informant Fan200408.

Fig. 4.4 The hospital of Long Village

Education Villagers in Fan Township also have some education subsidies. The villagers only need to pay 50 % of the fees for their children's education in kindergarten, and students in primary schools don't need to pay any fees other than the cost of books. Construction costs and other subsidies to the primary schools are paid by the collectivity. In Zhu Village, the village administration provides free education programs for the villagers. The courses are provided at night, three times a week. The villagers get subsidies if they attend the courses.[28]

Tourism

It is popular for villagers to go out on organized tours in many villages of Fan Township. In Long Village, such tours have been organized many times. An informant told me that:

> For example, we recently visited Chongqing. Sometimes, the village arranges for the old people of the village to go out for a tour. We don't need to pay any money. Of course, you have to pay if you want to buy something on your journey. We have been a lot of places, such as Hainan Island, Yunnan, the Three Gorges, and so forth. The old persons who are sick or too old to go out will be given 500 yuan in compensation. (Informant Fan200408)

[28] Informant Fan200422.

Work Opportunities and Insurance

Without farmland, many villagers have lost their jobs in agriculture. For those villagers who have no good educational backgrounds, finding a new job is difficult. As a result, the village administration tries to generate more work opportunities for those people. In general, these jobs are cleaning, driving, security, etc. A village leader:

> Yes, we have considered it before. We (the natural village) have several factories. We always try to arrange some jobs there for the villagers. We tried any way we can. But the working hours are too long. Women generally have to take care of their children. Lots of work in turn wouldn't be suitable for them. In this year, I have arranged 4 people as overseers and cleaners. We set the wage first. The people who are interested in it must draw lots for the jobs. We select persons according to fair principals. (Informant Fan200409)

4.3 Intergovernmental Revenue Sharing and Cadres' Governance

One of the two main themes of this dissertation is how market penetration lowers the economic demands of the state and its agencies in rural society. In Chap. 3, we have seen how market penetration decreases the state's economic dependence on rural society. In this chapter, the empirical data of Fan Township will show us how market penetration lowers the local governments' surcharges on peasants.

As I pointed out in Chap. 3, the revenue of a township government is made up of three parts: the tax revenues, the fiscal transfers from higher government levels, and self-retained funds. The aggravation or relief of the burden on peasants depends on the township government's fiscal situation. A township with a good fiscal situation will not go too far in exploiting the peasant's surplus. Instead, good welfare policies will be provided in order to buy more political support. As a result, the village administration will also follow this procedure.

Firstly, the expanse of tax bases and changes of tax structures make tax revenue the major part of Fan Township's fiscal income. For one thing, accompanying the market penetration process, the tax bases of Fan Township expand dramatically; for another, after many years of development, the industry structure of Fan Township has mostly changed from agriculture to manufacturing and services business. This makes the tax collecting easier.

Secondly, because of the plentiful tax revenue, the fiscal transfer from higher government levels plays less important roles in Fan Township than in other townships located far from Guangzhou city center.[29] Local village administrations in Fan Township will not receive any fiscal transfers from superior levels most of the time. A village cadre complained to me about this:

[29] For example, in Lee Township, which I will discuss in the next chapter, the allocations from higher levels of government are very important to the township' revenues structure.

> We submitted 5 million in tax last year, but our villagers didn't share any welfare from the Guangzhou government. We built all public facilities by ourselves. We are taxpayers, but we can't enjoy our rights. All issues, like security, family planning, and so on, have to be handled by ourselves. We invested 40 million in the village rebuilding program, without getting any subsidies from higher government. (Informant Fan200407)

Thirdly, the government levels immediately above Fan Township—the Tianhe District government and the Guangzhou city government—are both in the core of the PRD region. The three levels of government share the revenue of expanding tax bases. Although higher government didn't allocate subsidies to the Fan Township government, it did not press much for tax collection from the latter either. The plentiful tax revenue of Fan Township greatly decreases the township governments' needs to place local surcharges in rural society. For one thing, the revenue from rural society is easily collected now that the industry structure of rural Fan has been changed. For another, the cost of levying surcharges is higher than the cost of enlarging other tax bases, both economically and politically. The central state's concern for the stability of the rural society also affects Fan Township and the levels of government above it. A village cadre explained to me that in order to implement the "three representative" ideas, the local strategy is to "let the peasants get interest and let the cadres get education (rang nonmin dedao haochu, rang ganbu dedao jiaoyu)."[30]

Like other rural areas in Guangdong, every individual family household of Fan Township still needs to pay agricultural tax, five township-pooling fees, and fees for three village-retained funds. These taxes and charges are easy to obtain in Fan Township because the land has been used for high-profit business: the agricultural and the local charges are deducted from the collective profits directly. In a word, the peasant doesn't need to take money out of his (her) pocket by his (her) hand for agricultural taxes and local charges anymore.

4.3.1 From Distributors to Managers: The Village Cadres in Fan Township

A key argument of market transition theory is the decline of the political officer's advantages. Mao's collective institutions were abolished overall at the beginning of 1980. However, this doesn't mean that the advantages of village cadres have vanished. In Fan Township, the village cadres still enjoy their advantages (this will be discussed in Sect. 4.3.1.4). What have been changed are the roles of the village cadres—from the redistributors in Mao's China to the managers in reform China.

[30] Informant Fan200407. This informant is a township cadre. His statement shows that local officials also realize that the political ideas of the CCP can be accepted by peasants only when peasants can benefit from learning the ideas and the process of implementing these ideas. This is why local cadres try to "buy" political peace by providing public goods when they achieve this fiscal capacity.

4.3.1.1 The Constitution of the Village Cadres of Fan Township

In Mao's China, political loyalties, educational background, status, and reputation were the selection standards for village cadres. However, in reform China, the constitution of the village cadres of Fan Township shows that the human capital—especially the experiences of economic management—have become the most important standard. For example, the director of Zhu Village is a successful businessman, the director of Long Village is a building contractor, and the associate director of Long Village is an owner of several shops.

In in-depth interviews with village cadres, I asked what they did before they became cadres. Their answers are presented as follows:

> *The director of the Economic Development Company*: "I was doing transportation business, owning a hauler company. I began my business in 1981. I am an adventurer of the reform. I carried goods from Huang Pu[31] Harbor to the railway station. I finished the business and turned back to the village in 1997, when the Huang Pu Harbor lost its important role in the competition with other harbors. I transferred my business to my partners under the condition that they give me some quotas of revenue every year."[32]
>
> *The director of the tenth natural village:* "I was once a fruit tree planter, and then I ran a chicken house" (Informant Fan200409).
>
> *The director of the eleventh natural village:* "I once was a building contractor" (Informant Fan200429).
>
> *The associate director of the first natural village:* "I was in schools for several years. Then I joined the army. One year after I retired from the army, I was appointed to work in my village" (Informant Fan200419).
>
> *The director of the seventh natural village:* "I was a hauler before I became a village cadre. I bought a truck and I was also the driver." (Informant Fan200427)

From the constitution of the village cadres of Fan Township, one point is noteworthy: the first generation of adventurers of the market reform has now become village cadres of the new cooperative economies. The adventurers mainly consist of four kinds of people: building contractors, haulers (drivers), special agricultural household (zhuanyehu) members, and retired soldiers. These four groups of people share one common feature: they are better at organizational and economic management than ordinary villagers.

First, the increasing needs of construction and transportation accompanying the market penetration of the PRD region have provided many chances for building contractors and haulers. Building contractors have experience of running a company, managing staff, and dealing with financial issues. When they give up their own business and try to work for the village, for different reasons,[33] they become good candidates for manager of the new cooperative economy. Haulers go around everywhere and have more chances to see and learn all kinds of business. As a result, they are better in management than most ordinary villagers.[34]

---

[31] Huang Pu harbor is the largest harbor in Guangzhou.

[32] Informant Fan 200435.

[33] These reasons can be various. For example, one told me that the business environments outside became worse and he saw the good opportunity for the village collective economy.

[34] In the early period of the reform, not every peasant had such a chance to travel, see, and learn.

Second, the specialist agricultural households in the village also improve themselves by organizing large-scale agriculture and contracting for fishponds, fruit trees, or farmland.

The third group is the retired soldiers. Every year, some young people in rural areas join the army. As soldiers they may learn special skills such as driving, computer operation, and communication technology, etc. Some of them even join the CCP in the military.[35] Living in the military gives them a chance to experience how the formal political hierarchy of China works.[36] All these four groups became the new political elite in rural Fan Township. This observation complies with the argument of market transition theory that the returns on human capital will be higher accompanying the market transition process. However, management experience, but not the educational level, is the suitable measurement for the human capital of these people.[37]

The economic success of rural Fan Township should be partly attributed to these new political elites. They got good evaluations when I asked the villagers about their performance. As one villager told me:

> Of course, those people who always hold his hoe are useless. That time is gone. A good cadre should sit down, supervising everything. Only when there are some difficult problems does he take the responsibilities and resolve them. Only this kind of people is good enough. Those persons who work all day from sunrise to sunset are not good now. (Informant Fan200403)

Take Long Village as an example. The party secretary of Fan Township praised the new village cadres:

> After the direct election, 70 percent of the former cadres in Long Village were replaced. When new cadres came to power, the economics of Long Village developed very quickly, with an 80 percent increase per year. The GDP of Long Village last year was 63,400,000 yuan. It will reach 80,000,000 this year and reach 0.1 billion in the next two years. (Informant Fan 200402)

Talking about their achievement, the new political elites are also proud of themselves:

> To be honest, the former cadres of our village were not good in business. Most of them worked on the farm, knowing nothing about market economy. How can they lead the villagers to make money? For example, there is a mineral water factory. The situation of the factory was good at the beginning. But they didn't know management, having no idea how to use the right persons. They employed the villagers who only know the work on farmland to be the managers of the marketing department. Those people know nothing and can easily be cheated. They sent out thousands of yuan of goods, taking back nothing in cash. (Informant 200435)

---

[35] In China, usually, being a CCP member is a precondition for becoming a cadre.

[36] According to Chinese Party policy, when soldiers retire from the army, only those from urban areas may be given jobs; those from rural areas have to go back to their original home areas.

[37] One noteworthy point is that very few young people who have obtained higher education will come back to work in the villages. This institutional background is a regressive feature in the relationship between cadre position and human capital (measure by the number of the years of education).

4.3.1.2 Coming to Power

Fan Township is located in the middle of the PRD region near the Guangzhou city center, where chances for economic development are increasing. As a result, the human capital of the above four kinds of people, especially the experience of business administration, has become the preferred selection criteria of village cadres. This meets the demands of both the township government and the peasants. For one thing, the township government wants village cadres with abilities to improve the village economy, since the economic performance of their rural areas is the main standard of achievement of the township leaders. For another, the villagers of Fan Township hope that village cadres can offer some help to village economic development, from which they can benefit.

As I mentioned in Chap. 3,, in order to gain more political support from the peasants, direct village elections were implemented by the central state in 1998. In Guangdong, direct village elections were implemented in 1999.[38] Before 1999, the selection of village cadres was not directly by villagers. Instead, the representatives of the villagers would be elected first. Then the representatives would vote in the directors of the villagers committee. In this procedure, the cadres in the township could play more decisive roles in candidate selection, as to persuade 80 representatives is easier than to persuade thousands of villagers. After 1999, when direct village election was implemented, the procedures were changed. The first step is now nomination, in which villagers who gain more than 20 villagers' nominations will become candidates. The second step is voting. The name-list of all candidates for different positions will be printed on the ballots. Voters can then select the candidates or fill in other names of people whom they want to vote for. The candidate who earns more than half of all votes will be the winner.

This institutional arrangement for village cadre election leads to dual constraints on the village cadres' behavior. First, since the collective assets play a very important role in villagers' lives, direct village election is closely related to the villagers' interests and peasants are attentive to the election. However, although the township government has thus transferred some decision-making power to the villagers, it still holds its influence on the village cadre election in three ways: (1) the winners of the direct election have to be approved by the party branch of the township government, (2) the village branch of the CCP still retains the highest political power in the village, and (3) if the elected director of the village committee is a party member, he (she) will be asked to be the secretary of the village branch of the party. In this way, the township government can still control the director through the party hierarchy, as they have always done in the past.

[38] Please refer to Chap. 3.

4.3.1.3 The Governance of Village Cadres in Rural Fan Township

The governance of village cadres is closely related to the life chances of the villagers. Other than through the direct economic achievements of village cadres, a township government or a village administration's way to implement policies is also a key factor in villagers' lives. A township government that implements policies by coercion will bring suffering to the peasants. However, in the villages of Fan Township, several institutional arrangements lead to the soft governance of the local governments.

Firstly, as I mentioned in Sect. 4.2, the market penetration in the PRD region provides the higher levels of government (the Guangzhou City government, the Tianhe District government, and the Fan Township government) with several formal channels to collect economic surplus. It lowers their needs to collect economic surplus through the village cadres. On the contrary, in order to gain more political support, the higher government levels tend to stop behavior that will harm political stability, such as coercion and other illegal behavior. What the party secretary of the township branch said shows the concern of the township government on this issue:

> …it is good if the villages can reach the goals of these two aspects (material and ideological). But most villages, even the good villages can only improve in one aspect, namely, the improvement of the material civilization, rather than the improvement of villagers' ideological civilization. (Informant Fan200402)[39]

Secondly, their direct election places dual constraints on the cadres' behavior, as explained above.

Thirdly, the institutional framework of the cooperative economy both constrains and facilitates village cadres' behavior. On the one hand, all administrative expenses of the village have to be approved by the Fund Committee, and some important economic decisions have to be discussed and authorized by the Committee of Representatives of Stock Holders. On the other hand, the sharing of collective revenues gives an economic lever to the village cadres to implement their policies. Some examples from Long Village serve as evidence for this point.

Familly Planning Policy Since the middle of the 1970s, family planning policies have been implemented in China. This soon became the most difficult job of rural governments, because the policy contradicts key traditional values.[40] Most of the conflicts in rural China have come from the enforcing of the family planning policy.[41] However, with the economic lever, this policy is implemented very well in Long Village. According to the Constitution of the Cooperative Economy of Long Village, the stock bonus of people who violate the family planning policy will be

---

[39] As I have explained in Chap. 3, the main goals of the central state are to gain both "economic development (the material part)" and "social stability (the ideology part)." It is also the main measurement of the achievement of local official leaders. This party secretary's statement shows that he is not satisfied with the work on ideology.

[40] As one of the key traditional value of China, offspring are considered to be the continuation of family and clan. Two proverbs illustrate this: "More children, more happiness" and "The greatest unfilial behavior is having no son."

[41] Please refer to Greenhalgh et al. 1994, pp. 365–95; White 1990, pp. 53–76.

stopped for 14 years and will be added to the collective welfare. The total amount of this penalty can be very high. As the following conversation between the CCP branch secretary of Long Village and the author shows,

Interviewee: Family planning is the most difficult thing under the sky. It is easier in a rich village. But our village isn't rich enough. It is still difficult. We cannot send possemen to arrest the violators like some villages did before. What we can do is to constrain it by rules and regulations, mainly by economic constraints.
Interviewer: How can you constrain it by using economic means?
Interviewee: The administrative unit of family planning will hold physical examinations for women of child-bearing age. If any woman of bearing age doesn't attend the check, we will assume that she intends to offend the family planning policy. If it is confirmed, her collective welfare for the next 14 years will be cancelled…it is a large amount of money, including the stock bonus, medical care subsidy, work subsidies. The richer the village, the higher the amount of this money. (Informant Fan200407)

With these great costs, few people in Long Village disobey the family planning policy, except those who are rich enough to neglect their deserved collective shares.

Conscription and Security The economic lever also is used in conscription and security. In the Constitution of the Cooperative Economy of Long Village, there is a series of items about these two issues. (1) If anyone tries to escape conscription into the army, his (her) stock bonus will be stopped for 1 year. (2) If anyone flees from the army, his (her) stock bonus will be stopped for 5 years and the deducted bonus will be transferred to the administrative village for village welfare. (3) If anyone breaks the law and is put in jail, his (her) stock bonus will be stopped during his (her) imprisonment. (4) If anyone breaks the law and is sentenced to death, his (her) stock and stock bonus will be transferred to the village for collective welfare. A village cadre told me that the 5-year-bonus could amount to 100,000 yuan.

Village Rebuilding During my ethnographic studies in Long Village, one important job of the village administration was the village-rebuilding program. Driven by the profits of the house rental market, the villagers of Long Village tried to build as many houses as possible. As a result, before the village-rebuilding program was implemented, the buildings of Long Village were really disordered, with high density. The local people call this kind of building "the shaking hand buildings (woshou lou)," referring to two buildings so close that a person in one building can shake hands with a person in the other. The disorder of the buildings led to big problems for fire control. In 2003, there was a fire in Long Village. The fire engine could not reach the fire because of the high density of the buildings, and eight persons died. This accident greatly shocked the government and the peasants. As a result, the village-rebuilding program was created by the township government and was implemented by Long Village. Two broad roads two miles long have been constructed through the village. Two hundred houses were torn down. The total investment for the program reached 50,000,000 yuan.[42] It was very difficult to handle this big

[42] Informant Fan200402.

program by the village administration. However, using the economic lever, the program was implemented very well. The secretary of the township party branch told me the details of the program.

> Just in one year, we build 2 miles of roads through the village and tore down 200 houses, with few appeals or resistance from the villagers. I think it is a successful case. There are two reasons for it: the first is the support of the district government. Secondly, we do things according to the interests of the villagers. Everybody is saying "Put people as the foundation (yi ren wei ben)". We place the villagers in the center. We don't harm their interests. On the contrary, we have to increase their interests. So, the key point is that we are doing things catering to the villagers' interests. Of course, some governmental behavior has to be implemented even though villagers don't like it, like the family planning policy. It is a basic national policy and there is no room for negotiation. But other things are negotiable, such as this rebuilding program. We explained the reasons to the villagers.... (Informant Fan200402)

According to his description, three procedures were implemented by the village administration. (1) *Persuasion*. They asked all cadres of the village to explain the necessity of the rebuilding program face to face, to tell how the program would be carried out and what kinds of benefits it would produce. (2) *Compensation*. All owners of houses that had to be torn down were compensated with money or were provided with new houses in new building areas. (3) Foreseeable *profit sharing*. In this procedure, village cadres tried to convince the peasants that great profits could be brought by village-rebuilding program: street lamps would be put up in the village, the sight of the village would become better, villagers' rental business would become better with higher unit prices and more leases, and both the life conveniences and security would be improved.[43]

4.3.1.4 Cadres: Their Positions and Returns

Parish and Michelson (1996) assume that the financial returns of cadres depend on their position. My empirical studies are in line with their argument. The cadres in village administration became the managers of the collective economy. The advantages of the cadres in management position consist of several parts.

1. *Salary*. The party secretary of Long Village didn't tell me his exact salary, but he told me that it was set by the district government and was in proportion to the gross income of the village, the economic situation of the village, and his performance, etc. In general, it is several times that of the average annual income of the villagers.
2. *Stock bonus*. Since almost all of the village cadres were original inhabitants of the village, they could get a stock bonus from the village collective economy. Furthermore, the cadres in management positions were in their middle age and had served the village for many years. As a result, they held a larger number of shares, which could lead to good returns. As the share quota of these cadres was

---

[43] Informant Fan200402.

proportional to their performance, they could get larger bonuses if they could improve the collective economy greatly.

3. *Private businesses*. Holding a position in the political administration doesn't mean losing chances in the market. On the contrary, most of the cadres had had considerable experience in private business and continued their businesses even after they came to village power. According to my interviews, most of the cadres of Fan Township held some houses or shops for leasing. Some of them had share quotas from their previous businesses. Still others went into the stock market.
4. *Privilege*. Village cadres in the new cooperative economy, especially those who hold administrative positions, can gain many privileges. As I have observed in Fan Township, village cadres in administrative positions have special cars. The village office building is large and well-decorated (see Fig. 4.5). The main village leaders, including the village director, the secretary of the village branch of the CCP, and the members of the village committee, can have a private office in this building. They also enjoy other fringe benefits, such as subsidies for cell phones, social activities (e.g., to have dinner or to go to karaoke with friends, relatives, etc.) at public expense, and so on. Moreover, as Nee and Cao (2002) assume, finding jobs for their relatives and family members are one of the advantages cadres in Fan Township have. This is clear from an interview with a villager:

Fig. 4.5 The office building of Long Village administration

> I live at the middle level. If we don't have houses to lease out, the 150 yuan work subsidy isn't enough. I don't have political power (quanli). All those people, who have close relationship with power holders, have found a job in village administration. We don't have this kind of relationship. So we just do our own jobs. Anyway, we are very better than the migrant workers. (Informant Fan200401)

5. *Corruption.* The corruption of village cadres (especially in rich villages) has become a critical issue, which has attracted the attention of political scientists and economists. One can assume that the larger the scale of collective economy, the greater the possibilities of the existence of corruption among the managers of the collective economy—the village cadres. A total of 41 village cadres in rural areas of Guangzhou were charged with all kinds of corruption from January to July of 2005.[44] Although this is not a large number compared to the incidence of cases of corruption in all of rural China, we need to consider the possibilities for village cadres to involve themselves in corruption.

First, misappropriation (zhan yong/nuo yong) of collective revenue. In new cooperative economies, collective institutions continue to play important roles in economic development. They manage the land compensation funds, distribute collective revenue, and run collective businesses. The village is now more like a company than an old-style collective institution.[45] As with other hierarchic organizations, there are problems of "information asymmetry" and "moral hazard" in the village administration. As I have presented in previous the sections, the rules for resource distribution—the institutions of new cooperative economy—are complicated and make it easier for "information asymmetry" to arise. In this kind of villages, the misappropriation of collective revenue is a convenient way for village cadres to take money. Walder (2003) has discussed the characteristics of assets and the opportunities of elites. He proposes that "liquid assets are easier to appropriate than tangible ones" (p. 904). Comparing the agriculture products in agriculture villages, the collective assets in new cooperative economies are more "liquid" and more convenient for village cadres to appropriate.

Second, brokerage from contracting out. Another possible method of corruption for village cadres is the brokerage from contracting out. For example, collective programs, such as road construction, office building construction, and some others, can be allocated to the family members, relatives, or friends of village cadres. In most of cases, the village cadres, who control program distribution, can get some brokerage from this.

I did not find much data concerning corruption in Fan Township. The informants also gave good evaluations of the village cadres. Although I will not assume corruption is absent in Fan Township, it is noteworthy that some institutional characteris-

[44] Please see http://www.mos.gov.cn/Template/article/display0.jsp?mid=20050914016079

[45] Actually, when I was writing this thesis, many villages of Fan Township have been incorporated into a company, of which villagers became stockholders. At the same time, the household registration statuses of villagers were changed, and the villagers became urban residents (jumin) of Guangzhou. The village (cun), as an administrative unit, no longer exists.

tics in New Cooperative Economy make corruption in them less severe than in some other townships.

1. Sources of earnings of village cadres brought by market penetration are greatly improved. Village cadres can get money from many formal channels instead of through corruption, and this increases the opportunity cost of village cadres' corruption.
2. The village is close to the center of local higher-level administration. Actually, the office building of the Fan Township government is located in Long Village, and it takes just 20–30 min by bus to go from the Tianhe District's office building to the administration buildings of most other villages in Fan Township. This makes the supervision by higher levels of government possible. Most of the time, the policies of the district are implemented together by these three levels of governments or administration (village administration, township government, and district government). When I did my ethnographic study in Fan Township, I witnessed how a show was organized by the district government, township government, and village administration. The show was held in Long Village. The Long Village administration provided its village plaza and was in charge of some services, such as carrying desks and chairs, providing security personnel, and so on. The township government was in charge of reception and publicity. The district government was in charge of providing the contents of the shows. Furthermore, as mentioned above, the resources distribution policies of Fan Township are also worked out together by the district government, township government, and village administration. Therefore, one can imagine that corruption is dangerous, with this close supervision by higher levels of government.[46]
3. Fan Township borders the city center. With the long-time influence of urban culture, the villagers in this new cooperative economy are not the peasants, who only use the "weapons of the weak" described by Scott (1985). On the contrary, they are aware of their own rights. They like to participate in village elections and know something about the policies of all tiers of governments. As a result, village cadres' corruption is more easily brought to light. On the contrary, corruption in remote areas must be more difficult to be discovered.
4. The timing. Land requisition and its compensation are the main issues which have led to conflict between cadres and peasants in recent years.[47] However, Fan Township experienced the main land requisition processes from the end of the 1980s to the beginning of the 1990s. At that time, the effects of land requisition were still unknown by people. The collective resource distribution was carried

[46] Of course, one can also imagine that opportunities for corruption are greater, if one assumes that higher levels of government are also corrupt, as opportunities for guanxi are greater. But I want to remind here that the higher levels of governments are rich and the economic demands on the village administration are less. As a result, the supervision of higher levels of governments will be a constraint to the corruption of village administration.

[47] A Hong Kong newspaper has quoted sources in Beijing as saying that conflicts over land requisition deals have accounted for 66 % of the total of unrest in rural China since 2004. Please see BBC Monitoring Asia Pacific. London: Aug 2, 2005.

out together by the cadres and villagers. Therefore, I was not able to witness such conflict cases as a result of land requisition in Fan Township.

4.4 The Stratification Results in Rural Fan Township

As mentioned above, accompanying the market penetration in the new cooperative economy, the increasing earning sources, good welfare policies, and soft governance of local government led to increased life chances for the peasants of rural Fan Township, even though the rural cadres still had advantages. When I asked my informants how the population of their villages was stratified, they gave me the following answers:

> In general, the persons with high income are village cadres and businessmen. The second level is the people having wage work. The persons at the lowest level are the jumin (residents).[48] But poor people are few, because the village and district government will resolve the difficulties of peasants' lives (Informant Fan200406).
>
> Surely, those people who go outside for construction business, machine trade, and construction contractors, have absolute higher incomes than I have. What we get is just the distribution of the collective economy (Informant Fan200405).
>
> Of course, the richest people are government officers, needless to ask.... Some people are poor. For example, in the family of one young couple, the husband only has 3 shares and the wife has no stock because she is from elsewhere outside the village.[49] It means that the share of the stock bonus is only 1,000 yuan per year, counting 300 yuan per share. If the wife has no job, the earnings of the husband would be the only source of family earnings. In some more extreme cases, both the husband and wife have no jobs. What the husband can do is to carry people by motorcycle, for several yuan per day...poor and dangerous... (Informant Fan200408).
>
> From the perspective of living standards, there are few poor people in this village, since most of them have houses to lease and stock bonuses. About 70 percent are in the middle level. More than 10 percent stay in a worse situation. More than 10 percent are richer people who could go into transportation, running companies at the beginning of the reform. (Informant Fan200402)

Together with these answers, my observation in Fan Township also tells that the stratification consists of three levels. (1) At the top level are the cadres in management positions and successful businessmen. Since most of the cadres in management positions have been successful businessmen, there is an overlap between these two groups. It shows that human capital plays important roles in both the political market and the economic market. (2) The middle level consists of ordinary cadres, ordinary villagers who have good opportunities for profit sharing, and ordinary villagers who have some stable sources of earnings from the leasing trade or other businesses. (3) At the bottom are the people who have lower stock bonuses, without job opportunities or other sources of earnings.

---

[48] This refers to those people who have no stock bonus.

[49] The amount of a villager's stock depends on the time he (she) has served the collective economy and whether he (she) is an original inhabitant of the village.

I didn't take migrants into account in the discussion of the stratification results, since most of them were not likely to stay in Fan Township for a long time. However, the life chances of migrants living in the villages of Fan Township are also noteworthy here. The immigrants in Fan Township were mainly from the mountain areas of Guangdong and other southern and western provinces such as Hunan, Sichuan, Fujian, Jiangxi, Guangxi, and Hainan.[50] In some villages, the number of immigrants is larger than the number of local villagers right now. They are the main part of the labor market in Fan Township. They contribute the economic development of Fan Township by several ways: renting the villagers' houses or rooms, providing some services for villagers (e.g., cleaning, house construction, store, and so on) and other immigrants, and taking all low-wage jobs in factories and other economic institutions. According to how they made their living there, they can be divided into three types. (1) *Wage workers (dagong zhe, dagong zai, dagong mei).* They worked for the factories and other businesses in the villages of Fan Township. Mostly, they were young boys and girls and lived in the dormitories of the institutions they worked for. This group of immigrants earned less (wages generally ranged from 700 to 1,300 yuan per month) and had high mobility. (2) *Business owners (shengyi ren).* They ran shops, restaurants, salons, or stalls in the villages. Most of them lived with their families in rooms rented from the villagers of Fan Township. They had a lower mobility than the wage workers. As businesspersons, they could earn more than the other two groups.[51] (3) *White collar (bailing).* This group of people was those with college degree or professional skills and worked in the office buildings near the villages. They lived in the villages, renting rooms from villagers and working outside. They would move out of the village once they got enough money to gain a better living condition. Their income varied according to their jobs. Mostly, it ranged from 2,000 to 5,000.[52]

---

[50] The household registration system is not a barrier for rural people's mobility anymore. For the most part, a male peasant can travel freely in the country with his ID card (except to Shenzhen, Zhuhai, and other cities located on the national borders—although, since the turnover of Hong Kong in 1997 and Macau in 1999, the entrance controls to Shenzhen and Zhuhai have been relaxed). However, a female peasant of childbearing age needs a certificate (liudong renkou hunyu zhengming, the certificate of the floating population's childbearing and birth plan) to show her status of having fulfilled the obligation of the family planning policy. A peasant, whether male or female, previously needed to register at the police bureau of the destination to get a temporary living certificate (zan zhu zheng) if he (she) wants to stay there for a long time, but in 2005 this requirement was canceled.

[51] But it is not easy to tell the range of their earnings since it varied greatly according to their businesses.

[52] According to the situation in Guangzhou, those who can earn 6,000 yuan or above can easily pay for a room in the city.

4.5 Summary and Discussion

This chapter has described the economic situation, local politics, and people's lives of Fan Township, a township located in the core area of the PRD region of Guangdong Province. In this study, Fan Township is selected as representative of a kind of economy—the new cooperative economy, which dominates in the rural areas of the PRD. The new cooperative economy is one of the "forms of integration (Polanyi 1965)" of institutions, of which some characteristics should be highlighted:

First, the new cooperative economy involves close access to market elements (such as FDI, orders for goods, and others), and the economy thereby has developed greatly. Close access mostly refers to the proximity between the local rural areas and market centers, but in some other areas, it can refer to better transportation conditions, greater number of overseas Chinese, and special relationships (e.g., traditions of craft and trade specialization) with regional markets or even the global market. The earning sources of peasants increase and are various. The revenue of local governments also increases greatly. Market penetration, namely, the appropriative movement of material elements from the core inland, makes a difference, and not just "market transition" but the transfer of resource distribution from redistributive institutions to the market (Nee 1989).

Second, the state has played an important role in the new cooperative economy. At the macro-level, the state's special policies in Guangdong produced more chances for development for rural areas of the PRD region in the first 15 years (1978–1993) of the Reform Era. More or less, these areas enjoyed some advantages (in taxation, in opening businesses, and so on) because of special policies. The discrepancy between economic liberation and the continuation of political authoritarianism has put constraints on both the central and local governments. After years of economic development, the central state's ability and intention to remedy the problems of rural society have increased. At the local level, market penetration has also increased the township government's and village administration's abilities and intentions to advance the community welfare. Village administration plays important roles in economic development, and village cadres become the managers of the collective economy. The close access to market opportunities, rather than local cadres' incentive to develop the economy, is the decisive factor in the economic development.

Social institutions, including clan system, of overseas Chinese are not salient in the new cooperative economy. Villagers in the new cooperative economy are more like urban residents. The large amount of immigrants becomes the outstanding social characteristic there.

References

Greenhalgh, S., Chuzhu, Z., & Li, N. (1994). Restraining population growth in three Chinese villages, 1988–1993. *Population and Development Review, 20*, 365–395.

Nee, V. (1989). A theory of market transition: From redistribution to markets in state socialism. *American Sociological Review, 54*, 663–681.

Nee, V., & Cao, Y. (2002). Postsocialist inequalities: The causes of continuity and discontinuity. *Research in Social Stratification and Mobility, 19*, 3–39.

Parish, W. L., & Michelson, E. (1996). Politics and markets: Dual transformations. *American Journal of Sociology, 101*, 1042–1059.

Polanyi, K. (1965). The economy as instituted process. In K. Polanyi, C. M. Arensberg, & H. W. Pearson (Eds.), *Trade and market in the early empires: Economies in history and theory* (p. 248). New York: The Free Press.

Scott, J. C. (1985). *Weapons of the weak: Everyday forms of peasant resistance*. New Haven: Yale University Press.

Walder, A. G. (2003). Elite opportunity in transitional economics. *American Sociological Review, 68*, 899–916.

White, T. (1990). Postrevolutionary mobilization in China: The one-child policy reconsidered. *World Politics, 43*, 53–76.

Zheng, B., Qinbing, F., & Zhongxun, S. (1996). *Chao qi Tianhe: Guangzhou Shi Tianhe qu nong cun gu fen he zuo zhi gai ge shi jian tou shi* [Tides in Tianhe: an perpective of the reform of Rural Economic Stock Cooperation in Tianhe District, Guangzhou City]. Hong Kong: Hong Kong News Press.

Zhuang, Y., & Zheng, Z. (2002). *Tianhe qu renkou baogao* (Report on the population of Tianhe district), Office of the Fifth Census (Ed.). Beijing: Economic Science Press.

Chapter 5
An Outskirt Economy

Market penetration in Guangdong has proceeded from the coast inland and from the city centers to the outskirt areas. In this process, an outskirt economy is a specific structure, whose two characteristics benefit the peasants. For one thing, the geographical proximity to the city center provides opportunities for agricultural sidelines and the surplus rural labor of the outskirt economy; for another, the higher government levels gain their revenue mainly from the enterprises in the urban areas and other townships in the economic core. They thereby tend to provide subsidies to the outskirt townships instead of extracting from them. As a result, the peasants of the outskirt economies avoid a heavy burden.

To illustrate these two points, Lee Township, about 70 km from the city center of Guangzhou, will be taken as an example of the outskirt economies. It is under the governance of Zengcheng District of Guangzhou City. An introduction to Lee Township will first be presented. Secondly, I will introduce the earning sources of villagers in Lee Township. Thirdly, the revenue sharing between village administrations and the levels of government above them will be depicted. Lastly, the behavior of village administrations and their effects on peasants' life chances will be discussed.

5.1 Lee Township and Its Market Penetration

Lee Township is located near the northern edge of the PRD region. Mountain areas and foothills occupy 70 %, while the plain areas take up 30 %. It is 30 km. to Zengcheng city center, 70 km. to Guangzhou, 120 km. to Dongguan, 130 km. to Shenzhen, and 150 km. to Hong Kong[1] (see Fig. 5.1). It is under the governance of Zengcheng City, a county-level city of Guangzhou. There are 31 administrative

[1] Hong Kong, Guangzhou, Shenzhen, and Dongguan are four core cities in the PRD region.

N. Chen, *State, Market and Life Chances in Contemporary Rural Chinese Society*, DOI 10.1007/978-3-662-45046-8_5

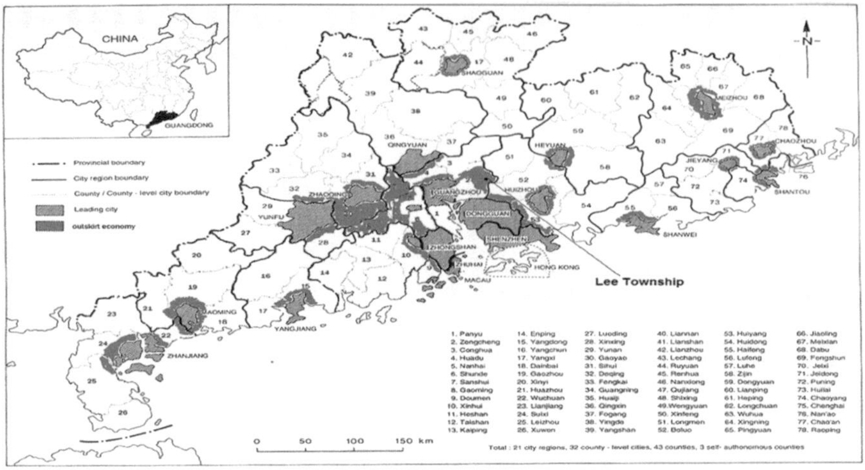

Fig. 5.1 The location of Lee Township

villages and 1 residence committee in Lee Township. The population was 52,728 in 2002, the rural population being 48,015 and the urban population 4,713[2]—about one tenth of the former.

Lee Township lags behind the townships in southern Zengcheng in market penetration. Table 5.1 shows that Lee Township is the lowest in rural investment of all the townships of Zengcheng City. The commodity market also lags behind that of the other townships in the core of the PRD region. The productive industry of Lee Township is in its elementary stage. It once consisted of granite mines and some manufactures for simple processing. In 1993, there were only 15 granite mines and 20 enterprises for flagstones, with a total investment of 450 million yuan and a gross output for the industry of the whole township of 112 million yuan, of which 15.25 million was from township enterprises, 12.20 million from village enterprises, 58.25 million from joint-household enterprises, and 26.30 million from private enterprises.[3] Ten years later gross industrial production value reached 663,610,000 yuan, some 5 times that of 1993. However, compared to that of the townships in the core areas, this increase is quite small. The average annual income of peasants was 2,398 yuan in 2003,[4] while the average annual income of peasants in Zengcheng was 4,725.7 yuan.[5] One can see that the annual average income of Lee Township in 2003 only constituted 10 % of that of in Fan Township in 2000 (please refer to Chap. 4). Moreover, according to my observations, almost all enterprises in Lee

[2] Figures from the 2003 government report of Lee Township (unpublished).

[3] Edition Committee of the Chorography of Zengcheng 1995, p. 79.

[4] The Report of the Work of Lee Township Government (unpublished), 2003.

[5] http://www.zengcheng.gov.cn/tongjiju/firstpage/tjfx/fx28.htm

Table 5.1 Investment in rural areas of the townships in Zengcheng City (thousands of yuan)

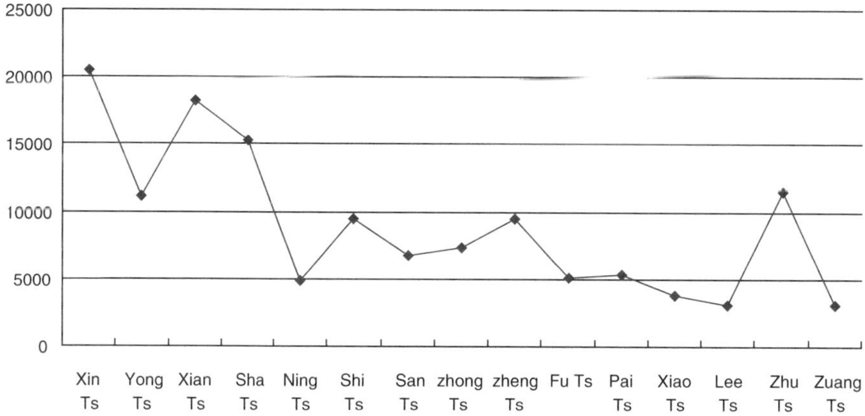

Source: Zengcheng government's webpage http://www.zengcheng.gov.cn/tongjiju/firstpage/lssj/lssj.asp

Township are small, except for one. Without the development of its commodity market, the labor market also lags behind. The number of people who come to Lee Township for work is smaller, but the number of those who go out for wage work is large.[6]

5.2 The Earnings of Peasants in Lee Township

With the lower level of market penetration, both the variety and quality of the earning sources of peasants of Lee Township present a different picture from those of Fan Township. In an undeveloped collective economy, peasants can share few collective assets. Peasants in Fan Township have many good opportunities to develop their own businesses (e.g., the leasing trade, the garages), while peasants of Lee Township have to go to the core cities of the PRD region to find the same opportunities.

Generally, the earning sources of the peasants in Lee Township are of two kinds: local earning sources and nonlocal earning sources. The former includes all kinds of family production in local areas, especially sideline products from vegetable gardens, fruit orchards, livestock husbandry, poultry husbandry, and local businesses (e.g., running a store in a village, hauling freight, running a construction team, and so on). The latter includes both migrant wage labor and migrant business operation.

---

[6] http://www.guangztr.edu.cn/gztr/jcjy/ccxxbj.htm

5.2.1 *Peasants' Earnings in Local Areas*

As noted previously in Chap. 3, an outstanding characteristic of the outskirt economy is the taking up of types of agricultural production, such as livestock husbandry, fishery, etc., which retreated from the suburban areas of the city centers. This is exactly what has happened in Zengcheng. The geographic proximity of Hong Kong, Guangzhou, Shenzhen, and Dongguan and the good conditions for agriculture make rural Zengcheng a main supplier of primary products to the big cities. For example, pig husbandry was prohibited in the suburban areas of Guangzhou and Dongguan in 2003; most of it moved to the rural areas of Zengcheng City. As far as agriculture is concerned, vegetable growing, which once was the major part of agricultural production in the suburban areas of Guangzhou, now is playing a more and more important role in Zengcheng. Lee Township, as one of the townships of Zengcheng, also participates in supplying vegetables.

In Lee Township, this agriculture, including sideline production, is very important to the economy. Table 5.2 shows that staples are still an important part of the agriculture of Lee Township, but vegetables are now in second place. Furthermore, the acreage of staples is decreasing gradually, while the acreage of vegetables is increasing dramatically.

Certainly, agricultural sideline production has been an important supplement for the material life of rural Chinese people for a long time. Especially since the reform, almost every peasant household has had some sidelines to vary its production. The most common sidelines are vegetables, fruit, livestock, etc. Most of this production

Table 5.2 The yields from agriculture and agricultural sideline in Lee Township

Agricultural products	Acreage (mu)	Average output (kg)	Gross output (Ton)
Staple crops	48,409	320	15,503
Spring	564	282	159
Summer	22,668	310	7020
Autumn	25,177	331	8324
Ordinary paddy	46,410	324	15,031
Summer	22,560	310	6994
Autumn	23,850	337	8037
High-quality paddy	25,835	326	8412
Corn	210	229	48
Sweet potatoes	1217	216	263
Irish potatoes	543	234	127
Soybeans	32	281	9
Sugarcane	56	5304	297
Peanuts	3540	158	561
Flowers	65		
Vegetables	10,917	1415	15,449

(Sources: Zengcheng government's webpage http://www.zengcheng.gov.cn/tongjiju/firstpage/lssj/lssj.asp)

has not been done on a large scale, as the degree of agricultural mechanization was very low. However, in an outskirt economy like that of Lee Township, market penetration provides opportunities for production specialization and agricultural mechanization. Some peasant families have become special households by contracting out the fishponds, fruits trees, and even the farmland of the collectivity, thereby enlarging the scale of agricultural sideline production. The rate of agricultural mechanization in Lee Township is quite high: 31.41 % for staples, 84.19 % for vegetables, and 62.55 % for fruits in 2004.[7]

Staple Crops

The main staple grown in Lee Township is paddy rice (see Table 5.2). In some villages of Lee Township, 50 % of the farmland is used for paddy. However, peasants cannot make much money from paddy. First of all, in the household responsibility system, the farmland is distributed according to an average for each household, according to population. As a result, the total acreage of farmland of each household is limited. The average farmland per farmer is about 0.44 acres in Guangdong.[8] Secondly, paddy production is not cost efficient. One informant explained the agricultural income of his family of four to me. The family had 2.5 mu of farmland, of which 1.5 mu was for paddy and the rest for vegetables and peanuts. He planted two crops of paddy per year. The yield of one *mu* of his paddy crop was about 400–500 kg, for annul yields of about 800–1,000 kg. Counting the unit price as 1.2 yuan per kg, the gross value of the paddy is about 960–1,200 yuan, before deducting the cost (per mu, per year) for agricultural tax (40 yuan per mu),[9] fertilizer (380 yuan per mu), seeds (60 yuan), and machine rental (140 yuan).[10] This cost-benefit analysis shows that the earnings of his household from staples were only about 340–580 yuan per year.

Thus, with the policy of the market economy, there are not many reasons for peasants to plant paddy rice. Explanations according to the moral economy may be better: rice is the main food of the peasant family and is thus the guarantee of the subsistence of peasants (Scott 1976). However, because paddy planting is not cost efficient, the acreage of paddy has decreased gradually in Zengcheng in recent years, from 71,270,000 in 1999 to 48,160,000 in 2003.[11]

Vegetable Growing

The profits from vegetable growing are much better than those from paddy rice. The average production value of one mu of vegetables is about 9,000 yuan, and the net

[7] January 29, in http://www.zengcheng.gov.cn/tongjiju/firstpage/tjfx/fx0502.htm

[8] Guangdong Agricultural Statistics Yearbook 1999.

[9] This is the agricultural tax since the tax-for-fee reform of 2004. The agricultural tax was much higher before, sometimes reaching 150–200 yuan per mu. From 2005 on, the agricultural tax has been totally canceled, as a provincial policy.

[10] Informant Lee200408.

[11] Lai Jieti, *A comprehensive development of agriculture, forestry, stock husbandry, and fishery; the agricultural economy reaches a new high level in recent years—the analysis of the agriculture production of 2004*, in http://www.zengcheng.gov.cn/tongjiju/firstpage/tjfx

profits can reach about 3,500 yuan per year. Vegetable growing plays a more and more important role in rural Zengcheng: from 2003 to 2004, the acreage of vegetables increased 10.5 % to 527,000 mu and gross production increased 11.4 % to 974,000 t,[12] while gross production value increased 14.9 % to 1.372 billion yuan. Not all vegetables are supplied to the four big cities of the PRD region: many peasants of Lee Township sell their vegetables in the local rural market or at the market center of Zengcheng, which is also a big market for the peasants in Lee Township.

Fruit Trees

Foothills occupy 70 % of Lee Township's territory and fruit trees are therefore common, mainly consisting of litchis and longans. A litchi tree begins to fructify when it is more than 5 years old. The fruit of a litchi tree of 6–7 years can reach 50 kg or more. Fertilizer and insecticide are the main expenses in growing litchis.

Forestry

To make a living by forestry requires much more investment than other sidelines. A special household (zhuanye hu) head, who owned 350 mu of forest, told me something about his business: he had planted more than 30,000 trees on his 350 mu of hillsides. The cost for fertilizer and weed killer was 25 yuan per day. After one more year, he could chop and sell parts of the trees.[13]

Other Sidelines

Pig and chicken husbandry are also popular in Lee Township. According to an informant, a peasant household can earn about 100 yuan from raising a pig successfully (see Table 5.3).

Local Businesses

Peasants' other earnings in local areas also include local individual businesses, such as stores, motorcycle taxis, house building for peasants' houses, carpentry, etc.

5.2.2 Earning from Migrant Wage Work and Migrant Business

The development of the PRD region not only provides a big market for Lee Township's agricultural products but also many wage work and business opportunities for the rural people of Lee Township. Most of them go to Guangzhou, Shenzhen, or Dongguan for wage work and businesses opportunities, while the rest go to other places all over the country. A village cadre told me that the township government had recorded data on the villagers who went outside for wage work and business when SARS broke out in 2003. The data shows that many cities, such as Qingdao and Shanghai, and provinces, such as Shanxi, Shandong, Wuhan, Hunan and Hubei,[14] were the destinations of the peasants of Lee Township. Another cadre told

[12] Ibid.

[13] Informant Lee200402.

[14] Informant Lee200414.

Table 5.3 The cost and profits of pig husbandry[a]

Cost	Descriptions	Value (yuan)
Young pig	250 yuan	250
Feeding period	4.5–5 months	
Feed	The first 3 months, 1 kg/day	594
	The last 2 months 3 kg/day	
Cost of manpower	500 yuan/person per month for raising 100 pigs	30
Tax and other		50
Sales value	About 115.5 kg	1,150
Profits		About 100

[a]Informant Lee200412

me how migrant wage work and migrant businesses play more and more important roles in peasants' lives.

> The main source of earnings is migrant work. This township isn't a good place to get rich. Several years ago, I thought that we should adjust our development plan according to local conditions: our township is a mountain township and the economic development can't reach our township. I had thought about the possibilities to develop our township's agriculture. But now, I think it is a blind lane. We can not earn much money from agriculture. Take longan growing as an example: we can get nothing when the yields are poor. Moreover, the price will decrease when we have a good harvest. I have grown longan trees for several years. I can't support my family if I depend on this solely. You can see, these years, people have bought all kinds of electric machines, motorcycles, and are building new houses. But the money wasn't from agriculture, but from migrant wage work or businesses. Almost for 20 years it has been like this. So, I think we should encourage more people to go outside for wage work. If a household has several people who go outside for work, the household can at least earn 10,000 yuan per year. The county government also has the same ideas as I have. So, they help us by offering work opportunities and providing free training courses. (Informant 200406)

Just as this informant said, the local governments also realized that migrant wage work can improve the peasants' earnings. When I was in the township for fieldwork, I saw how a recruitment fair for peasant workers was held in Zengcheng by the district government. The notices about the meeting were sent to the township governments. The township government asked the village cadres to give the peasant households this information. A bus was also prepared by the township government to carry the peasants who wanted to participate in the recruitment fair. The recruitment fair was part of the rural labor export program set up by the Zengcheng District Government. The government set up a special fund to support the program. In 2002 and 2003, the government invested a total of 5,600,000 yuan to facilitate the labor exchange.[15] The fund is to improve the communication between enterprises and rural surplus labor and to provide free training to the latter. In 2004, there were

[15]The money was used to hold a labor exchange fair regularly in the capital city of the district, to set up a labor exchange office in every township government, and so on.

12,793 peasants of Lee Township who went outside for wage work or business, which was 90 % of the total surplus rural labor.

However, the surplus rural labor of Zengcheng were not as good competitors for work in factories as young people from other, less-developed provinces like Hunan, Sichuan, Shanxi, and so on.[16] The wage positions available for peasants of Lee Township always consist of housekeeper, warehouseman, security, driver, and sales agent, etc.[17] As a result, migrant business operation is undoubtedly more attractive to the peasants of Lee Township, even though it is more difficult to do than migrant wage labor. Garages and automobile accessories are two main kinds of migrant business of peasants of Lee Township. Like many peasants' individual businesses, a social relationship plays a very important role in the formation of these businesses. For example, in Lee Township, a peasant, Zhang Bingxin, who succeeded in the automobile fitting businesses, asked more than 100 villagers of Lee Township to go out to work for him. Some of these people also became successful businessmen in automobile fittings later and, like Zhang Bingxin, they brought other villagers to go outside to work for them. Now, in many big cities, including Beijing, Tianjin, Chongqing, and so on,[18] some peasants of Zengcheng run their automobile fitting businesses in the same place, even on the same street, which then becomes the so-called street of automobile fittings of Zengcheng (Zengcheng qipei yi tiao jie).

The earnings from migrant wage labor and businesses have become increasingly significant in peasant family economies. For example, in 2004, the income from migrant wage work contributed a lot to the net-income increase of the peasants in Zengcheng.[19] Table 5.4 shows that the net income from wage work provides almost 60 % of the gross earnings of the peasants of Zengcheng, while the importance of family production (including agriculture product, sidelines, and even family businesses) in local areas has decreased gradually.

5.3 Revenue Sharing in Lee Township

The revenue sharing between Lee Township and government levels above it shows a specific structure of revenue sharing, in which fiscal subsidy or transfer plays a key role in the finances of local administration. The uneven market penetration in China makes fiscal transfer an important lever in the state's fiscal policy. Even in Guangdong Province, one of the most developed provinces in the country, this occurs. A report from the Development Research Center of the Guangdong Government shows that in 2003, the fiscal income of 67 counties (and county-level cities), which contained 83.3 % of the farmland and more than 60 % of population

---

[16] Those young people from the underdeveloped provinces can accept lower wages.

[17] *Zengcheng Daily*, March 24, 2005, Li ZiYuan.

[18] http://www.clz.gov.cn/clz/Art_3145.htm and http://business.sohu.com/2004/06/08/31/article220433169.shtml

[19] Unfortunately I can't find the exact data concerning Lee Township.

Table 5.4 Rural residents' net income and its constitution in Zengcheng, 1997–2003

Year	Average net income			1. Income from wage works			2. Net income from family production		
	Absolute value (yuan)	Rate of change (%)	Constitutes (%)	Absolute value (yuan)	Rate of change (%)	Constitutes (%)	Absolute value (yuan)	Rate of change (%)	Constitutes (%)
1997	4185.76	5.1	100	569.79	4.7	13.6	3163.76	5.1	75.6
1998	3987.94	−4.7	100	585.81	2.8	14.7	2927.61	−7.5	73.4
1999	4070.09	2.1	100	753.60	28.6	18.5	2843.75	−2.9	69.9
2000	4197.09	3.1	100	1506.92	99.9	35.9	2655.72	−6.6	53.3
2001	4329.40	3.2	100	1757.04	16.6	40.6	2508.77	−5.5	57.9
2002	4508.08	4.1	100	2264.89	28.9	50.2	1921.97	−23.4	42.6
2003	4725.70	4.8	100	2797.83	23.5	59.2	1514.22	−21.2	32.0

Sources: Zengcheng District Statistics Department, "Cong Zengcheng nongmin shouru bianhua kan xin jieduan nongmin zengshou wenti (Understanding the question of increasing peasants' income in the new phase from the changes of peasants' income in Zengcheng)." Available at http://www.zengcheng.gov.cn/tongjiju/firstpage/tjfx/fx28.htm

of the province, only accounted for 6.7 % of the fiscal income of the province. Only 5 counties did not need fiscal transfers from the provincial government. The other counties could not support the normal running of the administration without fiscal transfer. From 1996 to 2003, the provincial fiscal transfers to those counties increased ten times, from 0.58 billion to 6.79 billion.[20]

Table 5.5 gives us a clear picture of the constitution of the fiscal income of Lee Township. In 2001 and 2002, the tax revenue of Lee Township was less than 20 % of the total income of the township. A fiscal transfer and helping funds from above, including the Zengcheng government and all kinds of departments in Guangzhou City, accounted for 80 % of the fiscal income of Lee Township.

Both the Zengcheng District Government and the Guangzhou Government (see Fig. 5.2) have benefited a lot from market penetration. As Lee Township is located in the north of Zengcheng and is one of its poorest townships, these two higher government bodies do not try to take money from Lee Township but tend to provide more subsidies to Lee Township to buy support for their governance. Large fiscal transfers are related to the development strategy of the Guangzhou Government. According to this strategy, the south of Zengcheng will mainly be developed into a center of secondary industry and modern service industry. The north part will focus on the development of agriculture, tourism, and sustainable industry.[21] The goal of this strategy is to protect the natural environment of the north of the PRD region. A village cadre told me his feeling about this strategy:

> My heart was frozen when I heard the government report. (Why?) Because the government said that the mountain townships are not easy to be developed and the development cost is too high. They encourage us to go outside to other places to earn money and just keep the green mountain and clear water intact. They also said that mountain townships are the backyard of Guangzhou, which should not be polluted by industrial development. (Informant Lee200406)

To implement this strategy, the Guangzhou Government was trying to provide more subsidies to Lee Township's economy. One policy was to ask many of its agencies to provide helping programs to the villages in these townships (see Table 5.6).

The importance of fiscal transfer to Lee Township makes the other two parts of its revenue—local taxes and administration fees—less important. For one thing, it is difficult to increase the local tax revenue because the level of market penetration of Lee Township is low. For another, to increase fiscal income by collecting all kinds of surcharges comes with a high cost, since the peasants' appeals on such issues will do harm to the impression of superior government bodies of Lee Township, which will in turn do harm to the amount of fiscal transfers. To meet the demands of higher government is the key for gaining financial support, and how to fulfill the tasks assigned by the superior government bodies is really important to the township governments and village administration, because taking more subsidies from above seems to be easier than taking money from peasants' pockets. This makes the role

[20] *Nanfang Weekly*, September 22, 2005.

[21] Annual report of the Zengcheng government, on the webpage of the Zengcheng government.

Table 5.5 The constitution of the fiscal income of Lee Township

Year	Index	Number (million yuan)	Percentage (%)
2001	Fiscal income	21.342	100
	Allocation from city government	16.227	76
	Helping funds from the departments of GZ City	1.06	5
	Township pooling fee	3.655	17
	Fiscal sharing	0.40	2
2002	Fiscal income	21.90	100
	Allocation from city government	16.50	75.3
	Helping funds from the departments of GZ City	1.10	5
	Township pooling fee	3.80	17.3
	Fiscal sharing	0.50	2.3

Source: Ethnographic data collected in Lee Township

Table 5.6 Helping programs to Lee Township

Administrative village who receives the helping	The institutions who provide helping	Helping program
Shui Village	The Committee of Sciences of Guangzhou	Lumber mill
Bai Village	The Fiscal Bureau of Guangzhou	Forestry center
Peace Village	The United Front Department of Guangzhou	Buy shops for renting
Huang Village	The Committee of Agriculture of Gaungzhou	Vegetable-processing base
Liang Village	The Cultural Bureau of Guangzhou	Floriculture base

Source: Ethnographic data

of village administration different with what we saw in Fan Township, and I will discuss it in the next section.

5.4 From Redistributors to "Volunteer Firemen"

The village administrations in Lee Township are greatly different from their counterparts in Fan Township. Generally, in Fan Township, village cadres act like the managers of the village cooperative economy, while the village cadres in Lee Township acted like "volunteer firemen." In 1996, Parish and Michelson pointed out that many village administrations of China are "as fire departments in small U.S. hamlets and towns…most Chinese rural administrators fill this capacity only part-time" (Parish and Michelson 1996, p. 1043). They call such village cadres "volunteer firemen." I borrow this term here, highlighting not only the characteristic of "part time" but also presenting characteristics of the village administrations in rural Lee Township.

5.4.1 The Constitution of Village Cadres in Lee Township

In Fan Township, the village cadres are young and better equipped with management knowledge and skills. The number of cadres of a village in Fan Township is also large. Direct village elections are replacing the former cadres with new cadres, changing the nature of the cadre structure. However, the story is totally different in Lee Township.

First of all, the number of cadres in the villages of Lee Township is small. There are usually 5–7 persons in each village administration. These 5–7 persons belong to two institutions of village administration: the villagers committee (cunmin weiyuanhui) and the village branch of the CCP (dang zhibu). In each villager committee, the positions include the director, the associate director, the women's officer, the security officer, and the secretary (wenshu). In a village branch of the CCP, the positions include the branch secretary (cun zhibu shuji) and other committee members (zhibu weiyuan). This means that the positions are usually more than the number of elected cadres (see Fig. 5.2). As a result, some of the village cadres have to take two or even more positions. For example, if the director of the villagers committee is a member of the CCP, he (she) will also take a role in the village branch of the CCP.

Secondly, almost all of the village cadres in Lee Township are more than 40 years old. During my ethnographic study in the villages of Lee Township, I saw that most village cadres had held their positions for a long time. Some secretaries of village branches of the CCP had spent 30 years in their positions. Direct village elections did not bring great changes to the constitution of the village cadres in Lee Township. In fact, whether a villager wants to be a cadre depends on his (her) life cycle. Village cadres are either old, having spent many years in their positions, or middle aged. Middle-aged villagers have children of school age who need their parenting. Furthermore, being no longer young, they are less competitive in the labor markets outside their village. As a result, the position of village cadre is attractive only to those who do not want to leave the village for business chances elsewhere. The director of the villagers committee of Shui Village may serve as an example.

> I have a wife and several children. It is troublesome if I leave them at home and work in cities elsewhere. My family can not take care of each other, if I go to Guangzhou, Dongguan. Moreover, we need to take care of our children's education and their diets. We have to consider all these things. I won't be here as a cadre if I consider money only, because the salary of my position is only 450 yuan. To be honest, I can earn much more than I do now if I go out to work. (Informant Lee200421)

Thirdly, direct village elections did not change the constitution of the village cadres much—after it was implemented in 1998, the cadre structure of rural Lee Township almost remained intact. Because the stability of the village situation is a

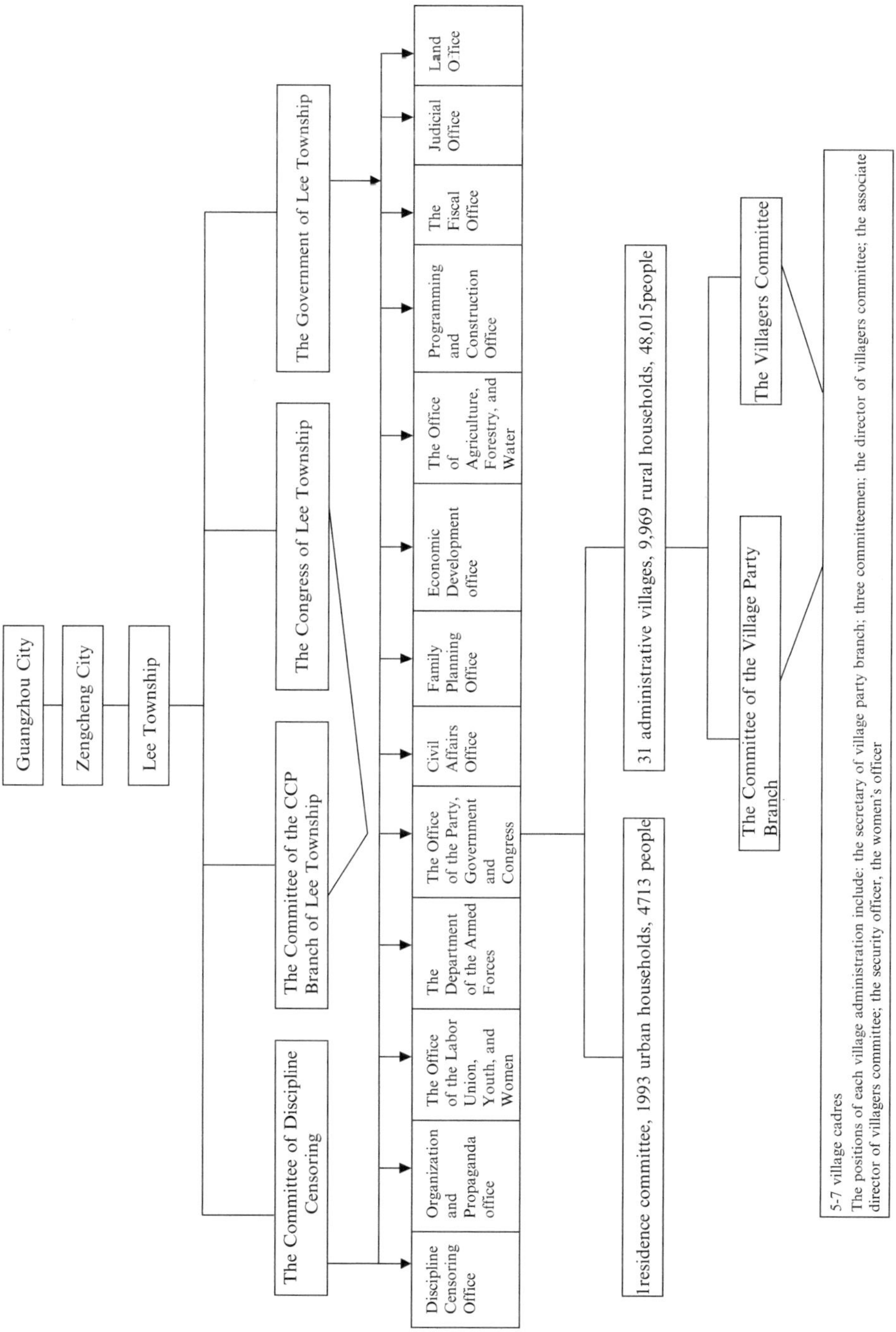

Fig. 5.2 The administrative framework of Lee Township

key factor for township governments when they plead for fiscal transfers and helping funds from above, the township government tends to keep control of the village cadres' election.[22] Although the Organic Law of the Committee of Villagers (cunmin wei yuanhui zuzhifa) requires that the direct village election be held openly, fairly, and rightly, there are still many ways for the township government to affect the election.

1. The highest power of the village is still the village branch of the CCP. The secretary and other officers of a village party branch are not elected directly by the villagers. Most of the time the township government asks the village party secretary to run for director of the villager committee, so that the township government can control the village administration through the CCP.[23] The director of Civil Affairs Office of Lee Township told me that:

   > Actually, I don't think that it (direct village election) had much effect and made much difference. Sometimes, some elected village directors conflict with village party secretaries. We learn some lessons from these issues and then we changed the policy so that the secretary of the village Party branch can also be the director of the villager committee. (Informant Lee200423)

2. The helping programs from higher government levels are attractive to the village administrations of Lee Township since the village economies lag behind. The township government thereby becomes the distributor of these helping programs, and good cooperation with the township government means better chances to benefit from these helping programs:

   > They (village cadres) can do nothing without the township governments. Because the economy of the villages is underdeveloped, they have to depend on the government for some supporting programs (Informant Lee200423).

3. The township government is the organizer of the village direct election. The steering committee is organized by the township government and the election results have to be approved by the township government. Like elections everywhere, there are some weaknesses in the election procedures, which can be used by the township government.

Fourthly, the positions of village cadres are not attractive to many villagers, since the economic benefits of the positions are trifling. A villager who has worked in Jiangmen[24]said:

[22] Unlike in Fan Township, where village cadres take care of their own economy and implement the policies very well by using economic levers.

[23] Actually, not just township government tends to do this. This kind of "overlapping policy" is even encouraged by the city government. I interviewed an officer in the Civil Affairs Bureau of the Guangzhoug Government, who told me that the Guangzhou government also asks that 70 % of the positions of villagers committee directors be taken by the secretary of the village Party branch (Informant GZ200401).

[24] One of the regional cities of the PRD region.

> In the townships in the south of Zengcheng, some people buy village office positions.[25] But in our township, no one wants to be village officers. (Why?) People can't get money from the position. So, nobody wants to take the job. Just several hundred yuan[26]! Who wants to take the position? The cadres should be changed every three years, but the cadres of our village are always those same people. (Informant Lee200411)

5.4.2 *The Jobs of Village Cadres in Lee Township*

There is a call-board before every village office of Lee Township bearing descriptions of the jobs of the party member in the villages, which can also be considered to be the jobs of village cadres.

1. *Economic development*: to lead the appointed households[27] to develop productivity and to guide and help them to do production and business scientifically and to achieve common prosperity (gongtong zhifu)
2. *Family planning*: to help the village party branch and the villagers committee to propagate and implement the family planning policy and to make sure all appointed households can fully obey the various policies of family planning
3. *Helping and relief*: to care and help the appointed households and to positively help the appointed households to solve the difficulties of production and living
4. *Tax and fee collecting*: to help the party branch and villagers committee to fulfill the all kinds of targets of taxation and fees and to lead and help them to pay the taxes and fees on time
5. *Security and mediation*: to improve the stability and solidarity of the appointed households, to interfere in the conflicts in the village, to make sure that the appointed households won't become estranged because of various clans, to prevent group scuffles between clans, to prevent them from appealing to higher government for help, and to create a stable and peaceful environment for production and living
6. *Environmental construction*: to improve the landscape and cleanliness of the environment, to lead the appointed households to follow the program for village construction, and to prevent any illegal private constructions
7. *Ideology helping*: to implement all kinds of strategies and policies of the party in rural areas; in various ways, to flexibly propagate and educate the appointed households; to lead them to think of the reasons for life changes and the ways to improve life; to make sure that all kinds of party policies are implemented by

[25] By buying the votes of the villagers.

[26] The salary of village cadres.

[27] According to a so-called "Party member responsibility system (dangyuan fuze zhi)," every Party member will be appointed to help several specific households.

the appointed households; and to propagate the law and prevent any illegal actions of the appointed households

8. *Science education*: to take the lead to learn sciences and use sciences; to lead the appointed households to believe in science, learn practical technology, and oppose superstition and heretical ideas; and to prevent any people of the appointed households to attend any organizations with heretical ideas
9. *Creating civilization*: to greatly improve civilization; to lead the appointed households to be civilized, polite, and healthy; to prevent any people in the appointed households from attending pornographic activities, gambling, or become drug users; to lead them transform the social tradition; to adopt the new form of wedding; to implement the cremation policy; and to encourage them to be a peasants with ideals, goodness, civilization, and discipline
10. *Supervision of public village affairs*: to pay attention to all kinds of public affairs of the village, to report the demands of the appointed households, to positively offer ideas to the party branch and village administration, and to supervise the running of village administration and the implementation of the openness of village administration

From this description, we can see that the duties of village cadres and party members include almost all aspects of peasants' lives. However, including everything usually means nothing special. In fact, the jobs of village cadres of Lee Townships are very flexible:

> Our jobs are flexible. It is hard to say that our jobs are more or less, "exist" or "do not exist". For example, there was a traffic accident on the first day of this year. We cadres had to go to the locale to deal with it. We had to interfere in the conflict; otherwise the accident could easily leads to quarrel or fighting. It is hard to say that rural cadres play very important roles. But it won't be good if there aren't rural cadres. There are a lot of small conflicts in rural areas. It would be a real trouble if these small conflicts accumulated together.... The jobs generally include family planning, agricultural tax collecting, implementing the other tasks assigned by the governments. For example, now we are facing the job of preventing 'bird flu'. So we should help villagers to vaccinate their chickens at this time. Another example: when SARS broke out last year, we mobilized villagers to clean the village, taught them the relavent information. If the peasants have something needing us to handle, we would go there. Our "office" is everywhere in the village. (Informant Lee200406)

Part-Time Workers

The village cadres do not need to be on duty in offices every day. Actually, they do not go to their offices often. Even when they go to their offices, they just come to have a look, to have a chat with their colleagues, and sometimes to play cards or mah-jongg in their office. Then they will leave the office to take care of their own family affairs. The office building and the facilities of the office are simple (see Fig. 5.3), without computers, fax machines, or copy machines. According to my observations and interviews, the village cadres of rural Lee Township do not play a very important role in villagers' everyday lives. For one thing, villagers do not have many expectations of the village cadres:

> (What do you need the village administration to help you with?) Nothing, the village administration is poor here. It is hopeless. The village administration needs somebody else

Fig. 5.3 A village office building in Lee Township

> to help them. Higher government gave them 120 thousand yuan, but no money was distributed to the production team. (Informant Lee200417)
>
> (Did you attend the direct village election?) Yes, but those things are none of my business. I don't care who the cadres of the village are. I just do my own business. I rarely contact the cadres. I don't need any help from them. I do not think cadres are necessary in our village…I don't want to care about those things (direct village elections and cadres' work). I won't be against what they do. I just want to earn money by myself. If his moral character and other things are OK, he is OK with me. (Informant Lee200419)

A retired village cadre told me his impression of the current village cadres:

> The cadres now are different from the former (pre-reform period) cadres. Now they are elected. What they do is just to prepare some financial bills or some document for higher government. When I was a cadre, the salary was only 240 yuan. All cadres of our village were only two men—me and the other person. We needed to do everything. On the contrary, the jobs of cadres right now are easier. They play mah-jong every day. (Informant Lee200417)

Passive Task Receiver

More data from my ethnographic study can show the work methods of the village administration of Lee Township. Village cadres in rural Lee Township do their work as passive receivers, by which I mean that most jobs of the village administration are nonscheduled and are often set by the township government. For example, when I asked one village cadre why he wanted to be a village cadre, he answered:

> The old Party secretary of our village asked me to do it. Anyway, I don't have much to do at home in ordinary time. So I took the job to do something for the villagers…. (Informant Lee200409)

In Lee Township, there was a township cadre who showed me the way to the village office and introduced me to the village officers. This cadre was from the Office of Rural Central Works (nongcun zhongxin gongzuo bangongshi), which facilitates the work of township government in rural areas. This work of the township government follows a certain procedure. Propaganda and mobilization is one task. When there is an important task assigned by higher government, the township government will hold a conference of township cadres and village officers. The task will be explained and distributed to the village cadres in the conference. Also, according to the district responsibility system, every township cadre in the Office of Rural Central Works will be asked to be responsible for supervising the work of two villages.[28]

In this way, only when township government needs the village cadres to do something will the village cadres take action.

> When there are notices, duties from higher government which need to be transmitted by me to natural villages and peasants, I will deal with it. Usually we just maintain the stability of the village and all kinds of work. I just don't know what to say about our jobs. (Informant Lee200414)

Family Planning Policy

There are actually only two fixed jobs of village administration of Lee Township: to collect agricultural taxes and to implement the family planning policy. When I did my fieldworks in Lee Township, the tax-for-fee reform has been implemented there. Village cadres did not need to spend much time in collecting the agricultural tax since most peasants would directly submit the tax to the township's fiscal office. This meant that the only fixed job of village cadre in Lee Township was really to implement the family planning policy.

As I mentioned above, the township government does not need to extract much revenue from the rural society because of the large scale of fiscal transfer and helping funds. Without heavy pressure of economic development on the shoulders of local cadres, the implementing of the family planning policy becomes the most important measure of their work. It is closely related to the allocation and aids from higher government levels. As the director of the Civil Affairs Office of Lee Township said:

> The family planning policy is the most difficult job in the rural areas. It is a 'one-vote veto' item. It means that family planning is a decisive standard of whether a local government can be appraised as an advanced government through comparison. An advanced government, of course, can get more subsidies from higher governments. The cadres of an advanced government also face more promotion chances. On the contrary, an officer who can't meet the standard of implementing family planning policy will face the risk of losing his (her) official position. (Informant Lee200423)

In rural China, women of reproductive age are the objects of the family planning policy. A young couple has to apply for a childbearing certificate (zhunsheng zheng) before they plan to have a baby. After that, the wife should go to a hospital for a checkup and an estimation of the expected date of childbirth. If the wife gives birth

[28] Informant Lee200424.

to a boy, the couple needs to apply for single-child identification. If the wife gives birth to a girl, the couple has the right to arrange for a second pregnancy after 4 years.[29] To township cadres, the work of carrying out the family planning policy includes regular inspections, the distribution of contraceptives, the collection and tabulation of report figures from lower levels, and the fixing of annual birth quotas and their breakdown according to villagers. The most time-consuming and difficult work of the cadres are at the village level—namely, the administration of contraceptive measures and the supervision of women of reproductive age, the constant visits to women with unauthorized pregnancies and the concomitant efforts to persuade and oblige them to have abortions, the hearing of medical complaints and appropriate counseling, the proclaiming of village birth quotas and the handing out of licenses to applicants, the collection of fines from violators of the policy, and the gathering and filing of raw data on births, deaths, and marriages.[30]

A cadre of Huang Village of Lee Township told me how the birth control work is going in his village:

> All the year around, we should supervise the women of reproductive age. This work is heavy to us. In my village, every season, about 110 women are under supervision. Right now, the work is different compared to what it was in the past decades. On the one hand, the work is much easier because people are accepting the policies; on the other hand, the work is much more difficult because many of people go outside for work, beyond the control of the village. …the township government requires the 100 % fulfillment of the birth control job. It is really difficult. Like my village, we only can reach 98 %. If a village can not meet the standard of birth control quotas several times, the Party secretary will be fired. This is the 'one-vote veto.' (Informant Lee200409)

In Fan Township, family planning policy was implemented by economic levers. However, in Lee Township, the job has to be implemented by the village cadres' work.[31] In Fan Township, to implement the policy well means good work performance. In Lee Township, village cadres implement the policy well in order to achieve more subsidies from the higher level of authority. However, in some other townships, the family planning policy is used as the source of revenue of local authorities. This has happened in Chan Township. I will discuss this case in the next chapter.

This is the village office of Huang Village in Lee Township. It is a two-floor building of about 200 square meters. The words in red banner is "to implement the family planning policy, we should educate ourselves, manage ourselves, and serve ourselves."

[29] Only rural residents have this right. A couple in urban areas only has the right to have one child, no matter whether it is a boy or girl.

[30] Informant Lee200409; to see more about this, please refer to Thomas 2003.

[31] Although the penalty is also used to prevent the violation of the family planning policy in Lee Township, village cadres are afraid that high penalties will lead to an increase of the discontent of the peasants, which will not be propitious for Lee Township when it arks for fiscal transfers and subsidies from higher level of government.

5.5 The Stratification Results of Rural Lee Township

5.5.1 The Advantages of Village Cadres

Although the economy of rural Lee Township lags behind and the work of administration has a part-time characteristic, village cadres still can gain some benefits from their positions. The director of the Civil Affairs Office of Lee Township gave a good summary of the advantages of village cadres in his township:

> All kinds of money governed by the village administration can reach 80–100 thousand per year…he will be poorer if he were not a cadre…at least there are more chances for him to go to restaurants at public expense …to be a cadre also gives some conveniences to their own businesses…. (Informant Lee2004)

This summary tells us that the advantages of village cadres in rural Lee Township are three.

First of all, village cadres are paid salaries. The salary of a director of the villagers committee and a secretary of a village party branch can reach 450 yuan per month. The salary of other cadres also can reach 400 yuan per month. This money means something as a part-time job when the average annual income of a peasant is only 2,398 yuan per year in Lee Township.[32]

---

[32] From July 1, 2005, the salary of village cadres of Zengcheng increase to 700 yuan, "in order to implement the all kinds of the Party's directions and policies, to enforce the Party's governance, to improve the working positivity of rural cadres, to improve the stability of rural society." Available at http://www.zcic.gd.cn/zxzx/zwxx/t20051010_1544.htm

Second, the sentence "all kinds of money governed by the village administration can reach about 80–100 thousands yuan per year" points out the village cadres' management advantages. Although the collective assets of the villages of Lee Township are trifling comparing to their counterparts in the villages of Fan Township, they are still considerable to a village administration with 5–7 cadres. These collective assets not only include fishponds and forests, most of which are contracted out by villagers, but also the helping funds or programs from higher government. Take Bai Village as an example. The Fiscal Bureau of Guangzhou bought a shop in Zengcheng City to rent and gave the rent of 4,000 yuan per month to Bai Village. The village also owned about 2,000 litchi trees. Taking these two things together, the income of the village administration could reach about 60 thousand yuan per year (Table 5.7). Although it is dangerous for village cadres to put all this money into their own pockets, having the right to use the money gives village cadres some advantages, leading to the comment that "at least there are more chances for him to go to restaurants at public expense." "Go to restaurants" does not just mean that the cadres get fed—more importantly, it means that the village cadres have chances to make good relationships with the cadres of higher government by entertaining them with dinner. Good relationships with township cadres help the village cadres' own businesses, so that "to be a cadre also gives some conveniences to their own businesses." A village cadre talked about this issue in this way:

> You know the policies of our governments. It is OK if I don't disobey them. Nobody will take the job as a cadre, if the government doesn't help cadres when they face difficulties. The officers of township government will give us help if we do have some difficulties and let them know. Actually, it's just like the relationship between the boss and workers. If the boss is bad to the workers…I am not talking about money. No matter how much the money is, you can spend all of it…how can we finish our jobs if we can't support our lives? (Informant Lee200421)

Moreover, a good relationship with cadres of higher-level government usually means more chances for helping programs and funds. Even though the clientelism between the village cadres and peasants has almost vanished, the clientelism between the township cadres and village cadres still exists in rural Lee Township (Oi 1989)

With these advantages, it is easy to point out that to be a cadre is a better choice within a determined choice framework such as that of rural Lee Township, especially to those who are at the middle or old and do not want or cannot go outside for higher-paying jobs.

5.5.2 *Peasants' Lives in Lee Township*

Although village cadres can attain some advantages from their positions, the lives of peasants of Lee Township also become better and better for two reasons: for one thing, the burden on the peasants of Lee Township has been greatly relieved. Secondly, the proximity with urban center provides more earning sources for peasants in Lee Township.

Table 5.7 List of income and expenses of Shui Village

Income	This month	Accumulative total	Payout	This month	Accumulative total
Business income			Business payout		
Contracted-out and other received money			Administration fees	33,551.35	33,551.35
Leased-out shops			Salary to village cadres	7,800.00	7,800.00
Leased-out land			Reception fees	245.00	245.00
Leased-out houses			Administration costs		
Leased-out fruit trees			Water and electricity fees	36.78	36.78
Leased-out fishponds			Maintenance fees		
Yields of investment			Other	25,469.57	25,469.57
Others	51,037.00	51,037.00	Roads and engineering program		
Income from interest			Other payouts		
Appropriate money from higher government	20,500.00	20,500.00	Payout for interest		
Administration fee from family planning			Tax		
Other	30,537.00	30.537.00	Family planning		
Helping funds			Welfare fees		
Welfare funds			Welfare payout		
Total	51,037.00	51,037.00	Schools		
			Kindergartens		
			Welfare for old people		
			Conscription and training		
			Security		
			Medical care		
			Environment and cleaning		
			Entertainment and sports		
			Family planning		
			Subsidies to the family members of soldiers		
			Subsidies to "five guarantee" households		
			Others		
			Total	33,551.35	33,551.35

5.5.2.1 The Relief of the Burden on the Peasants

The specific revenue-sharing framework between higher government and Lee Township prevents the latter's heavy economic demands on rural society. As a result, when the central government began to take serious measures to relieve the burden on the peasants, this revenue-sharing framework encouraged the local governments to follow in the central government's steps, which in turn has lead to the relief of the burden on peasants of Lee Township. The ways to relieve the burden on the peasants has included the tax-for-fee reform, the decrease in the education fees, the "five-reaching program (wu tong gongcheng)," and others.

Tax-for-Fee Reform

Although the tax-for-fee reform has been implemented in all the rural areas of the country, the effect of the reform on the outskirt economy is distinctive from its effect on other types of townships. On the one hand, in some developed townships, such as Fan Township, the reform did not make much difference because the agricultural tax was not the burden of the peasants any more. On the other hand, in some underdeveloped townships, the cash-starved township government might possibly be impeded by the reform (such as Chan Township, which I will discuss in the next chapter). As for Lee Township, as I have mentioned in the previous sections, the income from the agricultural tax and other local surcharges are trifling compared to the transfer and helping funds from higher levels, which account for more than 80 % of the total fiscal income of Lee Township. As a result, the tax-for-fee reform has been well implemented in Lee Township:

> The agriculture taxes are much less right now. Before the tax-for-fee reform, we needed to turn in 250–300 kg of paddy while we just turn in 50–60 kg right now. 70–80 % of the taxes have been relieved.[33]

The Decrease in Educational Fees

Besides taxes and fees, expensive education is another main burden on the peasants of rural China. Accompanying the tax-for-fee reform, the central government issued the so-called "one fee policy" in order to reduce the education costs of peasants' children. The reason educational costs have stayed high is that the local governments, especially township governments, and the schools create all kinds of educational fees. By the "one fee policy," central government wants the provincial government to set a fixed fee to replace all other fees, in order to make the education fees simpler and controllable. As a response, Guangdong Provincial government issued the "one fee policy" in July 2002.[34] In Lee Township, I could see the effects of this policy:

> The central government and the province issue regulations to prescribe the fees for primary schools and middle schools. Before the regulation was issued, the education cost was about

[33] Informant Lee200415.

[34] http://www.gdhed.edu.cn/msgshow.php?bk=sys_bd_misc&newsid=ac698948f8996ac63c49374 07b06713f

1,300 yuan per semester for middle school (2,000 yuan for a boarder). Right now, the expense is 500 yuan (700 yuan for a boarder).[35]

As far as primary school is concerned, the fees are around 2–300 yuan per semester right now. Half of the fee has been cancelled. In the former period, it cost much higher. Nobody supervised and checked it. The teachers asked for something. The school asked for something.[36]

"Five-Reaching Program"

An ethnographic researcher in rural Guangdong like me can make use of very good facilities now, compared to the period when Fei Xiaotong did his famous research in Jiangsu. I rented a motorcycle and rode through all the villages of Lee Township looking for people who would talk with me. The roads of rural Lee Township are constructed quite well, of concrete. This is the effect of the so-called "five-reaching programs (Wu Tong Gongcheng)," which prescribe that roads, electric power, tap water, telephones, and cable TV should reach all villages in rural areas.

To improve the basic facilities of rural areas is one of the goals of "the tenth five-year plan" of the central government. It was not until recent years, and especially from 2002, that, along with the tax-for-fee reform, the central government listed these goals as part of its main work. The achievement of the goals, of course, also depends on the local governments' attitudes and policies. In 2003, the Guangzhou government proposed to achieve the "five-reaching programs." In 2004, the Guangzhou government invested 70,000,000 yuan in this program and the Zengcheng government added more than 5,000,000 yuan.[37] Right now in Lee Township, every administrative village has a concrete road to connect it to the main roads to Guangzhou. The tap water program was being constructed when I was there in January 2004. In order to finish these construction programs, village collectives have the obligation to contribute part of the costs. However, most peasants in Lee Township don't need to pay for these construction programs. For example, in Shui Village, the village director told me how they collect money for these construction programs.

To build this cement road, governments allocated 300,000 yuan and our village needed to add more than 100,000 yuan. Where should I get it? My colleagues and I held a meeting about this issue. We did not dare to collect money from our villagers. Let me say it in this way: if we collect too much money from our villagers, it is not good. There are many regulations to prohibit collecting money from peasants. Moreover, the central government is now propagandizing the "three representatives thought (san ge daibiao sixiang)" and proposing to relieve the burdens on peasants. So, we decided to raise funds from the people who go outside and get rich. (Informant Lee200421)

Labor Outputting

As I have discussed above, local governments, including both Guangzhou City Government and Zengcheng District Government, have realized that outputting the

[35] Informant Lee200415.

[36] Informant Lee 200416.

[37] http://www.gztv.com/channel/news/node_16/2004/03/15/10794095758113.shtml

rural surplus labor of underdeveloped townships such as Lee Township for wage work in the big cities is an important way to increase peasants' earnings. As a result, both Guangzhou and Zengcheng set specific budgets for this goal.[38] The budget was spent on several things: (1) *Free training courses*: in early 2004, the Zengcheng District Government issued an official document entitled "Concerning improving the work of transferring rural labor to go out for work." According to this document, in the coming three years, Zengcheng government will provide free or semi-free training courses to peasants and try to help 10,000 people to get training. (2) *Subsidies to work units hiring local peasants*: a work unit will be awarded 500–1000 yuan if they train a rural laborer to be a professional with a middle-level certificate (e.g., a certified electrician, carpenter, mechanic, tailor, etc.). (3) *Recruitment fairs*: Zengcheng District Government has held recruitment fairs specifically for rural laborers twice per year in the capital city of the district. Sixteen townships under Zengcheng District also were asked to set up recruitment offices to facilitate rural laborers to find wage work.[39]

Other ways to relieve the burden on peasants of Lee Township include the other helping programs I have discussed in the last section, helping of handicapped, and so on. As a villager in Huang Village has said:

> Guangzhou's policy for the handicapped is OK right now. The handicapped can receive some alimony from the government. The government also builds a house of 40–50 square meters for them. They deserve it, since they can't do many things and have to depend on others. (Informant Lee200415)

5.5.2.2 The Earnings and Lives of Various Households

Now we can give a clear life-chance structure for the rural people in Lee Township. Village cadres can get salaries and some other advantages, while they can still run their own production in local areas. Meanwhile, the peasants' earnings depend on cash capital, human capital, and the family life cycle.

First, obviously, the peasants who go to cities and make good economic gains gain much more money than those who work in local areas of rural Lee Township, including the village cadres and ordinary peasants.

Second, peasant households who have enough cash capital to engage in agricultural sidelines with commercialization and specialization can also earn more than village cadres do, even though local village cadres are still influential for them.

Third, while migrant wage work becomes the main source of earning of rural people in Lee Township, the number of family members who are of the age for wage work makes a great difference. The earnings of a household are closely related to

[38] In 2004, the Guangzhou City Government permitted an 11,000,000 yuan budget and the Zengcheng District Government also spent 5,600,000 yuan in outputting rural surplus labor. Please see http://www.investchina.com.cn/chinese/zhuanti/jybg/1006286.htm

[39] Zen Hua, Zhi Qiang, *Zengcheng Daily*, March 2, 2004.

the family's life cycle: the larger the number of adult laborers, the higher the chances for the family to earn more money from migrant wage work.

At the lower level, there are households with children studying in school and households with handicapped or illness members.

5.6 Summary and Discussion

This chapter describes the various aspects of Lee Township, which is selected as a representative of outskirt economies. Compared to Fan Township, Lee Township presents another form of institutional arrangement. As the name implies, the salient characteristic of the outskirt economy is the proximity to cities, which means proximity with market center and government centers.

1. Proximity to market centers. This provides chances for rural people in the outskirt economy to develop high-profit agriculture with greater specialization and commercialization. This increases the local earning sources of rural people. The proximity to market centers has allowed the peasants in Lee Township to be the first group of the province to go out to find wage work and business chances in the city center.
2. Proximity to government centers. This leads to the specific revenue-sharing framework and specific roles of local government of outskirt economies. This proximity—Lee Township is 70 km. From Guangzhou—means its political, economic, and social situation is most heavily influenced by higher-level government's administrative performance. Work in Lee Township cannot by supervised only by local cadres (which is what happens in Fan Township). For higher government, the fiscal transfer thus becomes the most important way to "buy" the dependences of local governments in outskirt areas. As a result, in an outskirt economy, the salient characteristic is that fiscal transfer and subsidies play the most important role in local governments' revenue structures: around 80 % of the government income in Lee Township.

For higher-level governments in the cities, who derive good revenue from the urban areas and other nearby developed areas, fulfilling political goals instead of economic extraction from outskirt areas is more important. As a result, the important performance targets of local governments in the outskirt economy consist of fulfilling the political duties assigned by higher levels of government (in Lee Township, those political duties include implementing the family planning policy, decreasing the possible discontent of peasants, and outputting rural surplus labor). This fiscal dependency and these performance targets decrease the township government's incentives to boost local economic development, because developing the local economy is more difficult than asking for greater fiscal transfer. This strategy also decreases the township government's extractions from rural society since greater extraction would lead to greater discontent among the peasants, which would harm the performance of the township government and thereby affect support from higher levels of government (e.g., fiscal transfers, subsidies, and helping programs).

Although village cadres still hold some local advantages, cadre positions are only fit for those people who cannot or will not go out for wage work or business. Village cadres do their office jobs in part-time mode, as passive task receivers. Without the pressure to extract from rural society, the tax-for-fee reform has been implemented well in the outskirt economy, and the peasants' burden has been greatly relieved.

3. Although peasants in outskirt economies can benefit from higher-profit agricultural production, many young people (especially rural surplus laborers) there have gone outside for wage work or business chances in the cities. Social networks are important to the peasants who want to find or are having a wage work or business chances in city centers. Clan system doesn't play a salient role in village affairs.

References

Edition Committee of the Chorography of Zengcheng. (1995). *Zengcheng xian zhi* [The Chorography of Zengcheng]. Guangzhou: Guangdong renmin chubanshe.

Li, L. C. (2005). Understanding institutional change: Fiscal management in local China. *Journal of Contemporary Asia, 35*, 87–109.

Oi, J. C. (1989). *State and peasant in contemporary China: The political economy of village government*. Berkeley: University of California Press.

Parish, W. L., & Michelson, E. (1996). Politics and markets: Dual transformations. *American Journal of Sociology, 101*, 1042–1059.

Scott, J. C. (1976). *The moral economy of the peasant: Rebellion and subsistence in Southeast Asia*. New Haven: Yale University Press.

Thomas, S. (2003). *Birth control in China, 1949–2000: Population policy and demographic development*. New York: RoutledgeCurzon.

Chapter 6
A Local Economy

This chapter examines the effects of market penetration on social stratification in local economies, by which I refer to townships with the lowest market penetration level in the province, located in mountain areas of rural Guangdong. Chan Township, which is located in the western mountain areas of Guangdong Province, is selected as being representative of local economies. Two characteristics of the local economy will be highlighted in this chapter. First, cash-starved local governments tend to create many ways to collect money from rural people, even though the central government has issued policies to relieve the burden on peasants. Second, the low level of market penetration in the local areas limits sources of the earnings of peasants. Migrant wages and businesses are the main support of the peasants' lives.

6.1 Market Penetration in Chan Township

Chan Township is located in the western mountain areas of the province and is under the jurisdiction of Huazhou County, Maoming Prefecture (see Fig. 6.1). The acreage of the township is 179.3 km^2, most of which are in foothills. The population of the township was about 70 thousand in 2004. The township governs 1 residential committee, 30 administrative villages, and 322 natural villages. It is 60 km. to the county town and about 500 km. to Guangzhou, the capital of the province.

Chan Township was a township with good records for agricultural output and was a so-called "big agriculture township (nongye da zhen)" during the first period of the Reform Era. Since the reform began in 1978, the agricultural production of Chan

Township, like that of many other townships in rural Guangdong, recovered quickly from the chaos of the Cultural Revolution. With 20 years of reform, the

N. Chen, *State, Market and Life Chances in Contemporary Rural Chinese Society*, DOI 10.1007/978-3-662-45046-8_6

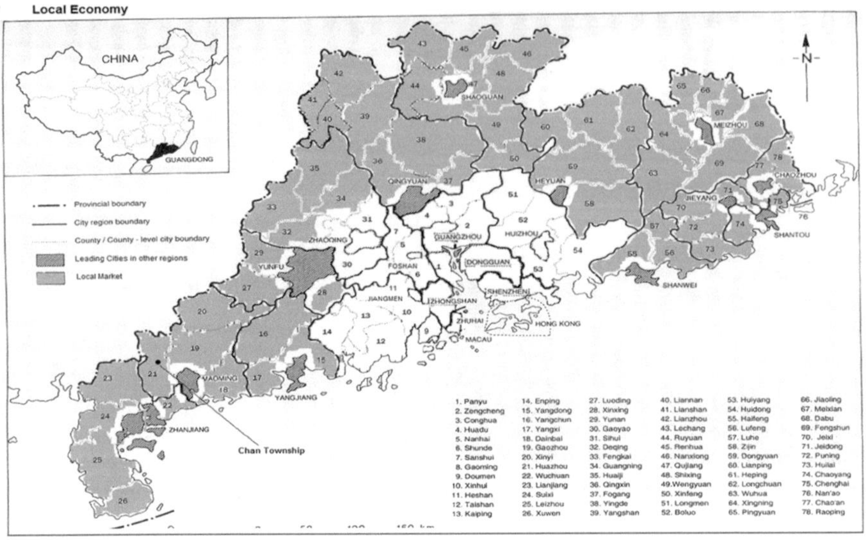

Fig. 6.1 The location of Chan Township

lives of peasants of Chan Township obviously have improved. As the director of the Qian Villagers Committee said to me:

> The living of peasants has improved a lot right now. Almost 90 percent of peasants can get enough to eat and get a house to live in. Only those who cannot go to elsewhere for work or are less competitive in earning money still face low levels of living standard. But, of course, it is better than before. (Informant Chan200406)

However, the situation appears differently when we compare Chan Township to Fan Township and Lee Township. The development of the commodity market and the labor market is still quite limited in Chan Township. Agriculture still lies at the core of the township's economy. The director of the township government told me the structure of the township's agriculture: there are 38,000 mu of cultivated land in the township, of which the acreage for mulberries is 20,000 mu, the acreage for paddy rice almost 10,000 mu, and the acreage for banana trees is 8,000 mu. In addition, fruit tree growing is an important part of the township's economy. There are two large fruit tree enterprises in the township. One owns 50,000 mu of longan trees and the other owns 40,000 mu. The acreage in fruit trees owned by ordinary peasants reached 100,000 mu in 2003.[1] It is noteworthy that the two large fruit enterprises have played a specific role in the economy of the township. However, these two enterprises collapsed in 2002–2003. I will give detailed descriptions of this in the next section.

Chan Township resembles Lee Township in having good natural conditions for agriculture. However, the advantage of Lee Township—the proximity with the eco-

[1] Informant Chan200402.

nomic core—provides the peasants of Lee Township a market for their agricultural products. As far as Chan Township is concerned, the marketing of agricultural products has been a problem for a long time, with the long distance to economic core, both geographically and economically.

Secondary industry is underdeveloped in Chan Township compared to that of Fan Township and even of Lee Township. According to my observation, the only profitable manufacturing enterprises in the township are two small brickfields. In 2003, only nine enterprises existed in the township: three lumber mills, three enterprises for arts and craft producers, and three quarries.[2]

Very few people from other places come to Chan Township for work. On the contrary, most young people of Chan Township go to the major cities in the PRD region for better-paying wage work or business. This is common for the mountain areas of the province.[3] Wives, old people, and children are left at home. A statistical review of Huazhou County presents this point: in 2004, the number of peasants of Huazhou County who went to other places (mostly, the cities in the PRD region) for wage work or business reached 227 thousand, 40.3 % of the total labor in the rural areas of Huazhou County.[4]

6.2 The Village Cadres as Assistants of Predators

In previous chapters the cadres in Fan Township were considered to be the managers of the cooperative economy and the cadres in Lee Township were considered to be "volunteer fireman" of the collective economy. The cadres in Chan Township play another role, that of "assistants of predators" who prey on the peasants. By this term I want to present how village cadres, driven by the cash-starved township government and together with it, act in the manner of a predatory state, extracting revenue from rural society.

6.2.1 Revenue Sharing Between the Local Governments and Rural Society

Before I discuss the details of how township cadres and village cadres exploit the resources of peasants, three characteristics of revenue sharing between higher government and Chan Township will be presented. Firstly, the Chan Township government, unlike the Lee Township government, cannot access enough subsidies, funds, or helping programs from higher government levels. Chan Township is under

[2] Informant Chan200402.

[3] Please refer to Chap. 2.

[4] Chen Chunping, available in *Maoming Daily*, April 26, 2005.

the jurisdiction of Huazhou County, Maoming Prefecture. Both the Maoming Prefecture government and the Huazhou County government are cash starved. The GDP per capita of Maoming Prefecture in 2002 was the eleventh among the 21 prefectures of the province (see Table 6.1). The economic development of Maoming is thus in the middle level among the prefecture cities of the province. Agriculture plays the most important role in Maoming's economy, with the agricultural output of Maoming Prefecture being the biggest of the prefecture in the province. The number of FDIs invested in the TVEs of Maoming rank only 14th among the 21 prefectures of the province. This fiscal situation limits the capability of the prefecture government in providing relief to the rural society. The Huazhou County government, unfortunately, is also a cash-starved government and is also one that cannot pay its administrative costs without fiscal transfer from the province. This situation worsens Chan Township's fiscal situation.

Secondly, the helping funds from the provincial government have to be shared with the prefecture and county governments. The quota left for the township government is hence quite limited. On the contrary, township governments serve as fiscal resources for cash-starved local county governments. The township governments have to meet the tax quotas assigned by the county governments. This is also true for Chan Township.

Table 6.1 GDP of the prefecture cities of Guangdong Province

Prefectural city	GDP/Capita	Agriculture (%)	Productive industry (%)	Tertiary industry (%)
Shenzhen	46,388	0.8	54.7	44.4
Dongguan	43,401	4.5	54.9	40.5
Guangzhou	41,884	3.4	40.9	55.7
Foshan	34,850	6.1	53.2	40.7
Zhuhai	32,682	4	55.2	40.9
Zhongshan	30,693	6.3	59.3	34.4
Huizhou	18,641	14	57.6	28.4
Jiangmen	17,344	10.6	48.4	41
Zhaoqing	11,549	27.8	37	35.2
Shantou	10,268	9.4	47.7	42.9
Maoming	9,005 (11th)	27.1 (8th)	38 (13th)	35 (13th)
Chaozhou	8,698	18.6	45.1	36.4
Shaoguan	8,528	21	44.7	34.2
Yangjiang	7,965	34.6	33.1	32.2
Jieyang	7,597	18.8	50.3	30.9
Zhanjiang	7,539	25.5	37.3	37.2
Yunfu	7,399	32.8	35.6	31.6
Shanwei	6,749	31	32.3	36.8
Qingyuan	4,416	38.8	30.3	30.9
Meizhou	4,200	29.1	36.2	34.7
Heyuan	3,542	33.2	28.9	37.9

Sources: Guangdong Provincial Statistical Bureau (2002)

Thirdly, the underdeveloped capital markets and commodity markets limit the sources of earnings of local governments. As mentioned above, there is no successful enterprise in Chan Township. FDI is also quite limited since the township is too far away from the economic core region. Agriculture and sidelines are still the main parts of the family production of peasants in Chan Township. The main cash income of the peasants is from migrant wage work or migrant business. One can see that the sources of revenue of Chan Township are limited, as compared with those of Fan Township and Lee Township.

I interviewed the director of the Chan Township government. He complained to me about the strained fiscal situation of the township government. The income of the township government consists of three parts: administrative outlay from higher government, return tax income from higher government, and penalties on violators of family planning policies (shehui fuyang fei). The first of these, according to the director, is quite limited. The administrative outlay is calculated according to the authorized number of cadres, which is set by higher government.[5] For Chan Township the number is 52, to which less than 100 yuan per month per cadre was given as administrative outlay. One can see that this money cannot possibly meet the expenses of the township government. In addition, the actual number of officers of Chan Township is much larger than the authorized number, as the township government cannot carry out its duties with the number of authorized people and thus needs more workers, meaning heavier administrative expenses and wages.[6] Secondly, the township government will share tax revenue only when the total amount from the township is larger than the assigned tax quota, which is set by higher government. Without the development of the economy, it is difficult for the tax revenue of Chan Township to go beyond the assigned, so that tax returns are limited as well. Finally, I was surprised to learn from the director that penalties from family planning violations are also an important part of the township's income.

Some studies of Chinese local governments emphasize that economic development and tax-for-fee reform have provided incentives for local officials to be more active in economic development, turning officials into "born and bred businessmen."[7] The local cadres in those studies may be similar to the cadres of Fan Township; the local cadres of Chan Township find it hard to develop local industry due to shortages of capital, markets, and know-how. To find a lucrative way to increase the government's income is difficult. However, Chan Township does find some ways to make money, and these can be classified as three categories: (1) "local governments as industrial firms" (Walder 1995b)—I borrow this thesis to describe how local cadres act in the manner of businessmen—(2) taking assets from rural society, and (3) policy as a source of revenue.

---

[5] In China, the number (bianzhi) of the officers of a township government is set by the county government according to the population of the township.

[6] Informant Chan200402.

[7] Please see Oi 1995, pp. 1132–49; Walder 1995a, b, p. 263.

6.2.1.1 "Local Governments as Industrial Firms"

Obviously, the most effective ways to increase tax revenue is to promote local economic development. However, without enough investment from outside, such as occurred in Fan Township, or without proximity to the economic core, such as Lee Township, it is difficult for Chan Township to find a way to boost the economy quickly. Actually, many attempts of the township government to develop the local economy failed in the end; these included banana tree cultivation programs and fish program[8] and the short-term "success" of the thriving and downfall of the two large fruit-growing enterprises of Chan Township.

In 1997, two companies, both with names of the form "Guangdong XX Manor Co. Ltd," were set up in Chan Township. These two companies proposed a specific agricultural mode to attract investment from outside, which can be described as "renting the land together, programming together, developing together, sharing the profits together, and, once invested, sharing the profits at 2:8, with 50-year contracts for property rights owners." This sentence refers to the process of the developing mode: the companies rented the mountain land of the township to plant fruit trees (mostly longan trees), and anyone who invested 28,000 yuan in the business would share property rights in 5 mu of longan trees for 50 years, after which the company would take a 20 % share of the profits from the trees, while the investors would take 80 % shares. Under this scheme the company would take care of all administrative jobs, including the developing, planting, administration, and selling of the produce, while the investor would not need to pay any more money. The companies also promised that the property rights of the investors could be sold, transferred, or inherited. Attractive propaganda was produced by the companies. Both the township government and county government contributed a lot to the success of these two companies. However, the CEO of one of them had been the driver of the former township party secretary's government-assigned car[9]; the former secretary had helped him to rent the mountain land. Another example of what was really going on was provided in 1998, when similar fund-raising activities in other regions were discovered to be traps for investors. Because of this, the China People's Bank issued a document entitled "Urgent circular concerning prohibiting the use of manor development to collect money illegally." The circular pointed out that "the money collecting activities which use manor development as excuses are illegal and should be prohibited and shut down."[10] However, the local county and township governments did not comply with the circulars. Instead, in July 1998, in order to attract more

[8] These two programs are similar. Taking the banana program as an example, in the beginning of 2000 the government of Chan Township asked peasants to plant banana trees as an agricultural sideline. Unfortunately, the price of bananas dropped dramatically at harvest time, and most of the peasants involved lost.

[9] In Chinese local politics, a driver of an officer' government-assigned car often become the janissary of the officer.

[10] In 1999, the State Administration for Industry and Commerce, Ministry of Justice, Ministry of Land and Resources, and People's Bank together issued 4 documentaries to prohibit the illegal money collecting activities.

investment, a team consisting of the company's staff and the cadres of township and county governments went to Beijing, Southeast Asia, and other places to hold expositions of the manor economy. The presence and guarantee of the local governments won the trust of investors and the expos had a great effect: the companies attracted many investments from all over the world. For example, the company's expo held in Beijing attracted more than 10,000,000 yuan in investment in only a few days.[11] When these two companies collapsed after 2–3 years, most of the investment funds had been pocketed and spent by the owners of the companies.

Actually, the above agricultural mode seems to be a good idea for agricultural development and not necessarily a business trap. Some researchers of rural China have written articles to promote this mode.[12] However, while local government was the main force for attracting investment, the close relationship between the company and local government also became the main factor of the collapse of the company.[13] For one thing, the local governments treated the companies as their private bank: the money and assets of the company were freely taken by the local governments. For example, when the investors urged the administrators of the company to return the money, the administrators complained that much of money has been taken by the local governments.[14] Also, much of the money was spent in improving relationships between the companies and various levels of government. In this circumstance, both the administration of the companies and local cadres treated the companies as cash machines rather than as enterprises.

The intervention of local government in local enterprises also exists in small collectively owned enterprises. Another informant, once the director of a collective enterprise of Chan Township, told me how he was forced to leave his position because he wouldn't cooperate with the party secretary of the township government.[15]

The above ethnographic data show how local township government made money by intervention in local corporations. It also shows that the "local governments as industrial firms" view doesn't necessarily lead to the success of the local economy.

6.2.1.2 Taking Assets from Rural Society

The above stories show that it is not easy for local governments to increase their revenue by developing the local economy under a low level of market penetration. As a result, while the demand for financial resources keeps pressing the local officials, they have to try to find other ways to meet it. Of course, one available way is

---

[11] Please see http://www.c-cmag.com/shshshow.asp?zs_id=610

[12] Yu Jianrong, A study on China's Modern Manor Economy, available at http://www.chinaelections.org/readnews.asp?newsid=%7B335D4A39-50F6-42E3-B668-818CA7E8D6CD%7D

[13] *nanfang nongcun bao* (Southern Country Newspaper), August 17, 2005; also see *News Weekly* (*xinwen zhoubao*), October 13, 2005.

[14] Please see http://www.c-cmag.com/shshshow.asp?zs_id=610

[15] Informant Chan200411.

to collect money from the peasants, regardless of the political and social consequences. A retired township cadre described the relationship between cadres and peasants before the tax-for-fee reform:

> I have been a township cadre for a long time. In the past years, the relationship between the party and the people (*dang qun guanxi*), the relationship between the government and people (*zheng qun guanxi*) was really bad. They (peasants) called us robbers. I did not feel good about it. We were just doing our jobs, but they called us robbers…when the township cadres went to the villages, what we did was to collect fees and crops—e.g., education fees, township retained fees, agriculture taxes and penalties on family planning. All about money, so they call us robbers…if there are some people who do not have money to hand in, we would try some strong ways to take from them—for example, we would take all their crops away. That is why people called us robbers. At that time, the relationship was really bad.[16]

A villager of Qian Village also told me that:

> Anyway, if only they (local governments) have the rights to collect money, they can find all kinds of excuses or indexes…taking away our crops and pigs.[17]

Another villager of Qian Village told me what he had to submit to the township government before the tax-for-fee reform.

> In the early years, the township took much money from us: 21 yuan per capita was for the township pooling fees, more than the agricultural tax; the education additional fee, 30 yuan per capita. A peasant knows little about policies. In a word, a peasant has to submit money as local government wants. A peasant did not know how to be a peasant at that time. Moreover, the Rural Cooperative Foundation had been messed up by the cadres. It collapsed at last.[18]

As I mentioned in the second chapter, the burden on peasants lies in three aspects: the state's taxes, local charges, and other surcharges. In addition to the regular revenue income—agricultural tax and local charges—there are many ways or excuses for local township governments to collect money in rural society. Some examples follow.

Taking Money from Rural Cooperative Foundation

The Rural Cooperative Foundation (henceforth RCF) was set up in the middle of the 1980s with the encouragement of the central government. Accompanying the increase in peasants' incomes, the capital of the Rural Cooperative Foundation rose quickly. As a result, some cash-starved governments intervened in the operation of the RCF. However, many of the RCFs were taken as cash machines for the local township governments, and this happened in Chan Township. One informant told me how the Rural Cooperative Foundation of Chan Township collapsed at last.

> The township government set up an account in the RCF for some township cadres. The bonuses of those township cadres were taken from the RCF. If people wanted a loan, they had to develop a personal relationship with the leaders of the township, bribing, and sending gifts. Some people could get a 1,000,000 loan while nothing was allocated to enterprises.

---

[16] Informant Chan200401.

[17] Informant Chan200405.

[18] Informant Chan200403.

> The RCF actually became the wallet of the local township leaders. Like XXX, who was running an enterprise in Dongguan, could only take out 800,000 yuan from his 1,000,000 yuan of loan (from RCF).[19, 20]

The RCF of Chan Township collapsed in 1997 when some peasants learned the "inside story" of the RCF and rushed to the RCF counter in order to withdraw their money. The collapse of Rural Cooperative Foundations was common in the underdeveloped areas of rural China and brought about ripple effects, which attracted the attention of the central government. Later the central government instructed the China Agriculture Bank to handle the RCF cases to appease the angry peasants.[21] However, this wasn't the end of the story. In recent years the liquidation of the debt of the RCF became another round in the money-taking process of local governments. Some debtors were seized and locked up without first going through any court or other legal public security procedures. They could be released only when their family members repaid the debts for them. One thing was ridiculous: the repaid money was set arbitrarily, because the database of the RCF has been messed up by the local cadres and no one could calculate the exact amount of every deal.

> I had just taken out 500 yuan in loan. I was seized by the township government's lock-up. I was told that I had to repay 1,300, no negotiation. Only when the debt was repaid could I be released. (Informant Chan200403)

Education Fees

Education fees are another revenue source for local governments. Before the "one fee policy"[22] was implemented, education fees were collected in the name of construction fees, incidental expenses (*xueza fei*), and so on. After the "one fee policy" was implemented in Chan Township, the education costs were transformed into many small items: fees for breakfast, additional lessons (*buke fei*), test papers, books, etc.[23]

> Right now, the middle school of Chan Township collects much money. No one can make it clear. The parents have to hand in 2–300 yuan to arrange several weeks of additional courses. In general, 20–50 yuan per week is necessary. (Informant Chan 200407)

In addition to the two ways mentioned above, there have also been other excuses for the township government to extract money from rural society:

> **(Public Security).** One more thing: as the public security problem is concerned, the cops in the township police station are also robbers. Criminals can be released if they can pay

---

[19] In other words, the township cadres raked off 200,000 yuan from this loan.

[20] Informant Chan200409.

[21] Wen Tiejun, "nongcun hezuo jijinhui de xingshuishi (The History of the Thriving and Collapse of Rural Cooperative Economy)," available at http://www.usc.cuhk.edu.hk/wk_wzdetails.asp?id=432; also see Kang Xiaoguang, "lueduo yu qingsuan—zhuangxing shiqi nongcun jinrong de weiji yu fan weiji yanjiu (Spoliation and Liquidation: a study on the crisis and anti-crisis of rural finance in the transforming period)," available at http://www.usc.cuhk.edu.hk/wk_wzdetails.asp?id=3727.

[22] Please refer to Chap. 5 for the "one fee policy."

[23] Informant Chan200408, 200409.

> enough money. The police station is set for money rather than public security. (Informant Chan200407)
>
> **(Money from motorcycle checking).** Actually, they (local governments) do not care about the agriculture tax right now. They get money in other ways. For example, every motor-bicycle has to submit 260–300 yuan for governmental registration every year. Every village has 20–30 motorcycles. It is a lot of money. (Informant Chan 200405)

6.2.1.3 Policies as Sources of Revenue

As all over the country, the central state began to promote serious policies to relieve the burden on peasants. The tax-for-fee reform has been implemented over the whole country. Official propaganda focused on the topic of the relief of the burden on peasants. In this circumstance, arbitrary money taking meant great political risks. As a result, another way, policies as a source of revenue, became the main tricks of local governments for taking money from rural society. In Chan Township, two policies, the family planning policy and the funeral and interment reform, became the main sources of revenue for township government and village administration. These two policies share a common characteristic: they are both related to penalties. A villager in Qian Village:

> Now, the central government is emphasizing that ordinary people can resist the local governments' unreasonable policies. That is why the situations become better. However, there are still two things: birth and death. These two things are really unreasonable. Death makes people sad, but the cadres will rob money from it rather than feel sad for the death. The cost of a cremation has reached three or four thousand yuan now. Inhumation has been accepted by Chinese people for a long time and it is also hygienic. Cremation needs the building of incineration facilities, which are always with bacteria.[24] We oppose this policy. Moreover, as for family planning policy, it should be implemented by persuasion instead of penalties. Here, the policy is only for money…the one child policy is a "three-off policy (*san guang zhengce*)", which means taking all money, all assets. However, you can have as many children as you want, if you get enough money to pay the penalties. (Informant Chan200407)

Family Planning Policy

The family planning policy is a tough issue in all the three townships of this study, but the attitude and ways of local governments in implementing the policy are various. In Fan Township, local government implements the policy by economic leverage. The goal of implementing it is to control the birth rate. The policy is not related to the revenue of the local government. In Lee Township, local governments want to control the birth rate because their performance in controlling the birth rate is related to the fiscal transfers from higher government. The policy is implemented by the efforts of village cadres. However, in Chan Township, the goal of implementing the policy is to extract as much money as possible.

[24] According to the informant's view, the incineration facilities will pollute the environment, bringing all kinds of bacteria.

> Just like this: (according to the policy) a couple can only have one (a boy) or two (a girl first, and then another child four years later) children. But the actual situation is not like that. Instead, if a couple wants more children, they can hide away and give birth to their child. The cadres will turn a blind eye to it at that time. But after that, they will find them out and fine them. (Informant Chan200411)

As a result, what cadres do is not about how to control the birth rate but how to collect the penalties. That is why the director of Chan Township said to me that the penalties from the violators of family planning policy are parts of the main income of the government. Actually, the family planning policy had been a revenue source for a long time in Chan Township. The former party secretary in Chan Township was the harshest person involved in extracting money from the family planning policy. The director of the family planning office was his relative and accomplice in extracting money.[25]

The Funeral and Interment Reform

The family planning policy has been implemented for about 30 years. The resistance from the peasants is less and less, even though the transformation has been a suffering experience for them. However, the funeral and interment reform (*bin zang gaige*), which was put in practice in Chan Township in the last 2 years, has become a new source of revenue. The traditional way of interment in China was ground burial. After the founding of New China, the funeral and interment reform was set up in the name of land resource protection, transformation of social traditions, and the ecology of the environment. The reform was carried out step by step: it was first implemented in cities and then in some populated rural areas. Ground burial was permitted in areas where there was sparse population, such as secluded mountain areas with inconvenient communication. According to this step-by-step process, Chan Township was delimited as a reform area about 2002 even though Chan Township is located in a mountain area of the province.

The reform has included replacing ground burial with cremation, building public cemeteries, and other funeral facilities. The reform put an additional burden on peasant households. In the previous period, the location of ground burial was mostly the uncultivated land of the hills. This uncultivated land was free for peasants. Since the funeral and interment reform was implemented in Chan Township, the burden has included the transportation fee to the nearby crematoriums and the administrative fee for the crematoriums. Those who do not want to comply with the reform policies have to hand in a great amount of money to the local administrators of the reform.

> If someone dies and his (her) family members select ground burial instead of cremation, they have to hand over 10,000 yuan. It can be negotiated. If they know someone in the government, the amount can be less—for example, 8,000 or 5,000. (Informant Chan200403)

In my ethnographic study in Chan Township, almost every informant complained to me about this issue:

---

[25] Informant Chan200403.

> The family planning policy has been implemented for about 20 years. Most people can tolerate it now. But I can not understand the funeral and interment reform. Why? Family planning is about birth and the funeral and interment reform is about death. Both are closely related to human's lives. I do not understand why we need the funeral and interment reform. I do not know which level of government initiated this reform. The government said ground burial is prohibited and cremation is compulsory…but they also (the township government) leave the quota for ground burial…those who can give the government 10,000 yuan can be included in the quota for ground burial. (Informant Chan200401)
>
> As to family planning policy, no one needs to pay money if he (she) complies with the policy requirement. But as to the funeral and interment reform…everyone will die someday. It means that the cost is inescapable. (Informant Chan200410)
>
> People say birth means penalties and death also means penalties. Cremation costs several thousand yuan. The quota for ground burial costs more than ten thousand. The amount is terrible. (Informant Chan200411)

I also heard of a peasant resistance case concerning the funeral and interment reform. The township government planned to build an ash pagoda in the middle of the township. They began the construction program after a discussion with village cadres. However, the peasants who lived near the project location knew about it and went to the project location together to oppose the construction. The tractors and bulldozers were overturned and the construction program had to stop. The concerns of the peasants involved two matters. The first one is about ideology: they believe that living near an ash pagoda will lead to bad luck. The second concern is about economy: if the ash pagoda were built, it would be compulsory to let the pagoda to keep remains and ashes, which would mean monthly and annual administration fees. A villager also told me his ideas about this issue:

> Both the funeral and interment reform and the family planning policy require us to pay money. Our peasants are really dissatisfied about these two things of the Communist Party. Why can rich people be excepted from the policy? The policy should be uniform in the whole country. At that time, I also talked to a peasant. He said he would go to fight if someone asked him to go, even if the government did not build the ash pagoda. We have been under the pressure of the family planning policy and the funeral and interment reform for a long time. (Informant Fan200405)

6.2.1.4 The Village Cadres as Assistants of the Predators

In order to clarify the roles of township cadres and village cadres in Chan Township, the relationship between the two has to be presented here. Certainly, the leading actors of the local predator state are township cadres, who own the local governance apparatus. In Chan Township, in the process of extracting resources from rural society, township cadres decide the tasks of extracting, and village cadres are the assistants.

Direct villager election has not really changed the relationship among the township government, village administration, and peasants. As in Lee Township, the Chan Township government also has the intention to influence the local direct village election, even though the goals of these two township governments are different: Lee Township cadres aim to fulfill policy requirements, while Chan Township cadres want to collect money. Actually, Chan Township government has stronger motivation to intervene in the village election results since rural society is its source of revenue. The ways of township governments' control are three. The first two are similar to those of Lee Township—to control the village administration by the party hierarchy and to influence the results of the election in the organizational process. The third one, however, is economic: the income of village administration in Chan Township is from local charges and surcharges, and these are controlled by the township government.

Some examples show that the village administrations that do not cooperate with township government cannot do their jobs well. As the director of the township government told me, there were two village administrations that wouldn't cooperate with the township government. The first one was that of Gao Village, where the villagers elected an old clansman to be the director of the villager committee. The second was that of Chou Village, where the elected director of the villager committee wouldn't provide the name list of violators of the family planning policy to the township government. Neither of these village administrations could keep their positions in the villager elections for a second term. The township government director considered that their losing the elections to their work abilities. One other possible reason for their electoral defeats is that the village administrations cannot do their jobs without a good relationship with the township government. As the retired township cadre has said:

> The relationship is still close. Although the village cadres are elected by peasants, village cadres are still the subordinates of the township government. The subordinates should obey the superiors. In the general situation, village cadres have to follow the township cadres. On one hand, village cadres are facing peasants. On the other hand, village cadres also have to implement the policy of higher government. To resist the higher won't work. Take the funeral and interment reform as an example: although some of village cadres are unwilling to assist township cadres, they still have to execute the township government's order. (Informant Chan200401)

The characteristics of village administrations in Chan Township resemble those of their counterparts in Lee Township: the number of village cadres is small, and all village cadres are in middle or old age, with little, routine work and passive performances. To put it concretely, village cadres act as communicators and profit sharers. On one hand, part of the job of village cadres in Chan Township is to make the information from higher government levels known to the peasants. On the other hand, village administration has to report to the township government what has happened in the village, especially concerning those issues which are relative to family planning policy and funeral reform. The work of local township government in rural areas has to depend on the village administrations, since village cadres are the insiders of the village situation. Meanwhile, the village administration can share the profits from all kinds of surcharges of the township government. They can also ask the township government for other support.

> Major jobs of village cadres are just communicators between peasants and township government. There aren't mines, enterprises. Their jobs are implementing family planning and funeral and interment reform…The village cadres can share parts of the penalties. (Informant 200401)

> Now they don't care about our agricultural production. First, they pay attention to the agricultural tax. Second, they keep eyes on the implementing of the family planning policy, to see if there is any one who wants to have more children. The third is about the funeral and interment reform. If they haven't seen some old man (women) for a long time, they will check it out and report to the township. These jobs are important to cadres because they are related to profits. (Informant Chan200403)

6.3 Stratification Results in Rural Chan Township

6.3.1 The Advantages of Village Cadres

The village cadres' advantages are of three kinds.

1. *Salary and subsidies.* The average salary of village cadres in Chan Township is 300 yuan per month. The directors of villagers committees also can get 200 yuan in subsidies for cell phone communication. Only in some villages will the directors and party secretary be paid higher salaries. In a local economy like that of Chan Township, the salary and subsidies of village cadres really mean something.
2. *Village-retained fees and other income from township government.* Before the tax-for-fee reform was implemented, village-retained fees were an authorized local charge. The income of village administration at that time could reach several tens of thousands of yuan (see Table 6.2). The village cadres also could share the financial benefits of being assistants of local state predators.
3. *Pocketing collective assets.* Take the director of Qian Village as an example: according to his description, his earnings consist of three parts: (1) his salary of 300 yuan, 10 % of his total income; (2) his income from agricultural production—8000 yuan from mulberries in the previous year; and (3) remittances from his son, who is doing his business in Guangzhou.[26] However, in addition, according to the complaints of an informant, some other possible earnings of this director come from some "land reclamation fees (ken huang fei)."[27]

   > Those land reclamation fees are allocated from the Huazhou County government and the Maoming County government. The fees should be distributed to the natural villages or be used to construct a *tori.*[28] Nothing! The entire fees were pocketed by him (the director of Qian Village). (Informant Chan200403)

[26] Informant Chan200406.

[27] As the name implies, the "land reclamation fee" was for a specific fund for land reclamation. It was distributed by higher levels of government.

[28] *Torii (paifang)* is a special Chinese architectural structure which guides one to the main part of a building. *Torii* can be set before buildings such as temples and a group of palaces and even before some markets and stores.

Table 6.2 FDI in TVEs of the prefectures of Guangdong Province in 2001

Prefecture	(Thousands of USD)
Dongguan	6,092,980
Guangzhou	2,913,220
Shenzhen	1,682,070
Zhuhai	1,025,780
Jiangmen	675,920
Shantou	563,090
Foshan	434,520
Zhongshan	368,000
Huizhou	294,280
Zhaoqing	147,660
Chaozhou	100,350
Jieyang	90,230
Yunfu	79,790
Maoming	65,920
Shanwei	40,240
Meizhou	26,360
Qingyuan	24,460
Yanjiang	15,450
Shaoguan	8,620
Heyuan	6,760
Zhanjiang	5,850

Sources: Guangdong Provincial Statistical Bureau (2002)

I have reproduced the content of an income and expenses form of Qian Village (see Table 6.3) that was posted on the notice board of the village government building. Obviously, the form is not professional: no detailed record of expenses is given, only an amount. It is obvious that no one would read this. There is a financial supervision team (*caiwu jiandu xiaozu*) in the village, which consists of three people, but this supervision team doesn't help much to supervise the collective economy. One of the team members said:

> (laugh) What is supervision? What we need to do is to go to the office building, have a lunch and come back with 20 yuan of recompense. Not only me, other persons do this too. (Informant Chan200403)

All this data shows that there are possibilities of village cadres to pocket some of the collective assets.

6.3.2 The "Get" and "Lose" of Peasants in Chan Township

In this section, the "get" and "lose" of the peasants in Chan Township will be documented in detail. In Fan Township and Lee Township, the better or worse life chances of a villager mainly depend on how much he (she) can get. However, in

Table 6.3 The income and expense of Qian Village in December 2002

Income				Expenses			
Subjects	Money from previous month	Money from present month	Total	Expenses	Money from previous month	Money from present month	Total
The balance in 2001			2,785.41	Salary of village cadres			212.00
Village-retained fees			101.80	Expense for water adjusting			
Income from water supervision				Electronic bill			
Income for old school construction			419.6	Expense for security team			
Income for new school construction			7,717.00	Expense for security			
Administration fees for construction approval				Administration expense			
Water-adjusting fees			709	Board wages for conferences			
Income from contracting out programs			1,470	Board subsidies for cadres			
Income from house rental			3,456	Cadres' subsidies			
Penalties from security team			1,110	Moon cakes, umbrella			
Loans				Expense of mediating (tiaojie fei)			
Other			8,292.30	Administration expenses for military recruitment			
				Expense for election			
				Other expenses			
Total			26,061.11				27,583.82
Balance due							−1522.71

Chan Township, not only what a peasant gets but also what a peasant loses means a lot to the earnings of the peasants.

6.3.2.1 What the Peasants of Chan Township Get

The structure of the sources of earnings of peasants in Chan Township resembles its counterpart in Lee Township. It consists of two parts—family production and migrant work or business.

Family Production

As mentioned in the first section of this chapter, the main crop in Chan Township is paddy rice; the agricultural sidelines include fruit growing, sericulture, and pisciculture. Like Lee Township, Chan Township also has good natural conditions for agricultural production. However, while the proximity of Lee Township to big cities provides a big market for its agricultural products, the long distance between Chan Township and the provincial economic center limits the specialization and commercialization of the agricultural products of Chan Township. First, planting paddy rice is not profitable.

> Don't you know how to calculate? Let me tell you something that is ridiculous. Let me tell you how much grain one peasant will get if he cultivates one mu of farmland. The costs include the village-retained fees, the township-pooling fees, the county pooling-fees, fertilizer, and seeds. Taking all these costs into consideration, a peasant can not earn anything from the farmland. (Informant Chan200404)

Secondly, one special household which owns two fish ponds told me the importance of the specialization and commercialization of agricultural products.

> On average, everybody owns 0.5 mu of farmland. People can not make a living on farmland. Taking the tax into consideration, the earnings become less…so, peasants have to do some sidelines to increase the earnings…however, sidelines are also useless if the scale is small. The situation is the same in sericulture, fishery…for example; it will not be any help to a peasant's family economy if he just has several mu of fish ponds. It will be OK if a peasant can own a fish pond of 20–30 mu acreage; only with this scale can peasants support their families. (Informant Chan200405)

Migrant Wage Work and Business

With low level of specialization and commercialization, family production in local areas cannot meet the expenses of a family. As a result, like many townships located in mountain areas of the province, migrant labor or business becomes the pillar of the earnings of peasant households. In Huazhou County,[29] the average annual income from migrant wage labor was 1980 yuan per person in 2000. Since 1990, the average income from migrant wages has increased by 14.8 per year, while average annual income only increased by 7.2 % per year. The proportion of income from

[29] Unfortunately, I cannot find statistical data for Chan Township, but the data from Huazhou County can roughly represent the situation of Chan Township since variation among the townships in Huazhou County is slight.

migrant labor in the total family income increased from 28.2 % in 1990 to 46.1 % in 2004, while the proportion of income from family businesses decreased from 82.6 to 46.7 %. The cities in the PRD region, namely, Guangzhou, Shenzhen, and Dongguan, have become the main destinations of the young peasants of Chan Township. Their jobs include production line worker, apprentice or construction laborer, and so on. Compared to the young people from other provinces, they have one advantage: they can speak Cantonese. Some of them can find a job at better pay in the service industry—for example, as a waiter or chef in a restaurant or hotel, as an employee in a salon, and so on. However, running a business in cities is more attractive for them. These businesses are various: stores, stalls, booths in markets, taxis and motorcycle taxis, restaurants, petty services on city sidewalks, and even begging and scrap collecting.

> When I was in the third grade of middle school, I fought against a classmate and was expelled by the school. At that time, I did not want to go to the factory as a young worker (*dagong zai*) for 400–600 yuan per month. Some countrymen of mine had their businesses in Zhuhai and I went there to help them. One year later, I found a business—as a provider of meat and vegetables for a hotel in Huizhou.[30] The business was profitable. I earned my first 300,000 two years later. But unfortunately, some local people saw the profits of this business and they threatened me and forced me to leave. So I had to leave! Now I am in Shenzhen, running a factory, producing bulbs. In the district I live in there are many of countrymen of mine. They also are doing some business: running a restaurant, selling meat in markets, or factory owners. Some of them make much money and some of them are not so rich. Anyway, it is better than being a peasant in my hometown. (Informant Chan200404)

6.3.2.2 What the Peasants of Chan Township Lose

Not only what peasants get but also what peasants lose should be taken into consideration when we discuss the earnings of peasants in Chan Township. As mentioned above, local township governments and village administrations have created many ways to extract resources from peasants, which include all kinds of taxes, charges, surcharges, penalties, and all kinds of assets. Before the tax-for-fee reform was held, the burdens on peasants were of several kinds.

1. *Normal taxes and local charges*. These include township and village-retained fees (*cun tiliui* and *zhen tongchou*), 21 yuan per capita; education additional fees (*jiaoyu fujia fei*), 30 yuan per capita; and agricultural tax, 80 yuan per capita. As a retired township cadre has put it:

> Before the tax-for-fee reform, a family with 4–5 members needed a tractor to carry the grain which should be handed over to the government……you can imagine how much it is. A peasant family needed to hand over about 600 yuan per mu per year to the government. It means half of the harvest. Taking the cost of seeds, pesticide, and fertilizer into consideration, the output of land was only enough for the family's food. (Informant Chan200401)

[30] Another big city near Zhuhai.

2. *All kinds of penalties*. The administrative behavior of local township government is closely related to penalties since it is a good way to increase the government's income. As mentioned above, violators of all kinds of policies (public security, family planning policy, funeral and interment reform, and so on) will face penalties. For example, those who violate the family planning policy will be fined more than 10,000 yuan for the first time and more than 20,000 yuan for the second time. The penalties, rather than implementing policies, become the true goal of local township government.
3. *Others*. Some other ways local township governments extract money from peasants have been mentioned in the last section. When the large fruit tree-planting enterprises contracted the mountains out from the township government, peasants in Chan Township lost a great part of their natural production materials without sharing any profit from it. When local governments took all the money from the RCF, the peasants lost their years of savings. When local governments create many excuses for penalties, the peasants with low income also face heavier pressures.

After the tax-for-fee reform began in 2002, normal taxes and local charges greatly decreased. Only one kind of tax—the agricultural tax—was compulsory for the peasants in Chan Township, while the other taxes and local charges were canceled.[31] The fee-for-tax reform brought some help to the peasants in Chan Township. Like a peasant have told me:

> Since 1978, when the reform began, the most helpful policy is the fee-for-tax reform. (Informant Chan200405)

The retired township cadre also said so:

> After the tax-for-fee reform, there were no other charges anymore. As for the agricultural tax, it is easy right now. It is 27 yuan per mu per year. (Informant Chan200401)

The fee-for-tax reform lessened the burden on peasants of Chan Township by canceling the township and village-retained fees, the additional educational fees, and the special agricultural product tax (*nongye techan shui*). However, it did not prevent local township governments' other ways of extracting money from rural society. The penalties on violators of the family planning policy and the funeral and interment reform are still ongoing. The costs for children's education are still high. Peasants still face the risks that township government might take new policies as a source of revenues:

> So far as the family planning policy and funeral and interment reform become the sources of the revenue of the township government, these two policies can not be implemented with good effects. The central government should abolish these policies. To administrate the society with money will lead to bad results in the end. (Informant Chan200405)

[31] In early 2005, when I was writing my thesis, all taxes on peasants of Guangdong were canceled.

6.4 Summary and Discussion

Chan Township, representative of local economies, has been discussed in this chapter. The characteristics of its institutional arrangement are as follows:

Firstly, it is far away from market centers and with a low level of market penetration. It is hard for this kind of economy to attract FDI and other business chances. As a result, specialization and commercialization of agricultural products are limited. The outputs from family production can only meet the needs of the peasants for food. The alternative for peasants in the local economy is to go to the big cities in the PRD region for wage work or business, and these options gradually become the main sources of the earnings of the peasant families of Chan Township. Only those who go outside and achieve success in business can become better off than village cadres.

The second characteristic that should be highlighted is the cash-starved local governments and the heavy burden on peasants. With low level of market penetration, the township government cannot get much tax income from local areas. Higher levels of government, at the county and even prefecture level, are cash starved too. Therefore, fiscal transfers from county or prefecture are less. More than this, the fiscal transfers to the township government from the central government and the provincial government also have to be shared (or even bitten off) by the governments at prefecture and county level. In this case, self-retained revenue from rural society becomes the most available way to increase the township government's income. The ethnographic data from Chan Township show this point: in order to increase its revenue, the local township government acts as a predator on rural society. Besides the normal income—namely, the administration fees, taxes, and local charges—the cash-starved township government also tries all kinds of ways to increase its revenue. It acted as an industrial firm in order to boost the local economy but failed. It found many ways to take assets from local rural society directly. It also transformed the state's policies into sources of revenue in the way of penalties. This predatory behavior of the local township government led to a heavy burden on the peasants of Chan Township. The tax-for-fee reform by the central state only partly relieves the burden on the peasants. So long as the township government's financial constraints still exist, the incentives for local township government to extract resources from the peasants will continue. Village cadres, as assistants of township governments, can share in some of the income from this extraction process. They also have salaries and the opportunity to take money from collecting assets. One thing is noteworthy: located as it is in a remote mountain area, it is difficult for the economic extractions in Fan Township to be easily discovered.

Thirdly, the social changes in local economies are also noteworthy. Most of the young people have gone out for education, work, or business. Old people, housewives, and their children are left in the villages. The only evidence showing that the clan system is still in existence is that some old men organize some social activities at important festivals (e.g., Spring Festival). Kinship networks and social networks (relatives or friends) play an important role when peasants in Chan Township want to find wage works or business chances in the cities elsewhere.

References

Guangdong Provincial Statistical Bureau. (2002). *Guangdong tongji nianjian 2001* [Guangdong statistical yearbook 2001]. Beijing: Zhongguo tongji chubanshe.

Oi, J. C. (1995). The role of the local state in China's transitional economy. *China Quarterly, 144*, 1132–1149.

Walder, A. G. (1995a). China's transitional economy: Interpreting its significance. *The China Quarterly, 144*, 963–979.

Walder, A. G. (1995b). Local governments as industrial firms: An organizational analysis of China's transitional economy. *American Journal of Sociology, 101*, 263.

Chapter 7
Conclusions and Implications

In previous chapters, I have offered an explanation of how market penetration in rural Guangdong affects the life chances of village cadres and peasants. The historical and comparative data from ethnographic studies have been presented. In this chapter, I shall recount and reflect on some of the key themes. First, I will give a summary of the findings of this study. Second, main empirical findings of this study will be highlighted and interpreted. Third, I will discuss the implications of this study for future stratification studies of rural China and the transforming economy. Finally, the limitations of this study will be analyzed.

7.1 Summary of the Findings

Based on the evidence from Guangdong Province in China, this study presents how market penetration affects the life chances of village cadres and peasants by two ways. First, market penetration increases the varieties and qualities of earning sources and then the life chances of the peasant, even though village cadres are advantaged in regard to most of these earning sources. Second, market penetration lowers the burden on peasants and increases the investments of state bureaucracies for social welfare of the community, thereby indirectly increasing the peasants' life chances.

In exploring these two themes, several main empirical findings have been presented. Those related to the first theme follow.

1. The reform in Guangdong is a process of market penetration from the coastal areas (the PRD region) to the inland areas (the mountain areas), accompanying the development of petty commodity markets, capital markets, commodity markets, and labor markets.

N. Chen, *State, Market and Life Chances in Contemporary Rural Chinese Society*, DOI 10.1007/978-3-662-45046-8_7

2. Historically, with the market penetration processes, peasants' sources of earnings change from just one source (staple crops) to the thriving of agriculture, including agricultural sidelines and individual family businesses, and then to a combination of staple crops, agricultural sidelines, individual family businesses, collective revenue sharing, migrant labor, migrant businesses, and so on (Chap. 3).
3. Comparatively, the higher the level of market penetration, the better the earning sources of peasants, even though returns to village cadres increase too.

First, in rural areas of the PRD region, which have experienced the highest market penetration level and are labeled part of the new cooperative economy in this study, peasants' sources of earnings include sharing in collective profits, wage labor, private businesses, agriculture sidelines, and all kinds of welfare benefits. Village cadres' sources of earnings include salaries, stock bonuses, private businesses, privileges, and some assumed "gray income." Only entrepreneurs who own businesses of a certain scale can earn better than village cadres (Chap. 4).

Second, in the fringe areas of the PRD region and in the outskirt areas of big cities (labeled outskirt economies), where market penetration is at the middle level, peasants' sources of earnings include crops, agricultural sidelines (vegetable growing, fruit production, forestry, and others), local businesses, migrant wage work, and migrant businesses. Village cadres' advantages lie in salaries, management advantages for tapping collective assets, and good relationships with township governments.[1] Village cadres are disadvantaged concerning access to nonlocal earning sources, such as migrant wage labor and migrant businesses, since they can't leave their positions for jobs elsewhere. Special households (zhuanye hu) with large scale of agriculture or sideline products and the peasants who go outside to other cities and become successful businessmen can earn more than village cadres (Chap. 5).

Third, in the rural mountain areas of Guangdong, which have the lowest level of market penetration in the province and are labeled local economies in this study, family production—including staples, agricultural sidelines, and individual family businesses—brings in very low profits or none at all. Migrant wage work and migrant businesses are the pillar of the peasant family's earnings. Village cadres' advantages include salaries and management advantages concerning collective assets. Like their counterparts in outskirt economies, village cadres are also disadvantaged concerning access to nonlocal earning sources. Only those who go outside to other cities to become successful businessmen can earn better than village cadres (Chap. 6).

The empirical findings relating to the second theme are summarized according to four points.

1. Historical evidence presented in this study shows that market penetration increases the motivation and ability of the state (both at the central level and at local levels) to relieve the burden on peasants. For the central government, the persistent market penetration has greatly increased the revenue bases of the state. Secondly, the tax reform of 1994 led to an increase in the amount of the state's

[1] This means that they are more likely to be able to get larger fiscal transfer, subsidies, and helping programs. See Chap. 5.

revenue sharing. Finally, market penetration has led to changes in industry structure and decreased the proportion of agriculture tax in national tax income. For these three reasons, the political needs of the central government from rural society have come gradually to prevail over its economic needs. As a result, the central government has promoted a series of policies to relieve rural societies, including the fee-for-tax reform, direct village elections, and so on

However, changes in the policies of the central government do not necessarily mean that local governments will follow. The situation at the local level varies according to the extent of market penetration: the higher the level of market penetration, the more likely that local government takes care of community welfare and increases their public investment (Chap. 3).

2. In the new cooperative economy, like that of Fan Township, the township government gains good revenues from the expanding tax bases. As a result, it does not need to extract directly from the peasants. Instead, the peasants can benefit from all kinds of welfare policies (Chap. 4).
3. In the outskirt economies like that of Lee Township, the local township government's revenue is mainly from fiscal transfers, support, and subsidies from higher levels of government. Peasants there also benefit from all kinds of helping programs and funds (Chap. 5). To extract too much from rural society would risk losing support from higher levels of government.[2] As a result, local township governments tend to follow the central government's policies on the burden reduction.
4. In local economies like that of Chan Township, where both the fiscal transfer (from higher levels of government) and local tax income are low. Rural society is the most available revenue source for the township governments. As a result, the cash-starved local governments create many ways to collect money from the rural people, even though the central government has issued policies to relieve the burden on peasants (Chap. 6).

7.2 The Findings Intepreted

7.2.1 Earning Source Distribution and Rural People's Access Patterns

Vigorous but inconclusive debate of stratification studies of rural China is that concerning the returns to cadres and peasants. This study contributes to this debate by exploring various earning sources created by the reform and by presenting rural people's access patterns to them.

[2] This has been discussed in Chap. 5. Higher levels of government—the Zengcheng District Government and Guangzhou Government—have gained good revenue bases because of the economic development in core areas of the PRD region. Lee Township is in the fringe areas of the PRD region and is a main provider of agricultural products. As a result, the Zengcheng Government and Guangzhou Government subsidize the Lee Township Government by fiscal transfer and helping programs, in order to maintain social stability and the natural environment there.

7.2.1.1 The Role of, and the Returns to, Village Cadres

The variety of roles of village cadres in rural Guangdong is consistent with the arguments of Parish and Michelson (1996). Village cadres in the new cooperative economy can be the managers of collective economy, as their counterparts in the studies by Oi (1992, 1999) and Walder (1995b). However, village cadres can also be part-time workers, as village cadres in outskirt economies or local economies are; while village cadres in Chan Township play another role—that of assistant to predators.

Research on social stratification in rural China is preoccupied with the question of cadre advantage. With the exception of Nee's study (Nee 1989) of the early period of the reform, most studies observe some advantages for cadres. These advantages are of various forms: high salaries and bonuses for cadre positions as managers of collective industry (Oi 1992; 1999; Walder 1995a, b; Whiting 2001); salaried positions and managerial posts for family members, relatives, and friends (Parish and Michelson 1996; Parish et al. 1995); lucrative alliances with private entrepreneurs that they favor in regulatory and tax matters (Chen 1999; Wank 1999); and even family businesses (Lin and Chen 1999) that benefit from the advantages of their positions. As a result, the further issue becomes "how large are the current advantages and how long they can be expected to last" (Walder 2002a, p. 357). The findings from the comparison of the three townships in this study are consistent with Walder's conclusions drawn from the national survey in 1996 (2002a). That is, the cadres' advantages will last for a long time. At the least, the evidence of this study shows that village cadres' advantages didn't decline in rural Guangdong in 2004. Many earning sources of cadres mentioned by earlier studies have been observed in Fan Township, including salaries and bonuses and salaried positions for family members or relatives. No direct evidence shows that rural cadres benefit much from lucrative alliances with private enterprises. However, it is obvious that cadres themselves can own businesses. From Chan Township and Lee Township to Fan Township, the returns to village cadres are increasing, accompanying the increase of market penetration. The evidence reported in this study can explain this: the reemergence of family farming and the other reform processes doesn't necessarily mean the vanishing of the collective characteristics of rural Guangdong. In all three townships of this study, we can see the preservation of the collective economy. More than that, the more developed the village economy, the larger the scale of the collective assets: in Fan Township, the richest of the three townships in this study, the collective economy has once again become the pillar of the rural economy. Even in Chan Township, the undeveloped township, the collective assets are still valuable in relation to ordinary peasants' incomes. One thing is noteworthy that village cadres are disadvantaged in access to nonlocal earning sources—namely, migrant wage work and migrant businesses (Chaps. 5 and 6)—since they cannot leave their positions for jobs outside the village.

The intergenerational inheritance of cadres' positions should also be discussed here. Walder (2002a, p. 357) proposes that a valid indicator to measure the advantages of cadres is whether they can pass their status on to their offspring. However, none of the cadres at the village level in my three townships had this large advantage, as they remain under the constraints of township supervision and the direct village election policy.[3] While other studies (Walder 2003; Zhao and Zhou 2002) found that management experience is the most important predictor of private entrepreneurship, this study finds management experience is also a determining factor for whether a villager can be a cadre, at least in Fan Township (Chap. 4). As for Lee Township and Chan Township, most village cadres had held cadre positions for many years, so that the factors which determined their cadre position cannot have changed too much.

7.2.1.2 The Returns to, and the Burden on, Peasants

To measure the returns of peasants in rural China is a challenging task. Many current stratification studies of rural China use national survey data sets, in which returns to peasants are measured according to their incomes (Keister and Nee 2001; Matthews and Nee 2000; Nee 1989; Nee 1991, 1996; Parish and Michelson 1996; Parish et al. 1995; Peng 1992). Ethnographic data in this study contributes some points to this literature: this study presents not only what peasants "get" but also what peasants "lose" and what this means to their lives. The former depends on the opportunities brought by market penetration, while the latter depends on the changes of the needs of the state (both at central level and local levels) on rural society; and these are in turn affected by market penetration.

In this context, some points should be highlighted. For one thing, evidence reported in this study shows the strong and durable effect of structural factors on life chances. Peasants' earnings are still greatly constrained within the earning distribution frameworks created by the market penetration process. These are related to the location of peasants—the second structure factor: peasant identity in the PRD region often means good earnings from collective revenue sharing (Chap. 4), while in mountain areas it means greater difficulty in making a living (Chap. 6). The earnings of peasants are still brittle and easily affected by central state and local governments' policies for extracting from or remedying rural society. In some areas, e.g., Chan Township, all kinds of local surcharges can lead to a heavy burden on the peasants.

This study considers that the burden on peasants consists of state taxes, local charges, fees, fundraising, fines and property confiscation, and other hidden economic burdens. The "hidden" ways for local township government to extract money or assets from rural society include the use of policy as a revenue source, the transfer of collective assets to family members or allies, and even the direct illegal appropriation of collective assets (Chap. 6)—thus, the lower the level of market penetration, the more aggravation of the burden of peasants. For example, in Fan Township, peasants don't need to pay taxes or other local charges from their own

[3] One exception in Guangdong is Nanshan Village, located in Shenzhen City. It is considered the richest village in Guangdong. The former village leader took a key role in the success of the village economy. His son, however, got his position through direct villager election.

pockets but on the contrary gain many welfare benefits (Chap. 4). The situation in Chan Township is the reverse.

7.2.1.3 Earning Inequality in Rural Guangdong

The advantages of rural cadres don't mean larger inequalities between village cadres and peasants, since peasants also benefit from new earning sources and burden relief. The findings of this study are consistent with those of Byrd and Gelb (1990), which show that market penetration is advantageous both for rural communities as a whole and for the cadres who oversee them. Accompanying the market penetration process, village cadres have the chance to increase their own returns by developing the whole economic situation of the community. In this case, the relationship between local cadres and rural residents is itself becoming less vertical. For example, peasants in Fan Township are more satisfied with their lives and give higher evaluation to their village cadres. However, peasants in Chan Township have more complaints about their lives and village cadres' governance than Fan Township. As a result, the key question for rural earnings inequality is not "cadres or peasants, who benefits most?," but the question of "has market penetration provided enough alternatives for both cadres and peasants?"[4]

In many earlier studies, a comparison of the incomes of cadre households and entrepreneur households is a main index for measuring rural inequality (Nee 1996; Walder 2002a, b). However, entrepreneur households are broadly defined by these studies. In Nee and Matthews' study (1996), entrepreneurs are defined as "simply households that started up small businesses after institutional change made self-employment legitimate, like entrepreneurs, self-employed professionals, middlemen, merchants, peddlers, and workers in the private sector" (1996, p. 422). In Walder's study it is defined as "drivers who own their own vehicles and operate them hauling goods and passengers; the owner of a retail shop, restaurant, guest house, or wholesale business; or an owner of a manufacturing enterprise" (2002a, p. 260). The findings of the present study show that these definitions are not suitable for comparison. Firstly, village cadres can also engage in new sources of earnings even when they are in their cadre positions. For instance, a village cadre can also be a special household or a store owner in local economies (Chap. 6). Secondly, in developed areas, only the entrepreneurs who own good businesses, namely, the owners of factories or companies, can achieve more than do village cadres in administrative positions (Chap. 4). In less developed areas, like Lee Township and Chan Township, only those people who run large-scale special production facilities and successful migrant businessmen can earn more money than village cadres do.

[4] Here I am talking about the intra-village inequality. However, the intervillage inequality may be larger, especially the inequality between the businessmen, some of whom are cadres, near the city, and the peasants, and even the cadres, in the countryside. But the

7.2.2 *Beyond Guangdong*

I do not intend to generalize the conclusions of this study, which are drawn from Guangdong experiences, to the whole country. However, the terms new cooperative economies, outskirt economies, and local economies not only point to the different situations of the three townships but also to three distinctive institutional arrangements in which society, economy, and the state are integrated and affect the life chances of rural people in them. From this perspective, trying to understand rural China as a whole through the lens of the Guangdong case can still be helpful for future stratification studies of rural China, by giving a possible variation of institutional arrangements.

First, new cooperative economies in rural Guangdong resemble those in most rural areas in developed provinces like Shanghai, Jiangsu, Zhejiang, and even Shandong. They share some common characteristics:

1. Most of these rural areas are located in coastal regions, which means close access to FDI and market centers. Capital markets, commodity markets, and labor markets are thriving, although in various different ways.[5]
2. Collective institutions have once again become important, even though they are playing different roles in local economies. For example, in the new cooperative economy of Guangdong, village collective administrations act like companies, of which villagers are stockholders. Village administrations are the managers of the collective economy. However, in some rural areas of Zhejiang, village administration act like a guild, of which individual entrepreneurs are the members. Village administrations maintain the business environment and social order. The revenue bases of local governments, especially township governments, have greatly increased accompanying the thriving of the local economies. Township governments don't need to press village administrations to collect money from the peasants' pockets.
3. The earning sources of the rural people have increased greatly during the years of reform, even though they have varied across different regions. Village cadres in these rural areas are undoubtedly rich, while peasants there can also find a good living. Especially, the peasant burden—which mainly arises from the improper levying of fees (luan shoufei), arbitrary fines (luan fakuan), and forced apportionment of funds (luan taipai)—is absent there.
4. In these rural areas, the key things for improving the life chances of rural people are how to maintain economic development and how to formulate better institutions of resource distribution.

Second, the situation of local economies in Guangdong resembles that of many townships located in northwestern and southwestern areas of the country. Common characteristics shared by these areas are as follows:

[5] For example, rural industries in rural areas of Wenzhou are dominated by little individual enterprises, while the rural areas of Jiangsu are occupied by large-scale TVEs.

1. They are not only far away from market centers but also lack other ways to access market chances.[6] After several years of the thriving of agriculture production brought on by family farming during the first period of the reform, the local economies in these areas have become stagnant
2. Local governments may look for ways to develop local economies. Some of these have been successful but most have failed, especially in those areas without close access to markets, traditions of craft or trade specialization, and qualified people with business knowledge. Local governments that have failed in developing local economy face two choices. As happened in Chan Township, the township government can become predatory on the rural society and village administration can become the assistant of the former. Peasants will then become the main source of revenue for the township governments, and various ways will be made use of to collect money from the peasants' pockets. The other choice is that, without enough revenue, the township government or village administration will be trapped in debt and barely be able to maintain their operations.
3. Peasants in such areas find it difficult to make a good living in local areas, especially with the persistence of low prices for agricultural products. The burden on them can be heavy some times. As a result, most peasants in such rural areas go outside for a better living. In this case, most of the villages are left destitute.
4. In these rural areas, critical ways to improve the life chances of rural people there may include some of the following. First would be to "shorten the distance" between these areas and market centers. This can be achieved by providing special policies for these rural areas to make them more attractive to investors, by improving transportation conditions and even by introducing people with extensive business experience.[7] Second, the central government or provincial governments could increase the fiscal transfers to these areas and make sure that the transfers actually reach the local economies and the local people. When the local government can benefit from fiscal transfers, the burden on peasants will be indirectly relieved.

Thirdly, accompanying the process of urbanization, the scope of outskirt economies will be enlarged quickly. For the rural people of outskirt economies, how to benefit from the thriving of city market centers becomes most important.

7.2.3 *Structure and Life Chances in Transforming Economies*

Studies of transitional societies now address theoretical issues that trace back to the classical themes of modern social science. In this study, structural changes and individual life chances have been highlighted. The findings of this study remind us how life chances are embedded in given structures, in institutional arrangements which

[6] In some remote areas, the function of local elite, or the traditions of craft and trade specialization, can compensate for the distance between the local areas and market center.

[7] Actually, some of these methods have been employed during recent years since the central government has issued the policy of "xibu da kaifa (the great development of the west)."

include those of the state, market, and society. Existing studies of social stratification in rural China have provided various explanations by focusing on various aspects of the facts.

1. *Explanations focusing on state institutions.* These focus on the relationship between changing revenue-sharing arrangements and local governments' incentives to develop the economy (Oi 1992, 1995, 1999; Walder 1995a, b; Wank 1999; Whiting 2001; Wong 1992, 1988),[8] regime changes (Walder 2003), the cadre evaluation system (Whiting 2001), and the state's special policies for a given region (Lau 2000).
2. *Explanations focusing on market institutions.* The first, of course, is market transition theory (Nee 1989), which emphasizes the incentives and opportunities brought by the market transition (from plan to market). Some sequential studies have extended this explanation further to include the rearrangements (Nee 1996; Oi and Walder 1999; Walder 1992, 1996) or the unit forms (Liu 1992; Peng 1992) of property rights. Other studies have highlighted the proximity of villages and urban markets, local natural resource endowment, transportation conditions, and density of economic institutions (Johnson 1994; Nee and Su 1990); good access to market chances, such as FDI (Zeng 2000) or business contracts; traditions of craft and trade specialization and access to nonagricultural wage employment (Luong and Unger 1998); industry structure (Walder and Zhao 2003); scale of firms (Zhao 2004); and development of market factors (capital market, labor market, commodity market, and others) (Szelenyi and Kostello 1996; Nee and Matthews 1996).
3. *Explanations focusing on institutions acting as "the lens of society."* These explanations highlight the positive effects of overseas Chinese (Buckley et al. 2004) and the existence of local business elites (Xiang and Zhou 2001), clan system (Peng et al. 2003), and social networks (Tsai 2006; Zhang and Li 2003) on economic development or life chances.

However, "a way of seeing is also a way of not seeing—a focus on object A involves a neglect of object B" (Merton 1949, p. 252). This is why the new institutionalism perspective criticizes the state-centered studies' neglect of the society (Nee and Matthews 1996). This study, in describing the changes, which have happened in rural Guangdong, provides a means of measurement of the effect of the abovementioned institutions on the life chances of rural people.

7.2.3.1 State Institution Measurement

First, the findings of this study show the effects of the state's special policies that gave Guangdong the chance to go "one step ahead." These directly facilitated the economic development of the PRD region and the life chances of rural people there.

---

[8] Both Oi's "local state corporatism" model and Walder's "local governments as industrial firms" belong to this group.

However, the effects of the state's special policies came only in the early period of the Reform Era (Chap. 3).

Second, this study finds that the effect of the local governments' incentives for economic development has been exaggerated. In reviewing the market penetration process in rural Guangdong, we see that the "local state corporatism" model makes sense only in rural areas with new cooperative economies. For example, I observe the cadres' positive roles in the development of the economy in Fan Township (Chap. 4). However, the efforts of cadres in Chan Township to boost the local economy did not bring positive results (Chap. 6). This comparison shows us that local governments' incentives to develop the economy do not always lead to success. Moreover, since outskirt economies and local economies cover most of the rural areas of Guangdong, one can see that the effect of "local state corporatism" has been exaggerated.

Third, the findings of this study are in line with Susan Whiting's studies (2001), which highlight the effect of the cadre evaluation system on local government behavior and thereby affect the life chances of rural people. Generally, three interrelated aspects will determine a local cadre's (e.g., township leaders) level of remuneration and influence his (her) tenure in office and opportunities for promotion: local economic development (GDP), social stability and harmony, and personal relationship with official leaders in higher levels of government. However, the results of this type of evaluation vary according to the various characteristics of local areas. Local cadres are aware at all times of where they stand in terms of fulfilling their key performance targets. In Fan Township, representing the new cooperative economy, where achieving economic goals is not a difficulty anymore, the more important performance target is to maintain social harmony. As a result, villagers can gain a better welfare system (Chap. 4). In outskirt economies—Lee Township—economic development is not the key target of township leaders. Instead, how to meet the targets of higher levels of government, such as those of the family planning system, environmentally sustainable development, and social harmony, becomes more important. This explains why state extraction and the peasants' burden are less there (Chap. 5). In Chan Township, the township leaders' key performance target is to meet the economic goals of the cash-starved county government and maintain the township government's operation at the same time. Without the development of the local economy, extracting money from peasants seems to be a rational action for the township leaders. This explains the heavy burden on the peasants of Chan Township (Chap. 6).

Fourth, this study also reveals the effects of proximity to government centers. This proximity not only explains the greater subsidies (such as those for Lee Township) but also the stricter supervision (such as in Fan Township) by higher levels of government. On the contrary, Chan Township is far away from the government center (about 500 kms. from the location of the provincial government), and this partly explains why the township government's extraction from rural society is heavier.

7.2.3.2 Market Institutions Measurement

First, the findings of this study devalue the effects of market transition—namely, the transition from redistributive institution to market institution. As Walder (2002b) points out, the reform in rural China is not only a transition from plan to market but also from a stable agrarian economy to a growing industrial-commercial economy. Strictly speaking, in rural Guangdong, only the introduction of the household responsibility system is directly related to the transition from plan to market. The development of rural areas of the PRD should first be attributed to the FDI. The migrant wage labor and migrant business are also directly due to the loosening of household registration policy and the chances available in the PRD region. This study also takes note of the unit form of property rights of rural enterprises in Guangdong, although this obviously isn't a decisive factor.

Second, evidence presented in this study supports the effects of proximity to urban market (Johnson 1994; Nee and Su 1990).[9] This factor plays its role in conjunction with other institutional factors. For one thing, proximity to an urban center means easier access to foreign direct investment, which is the driving force to boost the petty commodity market to go further—as Fan Township (Chap. 4). Proximity to the urban center also means close access to higher government support and helping programs (Chap. 5). On the contrary, the long distance from the urban center means a lack of FDI, business chances (Chap. 6).

Third, the findings of this study question the explanations which focus on industrial structure (Walder and Zhao 2003) and scale of firm (Zhao 2004). In rural Guangdong, rural industries have developed in various ways. For example, Dongguan's rural economy is dominated by "three supplies, one compensation (san lai yi bu)" enterprises, while in Shunde and Zhongshan, large collective enterprises play more important roles, so that the villages in these townships can be considered as belonging to the category of "industrial villages." Another example is Nanhai, where the rural economy consists of lots of small family enterprises, so that villages there can be put in the category of "entrepreneur villages" (see Chap. 3). Although the ways for rural industrial development are various, villagers benefit from rural industry similarly, according to three main sources of income: the collective revenue sharing, the available of wage work, and the chances for individual businesses (Chap. 3).

The data presented by this study cannot give an appropriate measurement of the effects of local natural source endowment and traditions of craft and trade specialization, since the three townships selected do not have these characteristics. However, one can argue that these two institutions are more important in remote areas, in which the existence of local natural resources and traditions of craft and trade specialization can undoubtedly compensate for the distance between the local areas and regional market centers.

---

[9] Nee and Su's (1990) regression analysis shows that access to local marketing and county town markets does not appear to have a significant effect on economic growth. Only proximity to the urban market can make a difference.

7.2.3.3 Social Institutions Measurement

First, this study supports the effects of social networks in improving life chances. Consistently with previous studies, social networks are shown to be a way for the peasants of Guangdong to find wage work or business chances in cities (Chaps. 5 and 6).

Second, this study does not find much effect of clan system on local economic success and life chances. Fan Township is bordering the city center and Lee Township is near cities. Clan system is not important anymore, thanks to the long-time influence of city civilization. In Chan Township, clan system may more easily play important roles; however, most of the young people have gone outside and the local economy is stagnant. There are no strong incentives for clan system to take the center of the stage.

Thirdly, the historical data of this study show that the large number of overseas Chinese directly (by donation) or indirectly (by investment) have played roles in the development of the whole Guangdong economy (Chap. 3). However, because the three selected townships are not important hometowns of overseas Chinese, the effects of the number of overseas Chinese on the life chances of rural people cannot be well measured. In Guangdong, Jiangmen is the most famous qiaoxian (a village or town inhabited by relatives of overseas Chinese and returned overseas Chinese). I have visited two counties there, Kaiping and Taishan. The level of market penetration in these two counties is lower than that in Shunde and Nanhai, two counties of Foshan Prefecture. It seems that the number of overseas Chinese has not been a decisive factor in the local economy development and the life chances of rural people. According to my observation, overseas Chinese will help their hometowns in two ways. First, the donations of overseas Chinese are invested in improving transportation conditions and education facilities (e.g., middle school, primary school, library, and so on) of the local areas. Second, local people there who want to start a business will more easily be able to borrow some money from overseas Chinese. Although many overseas Chinese have donated much to their hometowns, this does not mean that they will invest their money in running enterprises there, since businesses should be cost-effective investments.

Fourthly, in the three selected townships, no evidence shows salient effects of local business elites, either in the richest village or the poorest one. This is partly because of the sample bias of this study.

Although the effects of these institutions and factors have been discussed one by one, they interact and play their roles together in various forms. In this study, these forms are labeled new cooperative economy, outskirt economy, and local economy. Most importantly, in regard to the state-market interaction view, this study argues that the discrepancy between economic liberalization and continued political authoritarianism is the main form of institutional interaction in reform China.

The state-market interaction view has been emphasized by several scholars (Bian and Zhang 2002; Lin 2001; Parish and Michelson 1996; Wu and Xie 2003; Zhou 2000a, b). There are two points that need to be discussed: For one thing, this study focuses on rural areas of China while almost all previous studies employing the state-market interaction view focus on urban China. This is important not only because it remedies the neglect of the earlier studies but also because peasants in rural areas are still more easily affected by structural conditions than urban residents. For another, the existing studies failed to bridge the state-market interaction with individual life chances. For example, the study by Bian and Zhang (2002) stresses two points: (1) marketization is a multifaceted historical process and (2) the transformations of the Communist Party-state occur because it wants to protect its interests and retain its influence. However, these two points don't tell us how market and state interact, why the state adopts some actions and issues some policies but not others, or how these changes of state action and policy affect people's life chances.

By taking the needs of the state and its agencies into consideration, this study bridges the interaction between the state, the market, and the peasants' life chances. The state and its agencies have two needs: to extract enough revenue and to maintain political support. These two needs are contradicted in a transforming socialist state like China (Chap. 3). On the one hand, in order to improve the tax base and guarantee their revenue, the state tends to loosen its control of the market; on the other hand, the new structural incentives for opportunism and malfeasance created by the market can in turn erode the effectiveness and legitimacy of the state. One way to solve this contradiction is for the state to try to institute more welfare policies to "buy" people's support. According to this logic, peasants become the first target of the state's compensation policies, while the market penetration improves the ability of the state to remedy rural society. This is for three reasons: (1) peasants consist of almost 60 % of the population of China; (2) peasants were the main force and support of the CCP's coming to power and the main source of the CCP's legitimacy in the PRC; and (3) market penetration decreases the dependence of the state on the tax income from rural society (Chap. 3).

According to this logic, this study highlights how market penetration gradually increases the state and its agencies' intentions and abilities to relieve the burden on peasants. For example, in rural areas with a considerable extent of market penetration, such as Fan Township, the township governments and village administrations can gain much revenue from the thriving of markets and urban areas. Political support from the peasants, rather than economic surplus, becomes more desirable to local governments. As a result, they intend to provide more welfare, subsidies, and implementing policies in soft ways, which thereby benefit the life chances of the peasants. On the contrary, for the cash-starved local governments in the rural areas with low levels of market penetration, like Chan Township, rural society is their sole source of revenue. The local governments are more interested in the economic resources than in the peasants' political support.

Moreover, these findings remind us of the effect of political continuity on life chances in China. This topic has been intensively discussed. For example, Burawoy (1996) points out that the continuation of the CCP's powerful control in China has lead to the relaxation of redistributive imperatives, while the Russian state has reasserted central redistribution of economic resources in order to maintain political order without the party. Another example is Walder (2003), who emphasizes the effect of the extent of regime change on the political elite's opportunities to access various assets. The findings of this study add another point to this line of literature: the contradiction between political continuity and economic liberalization makes political legitimacy the main concern of the Chinese state. Peasants, as the main source of the political legitimacy of the CCP, thereby, can benefit from this situation, especially when the state's increasing revenue makes the policy of "buying" support from peasants possible.

7.3 Limitations

First, the three stages and kinds of rural economies of Guangdong will unavoidably be considered a simplification, even though I don't assume that the transition from one to the other is necessary. Although this study emphasizes the reform as a market penetration process from the core to the periphery, I can't deny that some townships located in mountain areas have good economic development. However, most of these townships have achieved their economic success because of local economic elites whose capability to connect local products with the big market outside in the economic core have made the township's economic success. The functions of such a local elite compensates for the distance between the village and the market center.

Second, it is also difficult to say that the three townships selected for this study can exactly present the situation of the areas in which they are located. For example, the sources of earnings in rural areas of the PRD region must be more complicated than what I have seen in Fan Township. However, I can be sure that these three townships do represent three main resource distribution frameworks by which researchers can explain most of the variations in rural people's earnings in rural Guangdong.

Third, Walder and Zhao's study (Walder and Zhao 2003) has provided categories for the village economy: agrarian village, industrial village, and entrepreneur village. Drawing from a national survey, these categories must be more applicable to the whole country than are the three categories developed in this study, namely, new cooperative economy, outskirt economy, and local economy. However, my categories should be more useful in two ways. Firstly, they include not only the market context but also the resource distribution framework—namely, the opportunity structure. Secondly, as far as rural Guangdong is concerned, Walder and Zhao's categories are not suitable, as evidence in rural Guangdong shows that peasants in industrial villages and entrepreneur villages benefit from the market similarly (collective revenue sharing, businesses chances, and wage work), even though industrial villages and entrepreneur villages have different industrial frameworks (Chap. 3). Finally, both industrial villages and entrepreneurial villages in Guangdong are located in the PRD region. If we consider the rural mountain area agrarian villages, then Walder and Zhao's definitions neglect outskirt economies, which have been proved to be a special type of economy in this study.

References

Bian, Y., & Zhang, Z. (2002). Marketization and income distribution in urban China, 1988 and 1995. *Research in Social Stratification and Mobility, 19*, 377–415.

Buckley, P. J., Clegg, J., & Wang, C. (2004). The relationship between inward foreign direct investment and the performance of domestically-owned Chinese manufacturing industry. *Multinational Business Review, 12*(3), 23.

Burawoy, M. (1996). The state and economic involution: Russia through a china lens. *World Development, 24*, 1105–1117.

Byrd, W. A., & Gelb, A. (1990). Why industrialize? The incentives for rural community governments. In W. A. Byrd & Q. Lin (Eds.), *China's rural industry: Structure, development, and reform* (pp. 358–387). New York: Oxford University Press.

Chen, Minjin. (1999). *Gaige kaifang ershinian chengjiu huigu* [Reflections on the achievements of twenty years of reforms and opening to the outside world]. Guangzhou: Guangdong Nianjian Press.

Johnson, G. E. (1994). Open for business, open to the world: Consequences of global incorporation in Guangdong and the Pearl River delta. In T. Lyons & V. Nee (Eds.), *The economic transformation of south China* (pp. 55–87). NY: Cornell University Press.

Keister, L. A., & Nee, V. (2001). The rational peasant in China: Flexible adaptation: Flexible adaptation, risk diversification, and opportunity. *Rationality and Society, 13*, 33.

Lau, P.-k. (2000). Industrial structure and industrial policy in Guangdong province. In Y. S. Joseph Cheng (Ed.), *Guangdong in the twenty-first century: Stagnation or second take-off?* (pp. 79–102). Hong Kong: City University of Hong Kong Press.

Lin, Y.-m. (2001). *Between politics and markets: Firms, competition, and institutional change in post-Mao China*. New York: Cambridge University Press.

Lin, N., & Chen, C.-j. J. (1999). Local elites as officials and owners: Shareholding and property rights in Daqiuzhuang. In J. C. Oi & A. G. Walder (Eds.), *Property rights and economy reform in China* (pp. 145–170). Stanford: Stanford University Press.

Liu, Y. (1992). Reform from below: The private economy and local politics in the rural industrialization of Wenzhou. *China Quarterly, 130*, 293–316.

Matthews, R., & Nee, V. (2000). Gender inequality and economic growth in rural China. *Social Science Research, 29*, 606–632.

Merton, R. K. (1949). *Social theory and social structure*. New York: Free Press.

Nee, V. (1989). A theory of market transition: From redistribution to markets in state socialism. *American Sociological Review, 54*, 663–681.

Nee, V. (1991). Social inequality in reforming state socialism. *American Sociological Review, 56*, 267–282.

Nee, V. (1996). The emergence of a market society: Changing mechanisms of stratification in China. *American Journal of Sociology, 101*, 908–949.

Nee, V., & Matthews, R. (1996). Market transition and societal transformation in reforming state socialism. *Annual Review of Sociology, 2*, 401–435.

Nee, V., & Su, S. (1990). Institutional change and economic growth in China: The view from the village. *Journal of Asian Studies, 49*, 3–25.

Oi, J. C. (1992). Fiscal reform and the economic foundations of local state corporatism in China. *World Politics, 45*, 99–126.

Oi, J. C. (1995). The role of the local state in China's transitional economy. *China Quarterly, 144*, 1132–1149.

Oi, J. C. (1999). *Rural China takes off: Institutional foundations of economic reform*. Berkeley: University of California Press.

Oi, J. C., & Andrew Walder, G. (1999). *Property right and economic reform in China*. Stanford: Stanford University Press.

Parish, W. L., & Michelson, E. (1996). Politics and markets: Dual transformations. *American Journal of Sociology, 101*, 1042–1059.

Parish, W. L., Zhe, X., & Li, F. (1995). Nonfarm work and marketization of the Chinese countryside. *The China Quarterly, 143*, 1–29.
Peng, Y. (1992). Wage determination in rural and urban China: A comparison of public and private industrial sectors. *American Sociological Review, 57*, 198–213.
Peng, Yusheng, Zhe, Xiaoye, & Chen, Yingying. (2003). "Zhongguo xiangcun de zongzu wangluo, gongyehua, yu zhidu xuanze (The Kinship Networks, Industrialization, and Institution Selection in Rural China)." *Zhongguo xiangcun yanjiu (Rural China Studies) 1,* 251–71.
Szelenyi, I., & Kostello, E. (1996). The market transition debate: Toward a synthesis. *American Journal of Sociology, 101*, 1082–1096.
Tsai, Jenny Hsin-Chun. (2006). Xenophobia, ethnic community, and immigrant youths' friendship network formation. *Adolescence, 41*, 162:285.
Van Luong, H., & Unger, J. (1998). Wealth, power, and poverty in the transition to market economies: The process of socio-economic differentiation in rural China and northern Vietnam. *The China Journal, 40*, 61–93.
Walder, A. G. (1992). Property rights and stratification in socialist redistributive economies. *American Sociological Review, 57*, 524–39.
Walder, A. G. (1995a). China's transitional economy: Interpreting its significance. *The China Quarterly, 144*, 963–979.
Walder, A. G. (1995b). Local governments as industrial firms: An organizational analysis of China's transitional economy. *American Journal of Sociology, 101*, 263.
Walder, A. G. (1996). Markets and inequality in transitional economics: Toward testable theories. *American Journal of Sociology, 101*, 1060–1073.
Walder, A. G. (2002a). Income determination and market opportunity in rural China, 1978–1996. *Journal of Comparative Economics, 30*, 354–375.
Walder, A. G. (2002b). Market and income inequality in rural China: Political advantage in an expanding economy. *American Sociological Review, 67*, 231–253.
Walder, A. G. (2003). Elite opportunity in transitional economics. *American Sociological Review, 68*, 899–916.
Walder, A. G., & Zhao, L. (2003). *Political office, kinship, and household wealth in rural China* (Working paper series of Asia/Pacific Research Center of Stanford University).
Wank, D. L. (1999). *Commodifying communism: Business, trust, and politics in a Chinese city*. New York: Cambridge University Press.
Whiting, S. H. (2001). *Power and wealth in Rural China: The political economy of institutional change*. New York: Cambridge University Press.
Wong, C. P. W. (1988). Interpreting rural industrial growth in the post-mao period. *Modern China, 14*, 3–30.
Wong, C. P. W. (1992). Fiscal reform and local industrialization: The problematic sequencing of reform in Post-Mao China. *Modern China, 18*(2), 197–227.
Xiang, H., & Zhou, W. (2001). Nongcun jingji jingying yu cunmin zizhi (Rural Economic Elite and Villager Self-governances). *Society, 12*, 8–11.
Wu, X., & Xie, Y. (2003). Does the market pay off? Earnings returns to education in Urban China. *American Sociological Review, 68*, 425–442.
Zeng, K. (2000). Retrospect and prospects of foreign direct investment inflow: The case of Guangdong province. In J. Y. S. Cheng (Ed.), *Guangdong in the twenty-first century: Stagnation or second take-off?* (pp. 103–128). Hong Kong: City University of Hong Kong Press.
Zhang, X., & Li, G. (2003). Does Guanxi matter to nonfarm employment? *Journal of Comparative Economics, 31*(2), 315.
Zhao, Litao. (2004). Paths to private entrepreneurship: Markets and occupational mobility in rural China. PhD thesis, Department of Sociology, Stanford University, Stanford.
Zhao, W., & Zhou, X. (2002). Institutional transformation and results to education in urban China: An empirical assessment. *Research in Social Stratification and Mobility, 19*, 339–375.
Zhou, X. (2000a). Economic transformation and income inequality in Urban China: Evidence from a panel data. *American Journal of Sociology, 105*, 1135–1174.
Zhou, X. (2000b). Reply: Beyond the debate and toward substantive institutional analysis. *American Journal of Sociology, 105*, 1190–1195.

Appendix: Informant List

	Number	Characteristics
1	Fan200401	Female, a villager, 50-year-old
2	Fan200402	Male, a villager, 40-year-old, the party secretary of the township government
3	Fan200403	Male, a villager, 59-year-old
4	Fan200404	Male, a villager, 62-year-old
5	Fan200405	Male, a villager, 71-year-old
6	Fan200406	Female, 30-year-old, a resident
7	Fan200407	Male, the secretary of the village branch of CCP, Long Village
8	Fan200408	Female, 53-year-old, working in the village garden, Long Village
9	Fan200409	Male, 48-year-old, the director of the tenth natural village, Zhu Village
10	Fan200410	Female, 39-year-old, a villager, working in village's kindergarten, Zhu Village
11	Fan200411	Female, 26-year-old, a villager, a women out of work
12	Fan200412	Female, 35-year-old, a store holder
13	Fan200413	Male, a villager, 72-year-old
14	Fan200414	Female, a villager, 28-year-old, a family women
15	Fan200415	Male, 26-year-old, a secure of the village
16	Fan200416	Male, 22-year-old, a store keeper
17	Fan200417	Male, 18-year-old, a student of technical secondary school
18	Fan200418	Male, 79-year-old, a villager
19	Fan200419	Male, 33-year-old, the vice director of the first natural village, Zhu Village
20	Fan200420	Female, 13-year-old, a student of middle school
21	Fan200421	Male, 27-year-old, a security of Zhu Village
22	Fan200422	Male, 47-year-old, the director of the first natural village, Zhu village
23	Fan200423	Male, 50-year-old, a worker of railway
24	Fan200424	Female, 73-year-old, a keeper of the village's temple
25	Fan200425	Male, 60-year-old, a villager

(continued)

N. Chen, *State, Market and Life Chances in Contemporary Rural Chinese Society*, DOI 10.1007/978-3-662-45046-8

	Number	Characteristics
26	Fan200426	Male, 44-year-old, a holder of a garage
27	Fan200427	Male, 40-year-old, the vice director of seventh natural village, Zhu Village
28	Fan200428	Male, 28-year-old, a repairman
29	Fan200429	Male, 54-year-old, the director of the eleventh natural village, Zhu Village
30	Fan200430	Male, 65-year-old, a villager
31	Fan200431	Female, 23-year-old, a keeper of post office of village
32	Fan200432	Female, 46-year-old, a vegetable planter
33	Fan200433	Female, 42-year-old, the Director of Family Planning Office, Zhu Village
34	Fan200434	Female, 46-year-old, the treasure of the village office
35	Fan200435	Male, 47-year-old, the manager of village development company, Zhu Village
36	Fan200436	Female, a villager
37	Fan200437	Male, 48-year-old, a villager
38	Lee200401	Male, the director of Bai Village
39	Lee200402	Male, a holder of a forest center
40	Lee200403	Male, a disabled man
41	Lee200404	Male, a technical man
42	Lee200405	Male, an old man living alone
43	Lee200406	Male, the secretary of village party branch of Peace Village
44	Lee200407	Male, a director of natural village, Huang Village
45	Lee200408	Male, a villager
46	Lee200409	Male, the director of Huang Village
47	Lee200410	Male, a construction man
48	Lee200411	Male, a villager of Shui Village
49	Lee200412	Male, a special household raising chicken
50	Lee200413	Male, a village cadre of Shui Village
51	Lee200414	Male, the secretary of village party branch of Shui Village
52	Lee200415	Male, a villager of Shui Village, a retired soldier
53	Lee200416	Male, a retired cadre from the township bank
54	Lee200417	Male, a director of a natural village, Shui Village
55	Lee200418	Male, a director of a natural village, vegetable planter, Huang Village
56	Lee200419	Male, a villager
57	Lee200420	Male, a villager
58	Lee200421	Male, the director of Shui Village
59	Lee200422	Female, the keeper of a store
60	Lee200423	Male, the director of civil affair office of Lee Township
61	Lee200424	Male, a township cadre
62	Chan200401	Male, a retired township cadres
63	Chan200402	Male, the director of the township
64	Chan200403	Male, a retired director of natural village
65	Chan200404	Male, a young man go outside for business

(continued)

	Number	Characteristics
66	Chan200405	Male, special household of fish raising
67	Chan200406	Male, the director of Qiang Village
68	Chan200407	Male, a villager
69	Chan200408	Male, a villager
70	Chan200409	Male, the former director of a local factory
71	Chan200410	Female, a villager
72	Chan200411	Female, a villager

Bibliography

Brinton, M. C., & Nee, V. (1998). *The new institutionalism in sociology*. New York: Russell Sage Foundation.

Edition Committee of the Chorography of Guangdong Province. (1999). *Guangdong Shengzhi: jingji zongshu* (The chorography of Guangdong—The summary of the economy). Guangzhou: Guangdong renmin chubanshe.

Edition Committee of the Chorography of Guangzhou. (1996). *Guangzhou shizhi* [The chorography of Guangzhou]. Guangzhou: Guangdong renmin chubanshe.

Edition Committee of the Chorography of Huazhou. (1995). *Huazhou xian zhi* [The chorography of Huazhou]. Guangzhou: Guangdong renmin chubanshe.

Edition Committee of the Chorography of Tianhe District, Guangzhou. (1998). *Guangzhou shi tianhe qu zhi* [The chorography of Tianhe District, Guangzhou]. Guangzhou: Guangdong renmin chubanshe.

Granovetter, M. (1985). Economic action and social structure: The problem of embeddedness. *American Journal of Sociology, 91*.

Walder, A. G. (1989). Social change in post-revolution China. *Annual Review of Sociology, 15*, 405.

Wong, C. P. W. (1983). *Rural industrialization in China: Development of the "Five Small Industries."* University Microfilms International.

Xiang, Jiquan. (2003). *Fei gai shui: yichang wei wancheng de geming—dui nongcun shui fei gaige de zhengzhi fenxi ji houxu gaige de jianyi* (Tax-for-fee reform: An uncompleted revolution—the political analyses on fax-for-fee reform and the suggestions to the works in next steps). Available at http://www.usc.cuhk.edu.hk/wkgb.asp

Yu, Jianrong. A study on China's modern manor economy. Available at http://www.chinaelections.org/readnews.asp?newsid=%7B335D4A39-50F6-42E3-B668-818CA7E8D6CD%7D

Zhang, A., & Wenbo, B. (2000). Xiangcun 'san ti wu tong' de lilun, zhengce yu shijian (The theories, policies, and practices of 'Three Five Township-pooling Fees' and the 'Three Village-retained Funds'). *Zhanglue yu guanli (Strategies and Management), 1*, 37–40.

Zhu, Wenhui. (2003). *Zouxiang jing he—zhujiang sanjiazhou yu changjiang sanjiaozhou jingji fazhan bijiao* [Toward competition and cooperation—A comparison between the conomic of Pearl River Delta and Yanzi River Delta]. Beijing: Tsinghua University Press.

N. Chen, *State, Market and Life Chances in Contemporary Rural Chinese Society*, DOI 10.1007/978-3-662-45046-8

MIX
Papier aus verantwortungsvollen Quellen
Paper from responsible sources
FSC® C105338

If you have any concerns about our products,
you can contact us on
ProductSafety@springernature.com

In case Publisher is established outside the EU,
the EU authorized representative is:
Springer Nature Customer Service Center GmbH
Europaplatz 3, 69115 Heidelberg, Germany

Printed by Libri Plureos GmbH
in Hamburg, Germany